The Social Edges of Psychoanalysis

The Social Edges of Psychoanalysis

Neil J. Smelser

UNIVERSITY OF CALIFORNIA PRESS

Berkeley / Los Angeles / London

University of California Press
Berkeley and Los Angeles, California

University of California, Ltd.
London, England

Library of Congress Cataloging-in-Publication Data
Smelser, Neil J.
The social edges of psychoanalysis / Neil J. Smelser.
p. cm.
Includes bibliographical references and index.
ISBN 0-520-21489-7 (alk. paper)
1. Social sciences and psychoanalysis. I. Title.
BF175.4.S65S64 1998
150.19'5—dc21 98-46470
CIP

Printed in the United States of America
9 8 7 6 5 4 3 2 1

The paper used in this publication meets the minimum requirements of American National Standard for Information Sciences—Permanence of Paper for Printed Library Materials, ANSI Z39.48-1984.

Contents

PART IV: MICRO-MACRO CONNECTIONS

Preface

It is a pleasure to witness the appearance of my psychoanalytically informed writings in a single publication. Until 1990 these writings were few in number, scattered widely in diverse journals and books, and accessible to few readers. In the past several years, however, my writing on social applications of psychoanalytic thinking has accelerated. Moreover, in reviewing the writings retrospectively, I have found them conveniently assignable to definite themes—though I did not realize this while I was writing the individual essays. These themes constitute the titles of the four parts of this book.

By way of framing the material between these covers, I will address three topics in the preface: (1) a biographical account of my contacts and involvements with psychoanalysis, (2) a few general remarks on the relations between psychoanalysis and the social sciences, and (3) a brief note on the circumstances under which each essay in the volume was written.

Contacts and Involvements with Psychoanalysis

Psychoanalysis had a salient place in the culture of Harvard that I knew as an undergraduate (1948–52) and graduate student (1954–58). It infused much literary and dramatic criticism as well as social science work. Talk about psychoanalytic ideas and therapy was the unofficial but dominant currency at cocktail parties and other social gatherings, to say nothing of *New Yorker* cartoons and popular jokes. More immediately, psychoanalysis was a central ingredient of the culture of the Social Relations Department.

When I was an undergraduate, I took courses in clinical psychology with Henry A. Murray and Robert White, both influenced by strands of psychoanalytic work (Murray, 1938; White, 1948). (Even Gordon Allport's negative critique [Allport, 1937] revealed how salient that perspective was.) Clyde Kluckhohn, with whom I also studied, was professionally and personally close to psychoanalytic thinking. When I was in graduate school, the psychoanalytic presence intensified. Many of my mentors and teachers were taking advantage of the psychoanalytic training available at the Boston Psychoanalytic Institute—Talcott Parsons, Gardner Lindzey, Alex Inkeles, and Robert F. Bales. Parsons's deepest involvement with psychoanalysis was in the 1950s, and in 1954 I worked as a research assistant with him when he was writing for the book *Family, Socialization, and Interaction Process* (Parsons, Bales, et al., 1955), an apex of his psychoanalytic thinking. I identified positively with most of my teachers—and certainly did so with respect to their psychoanalytic interests. The fact that my older brother, Bill, was completing his doctorate in clinical psychology at Berkeley during those years only strengthened my interests in depth psychology. By the time I left Harvard to teach at Berkeley in 1958, I was committed intellectually to undertaking psychoanalytic training at some undefined time in the future.

The timing of the decision to do so was a personal, not an intellectual, matter. In 1962, my first marriage was cascading toward a painful end, and I was in need of help in coming to terms with my unhappiness. I decided to seek that help in the context of applying to the San Francisco Psychoanalytic Institute. I was admitted and began my personal analysis with Stanley Goodman immediately. My colleagues in sociology provided no support for this decision. Most of them were indifferent or unfriendly to psychoanalysis, and they wondered why I would be going off in a direction that would not help and might detract from my career as a professional sociologist. To seek training was thus something of an isolated personal decision on my part, made without reference to career considerations. To be sure, my career was advancing well at the time, and I was confident about that aspect of my future.

The training program at the Institute was both intense and prolonged. It was a nine-year experience consisting of a personal analysis, more than twenty theoretical and clinical seminars, and a long period of supervised analytic practice. The Institute was primarily Freudian in tradition and emphasis but lacked the orthodoxy that I predicted I would confront—and challenge—when I entered it. The experience had a decisive personal and intellectual impact on me. It benefited my personal life enormously. It improved my relations with professional colleagues. It proved a continuing source of intellectual engagement. I developed lifelong friendships with many of my teachers, especially Robert Wallerstein, Edwin Weinshel, Joseph Weiss, Haskell Norman, and Jerome Oremland, and with several in or near my cohort, especially Bennett Markel, Kay Blacker, and Mardi Horowitz.

The psychoanalytic institutes were in transition between 1962 and 1971, the year I graduated. When accepted, I had to sign a promise not to practice privately after I graduated (though my training was to be no different from that of my medically trained colleagues). By 1971, however, I was encouraged by the Institute to practice, and in 1979 I was licensed to practice psychotherapy in the state of California by an act of the legislature which included non-M.D. graduates of psychoanalytic institutes as bona fide practitioners of psychotherapy.

I chose not to continue to practice psychoanalysis, however, even though the practice associated with my candidacy was enormously rewarding. My reason was simple. By 1970, I was well established in my academic career, and that career entailed extensive traveling. I simply was not prepared to curtail my mobility in the way that a conscientious psychoanalytic practice demanded. I kept my hand in practice in two ways—first, by joining the University of California student health service as a part-time therapist for several years, thus gearing my practice to the academic calendar; and second, by serving as a clinical supervisor of students in the U.C. doctoral program in clinical psychology for almost ten years. I should also mention a sustained period of intellectual collaboration (Smelser and Erikson, 1980) and close personal friendship with Erik Erikson in the late 1970s and early 1980s, when he lived in the San Francisco Bay area after his retirement from Harvard.

As this brief account must indicate, the psychoanalytic experience became a significant part of my life; however, I never became anything like a personal or intellectual convert. Throughout my training and afterwards, I remained strongly critical of the scientific inadequacies of psychoanalytic theory and research. As the essays in this volume testify, my use of its content and methods has been selective, not wholesale. I did not curtail my academic career in sociology to practice psychoanalysis, and most of my scholarly research has continued to be at a macroscopic, social-structural level scarcely informed by psychoanalysis. In 1956, when I was a nonresident tutor at Harvard's Eliot House, John Finley, the master, remarked that I seemed to be a half-member of everything. I did not and do not accept that as an accurate description of myself, but it does seem fair enough as an account of my intellectual and personal relationships with the psychoanalytic world. When all is said and done, however, I have maintained a personal and intellectual contact with that world, and this book is its most tangible result.

Psychoanalysis and the Behavioral and Social Sciences

If readers will turn to the first few pages of chapter 10, they will discover some remarks on the difficulties of attaining an interdisciplinary marriage between psychoanalysis and the social sciences. The relevant points are as follows:

- Classical psychoanalysis, especially Freud's writing on civilization, develops a primarily dualistic and antagonistic rendition of the relations between human nature and culture, and it largely ignores the mediating influences of social institutions.
- Psychoanalysis, relying on explanation in terms of clinical constellations of intrapsychic forces, does not easily square with other social-scientific models of causation (behaviorism, social determination).
- Closely related, the units and levels of analysis of psychoanalysis and the social sciences differ fundamentally.
- Despite some efforts, it is difficult to reconcile models of unconscious motivation and conflict with other psychological models, such as rational choice and phenomenology.
- The identification of sources of change differs fundamentally between the psychoanalytic and social frameworks of analysis.

I also noticed that, despite these difficulties, the psychoanalytic tradition has found its way into social-scientific thinking in a number of ways—as a means for understanding nonrational aspects of social behavior and culture, as an analogy for social organization, in anthropological explanations of culture, as an explanation of socialization, as part of social theory, and as a critical method.

I review these remarks, published about a decade ago, with little to correct or add. I would like to make a few supplementary remarks in this preface.

It is still true that psychoanalysis is not a major force in the behavioral and social scientists' empirical research. It has declined considerably in academic psychiatry, having been systematically displaced by biological and pharmacological frameworks and applications. It has never found an institutional or intellectual home in psychology departments in universities, still dominated by the more empiricist traditions of experimentalism, learning theory, and social psychology that are hostile to psychoanalysis as "unscientific" and otherwise uncongenial with academic psychology. There is considerable student demand for psychoanalytic, humanistic, and personality psychology in universities' psychology departments, usually unmatched, however, by faculty enthusiasm for teaching courses with these emphases. In anthropology, the classical, psychoanalytically inspired "culture and personality" approach has been supplemented by a greater diversity of paradigms. Empirical workers in sociology and political science seldom employ psychoanalytic frameworks, and most economists may as well have never heard of psychoanalysis.

On the other hand, many social theorists and commentators over the decades have continued to confront the psychoanalytic tradition for various reasons: they continue to be attracted to it, they borrow from it selectively, they adapt it to their own agenda and purposes, or they find it offensive. Making no effort to give a review of the literature, I offer four illustrations:

- Early critical theory (for example, Adorno, et al., 1950; Lowenthal, 1949) applied psychoanalysis wholesale in its assault on fascism and critique of capitalism, and more recently Habermas treated the psychoanalytic method as wholly consistent with—indeed, part of—critical sociology (Habermas, 1973; see also Seidman, 1989).
- One line of confrontation might be described as a theological one in secular clothes: a continued assault on the "Augustinian" (original sin) aspects of Freudian psychoanalysis, and an effort to resurrect some variation of Rousseau's social theory (social corruption of the individual) in its place. The letters between Freud (instinctual origins of war and aggression) and Einstein (social origins) reflect this tension. Another version of the tension is found in

Marcuse's *Eros and Civilization* (1955), which acknowledged destructiveness in civilization but rejected its impulsive or instinctual basis and traced it to frustrations and injustices imposed by capitalist social organization. A more remote variation of the tension is found in the assault on Freud's account of incestuous seduction as a wish-generated fantasy and an insistence on the real, objective seduction of the child as the basis of trauma (Masson, 1983). This critique has manifested itself in the advocacy of recovered memories as real rather than fantastic, distorted, and defensive (see Prager, 1998, for an excellent analysis). A final example is the work of Alice Miller (1981, 1983, 1984), whose argument traces childhood suffering to the objective cruelties imposed on children rather than the dynamics of intrapsychic desire and conflict. I regard these polarized squarings-off as basically unproductive and as calling for new, interactive models of human experience involving both social and intrapsychic forces.

- The psychoanalytic perspective has found its way into contemporary feminist writings. In the 1970s the dominant tone was a hostile one, especially with respect to Freud's "anatomy is destiny" writings on female socialization and character. Since that time a more complex orientation has involved and has, more sympathetically, incorporated psychoanalytic insights. Examples are Chodorow's *The Reproduction of Mothering* (1978), Johnson's (1988) psychoanalytically informed accounts of contemporary gender roles, and Jessica Benjamin's (1988) reformulation of psychoanalytic ideas of domination and application of that reformulation to gender domination.

- Postmodern writers have selectively incorporated psychoanalytic principles into their work, again largely as a supportive adjunct to their larger commitments to a radical epistemological relativism, their preoccupation with hegemony, and their recurrent unmasking and debunking tendencies. The most significant contribution is that of Foucault (1978), who treated Freudian psychology as part of a larger, historically evolving discourse about sexuality and social control. Foucault, ironically, simultaneously both "objectified" and "subjectified" psychoanalytic claims. He made these claims an object for study and analysis, but in treating them as discursive, intersubjective strategies of domination, he implicitly undermined them as scientific claims to knowledge. In most cases (see Flax, 1990, 1993, for example) postmodernist writers reject classical psychoanalysis and suggest some radical reformulation in keeping with their own agenda.

Writing the Essays in This Book

The essays in this volume are organized not chronologically but according to four analytic themes, which reflect different preoccupations I have had over the years in thinking about psychoanalytic thinking on the one hand, and social process, social structure, and social problems on the other. These topics concern, in order, interdisciplinary knowledge and applications, the application of psychoanalytic thinking to sociological issues, the special place of ambivalence in social life, and the articulation of the microscopic and macroscopic levels of the human condition. In placing the contributions in context, however, I will consider them chronologically, and in each case give an indication of the intended audience and the intended messages, at least those of which I am aware.

The earliest essay, "Social and Psychological Dimensions of Collective Behavior," was written in late 1965 for presentation to the Ad Hoc Research Committee of the San Francisco Psychoanalytic Institute. As I reconstruct matters, I was carrying on three dialogues at the time. The first audience was myself. I had written a major work, *Theory of Collective Behavior* (1962), several years before. In characterizing the beliefs associated with episodes of collective behavior (panics, crazes, hostile outbursts), I had relied on an implicit but unacknowledged psychoanalytic logic, treating anxiety as the core ingredient in those beliefs. I assigned to anxiety much the same role as Freud did in his *Inhibitions, Symptoms, and Anxiety* (1959 [1926]) and regarded other belief-systems (hostile beliefs, reform and revolutionary ideologies) as combinations of anxiety with other affective and cognitive components. In my subsequent essay I wanted to make the psychodynamic underpinnings more explicit.

The second audience was my psychoanalytic colleagues. To them I was acknowledging the importance of internal psychodynamic forces in collective episodes but also reminding them that these could not be understood without simultaneous reference to the social-structural and cultural contexts in which they occur.

Third, I was speaking to the social turmoil (the Free Speech Movement and its derivatives) I had experienced firsthand in 1964–65. In particular, I had been recruited by Acting Chancellor Martin Meyerson to serve as his special assistant in the area of student political activity for most of the year 1965. In that capacity I became both negotiator with representatives of protest groups and strategic and tactical advisor to Meyerson on how the Berkeley campus should deal with these movements as well as the backlashes against them. It was an enormously educational experience for me. I appreciated the social context of these movements (described in Smelser, 1974) but also was impressed with the apparent psychodynamic forces involved, especially in the students' orientations toward academic administrators and faculty. Much of the discussion of protest movements in that essay derived from my efforts to sort out those social and psychological complexities.

The collaboration for the article "Psychoanalysis and Sociology: Articulations and Applications" was initiated by Robert Wallerstein of the San Francisco Psychoanalytic Institute, who himself had in turn been commissioned to write an article commemorating the fiftieth anniversary publication of *The International Journal of Psycho-Analysis.* Bob suggested the interdisciplinary theme. As it turned out, I had in the previous few years been asked to write on the nature and scope of sociology and its relations to the other social sciences (Smelser, 1967, 1969) and was ready to undertake this rewarding collaboration because it fit so well with my current interests.

The essay "Some Determinants of Destructive Behavior" was also commissioned, this time by Nevitt Sanford, director of the Wright Institute in Berkeley. The occasion was a symposium on "The Legitimation of Evil," organized by Sanford and several of his colleagues. The conference was held at the height of antiwar sentiment that engulfed many quarters of American society, especially its universities, in the wake of the My Lai massacre in Vietnam. The reference points of the conference were that massacre and the genocide it symbolized and the later Kent State and Jackson State killings. I was as appalled by these events as the next but can say that I experienced a distinct discomfort at what I regarded as Sanford's appeal to social science expertise as a cloak for partisan ideological protest against the war. Readers of my essay will note a muffled reluctance on my part to join this outrage and an attempt to take an analytic approach to destructive behavior (I chose those words instead of "evil") and thus set myself off from the chorus of disapproval that dominated the atmosphere of the conference.

For reasons not available to me, my psychoanalytic pen was inactive during the decade of the 1970s, the decade after I had graduated from the Psychoanalytic Institute. The main news of that decade was the development of my friendship and collaboration with Erik Erikson. Over a period of two years we conceived, planned, and organized the 1977 conference on "Love and Work in Adulthood," a conference meant to consolidate the best current psychological and social thinking on adult development. For my contribution I synthesized both old and emerging interests. My first major work was on the British working-class family in the Industrial Revolution (Smelser, 1959), and my interests in British education were already beginning to crystallize in the 1970s, but they had to wait more than a decade before seeing the light of publication (Smelser, 1991). In keeping with the conference's theme of work and love, I wrote a brief essay on the social structuring of labor and intimacy in Britain and the United States in the nineteenth century, this time emphasizing the penetration of the institutional side of life into these personal ranges of experiences. It appears as the chapter titled "Vicissitudes of Work and Love in Anglo-American Society."

In 1980 Jerome Oremland, a close friend in the San Francisco Psychoanalytic Institute, invited me to participate in a plenary session at the meetings of the American Psychoanalytic Association in San Francisco. He assigned me no topic. By coincidence I had been associated in a consultant role with a research project on California's history, economy, and culture at the Institute of Governmental Studies on the Berkeley campus, so the subject of California was on my mind. I conceived the idea of speaking to the assembled psychoanalysts as a means of demonstrating the power of both psychoanalytic and social ideas to account for a familiar myth—the myth of the good life in California. In carrying out this assignment I was so struck by both the utopian and the dismal elements in this myth that it was difficult not to interpret it in the context of ambivalence—a struggle between gratification and renunciation. This experience crystallized a focus on ambivalence that was to persist. The address sat around, unpublished, for a couple of years. In 1983, Samuel Oliner asked me to submit something of my choice to the *Humboldt Journal of Social Relations*, so I sent him that essay.

In the mid-1980s I became involved in a leadership role in a series of conferences sponsored jointly by the Theory Sections of the American Sociological Association and the German Sociological Association. The topic of the first conference was the analytic relations between the microscopic (social-psychological and personal-interactive) and the macroscopic (social-structural and institutional) levels of social life. My co-organizers asked me to contribute a paper. On this occasion I went back to something I wrote in the late 1960s. It was my thesis—a short paper, actually—required for my graduation from the San Francisco Psychoanalytic Institute. In that paper I tried to synthesize the sprawling psychoanalytic literature on the mechanisms of defense. It had also laid around unpublished for many years. For the German-American conference, held in 1984 at the Schloss Rauischolzhausen in Giessen, I resurrected that paper and extended it by arguing that there is a formal coincidence between mechanisms of defense involved in internal conflict and in coping with social situations. That essay appears as "Depth Psychology and the Social Order."

Twice during the 1980s I had co-taught a course with Bob Wallerstein at the University of California, San Francisco (his home campus) on the social applications of psychoanalysis. We asked students to read works on community disaster, bureaucratic organization, psychohistory, and literary criticism. I had in my possession extensive lecture and seminar notes, and when Jeffrey Prager asked me, sometime in 1990, to contribute to a volume titled *Psychoanalytic Sociology*, which he was co-editing for publication in England, I decided to develop a major methodological essay on the problematics of applying psychoanalytic ideas and methods to nonclinical phenomena. That essay appears in this volume under the ungainly title "The Psychoanalytic Mode of Inquiry in the Context of the Behavioral and Social Sciences."

One of my recurring intellectual interests is the sociology of higher education (see, for example, Smelser, 1974; Smelser and Content, 1980). As a by-product of this work I was asked to be involved in planning two conferences at the American Academy of Arts and Sciences on issues confronting research universities in the United States. These conferences were to lead to a special issue of *Daedalus* on the subject. My original intent and agreement with the other organizers was to write an article on the general mission of those institutions. At an advanced stage of planning, however, the other organizers of the conference approached me with a plea. They were having a great deal of difficulty in finding anyone to write on the subject of diversity (including multiculturalism and the "culture wars") and begged me to do so. The problem was that almost everybody else had declared himself or herself on this polarized set of issues, and, as a result, their contributions would bring nothing new. I decided to rise to the challenge, to cut through the polarization, and to write a more or less neutral piece that aimed to analyze and explain the issues and conflicts involved. In this connection the idea of ambivalence loomed large in my mind. The conflicts over diversity seemed to me to involve partisanship, to be sure, but many of the contending groups seemed to be pursuing several, possibly contradictory, objectives at once. Hence, under the title "The Politics of Ambivalence," I analyzed the special debates and conflicts that fall under the heading of "diversity."

Subsequently—and because a number of people had noticed my *Daedalus* essay—I was asked to contribute a paper on affirmative action at a Princeton conference on higher education that was held as a part of the celebration of that university's 250th anniversary in the spring of 1996. While that paper, "Problematics of Affirmative Action," is the least psychoanalytically explicit of any essay in this volume, I regard it as an extension of my preoccupation with ambivalence, as I attempt to explain—from cultural, political, social-structural, and social-psychological points of view—why affirmative action has experienced such an unsettled, nonroutinized existence since its beginnings in the 1960s. My motive, once again, was to be analytic rather than partisan. As a result, I felt myself somewhat marginalized in the midst of partisans at that meeting.

In 1995 I was elected President of the American Sociological Association. One of the honors associated with that office is to deliver a major address at the annual meetings of one's presidential year. At an early stage of reflecting on topics, I had about six in mind. I showed my list to Christine Williams, a former student of mine now on the faculty at the University of Texas–Austin, who happened to be a Fellow at the Center for Advanced Studies in the Behavioral Sciences in 1995–96. She urged me to extend the theme of ambivalence in theoretical directions and helped persuade me it was the best of the several ideas. In the meantime, I had, at various times in my career, struggled with the strengths and weaknesses of the principle of rational choice as a foundational idea in economics and other social sciences (Smelser, 1963, 1992). Jim Coleman once told me I had something of a love-hate relationship with that principle, and I suppose he was right. In any event, for my presidential address I chose to comment on the limits of rational choice as an informing perspective in the social sciences, and to develop a positive case for the idea of ambivalence as an alternative postulate. That address is printed here as "The Rational and the Ambivalent in the Social Sciences."

Finally I mention the essay "Erik Erikson as Social Scientist." Once again Bob Wallerstein was the instigator. He scheduled, through the San Francisco Psychoanalytic Society, a symposium on Erik Erikson's life and work in January 1995, about six months after Erikson's death.

He asked me to present, and, after reflection, I decided to undertake a sympathetic but critical assessment of the social-scientific contributions of that remarkable psychoanalyst. This was a welcome occasion, not least because it afforded me the opportunity to revisit and pay my respects to my departed friend.

When I look over my personal history of writing about the social edges of psychoanalysis, two observations strike me. First, in comparing the earlier (late 1960s) and the later (1990s) essays, I note that the former display a certain caution, which takes the form of hedging the substantive arguments in an ongoing gloss that relates those arguments to issues of theoretical and methodological significance. I suppose this might be called a form of "scientific correctness." In the later works this parallel conversation about theory and method fades into the background, and I tend simply to get on with the argument. I am not certain how to interpret this difference—discovered only when I was putting the essays together—but I would suggest that it might be attributed to a growth of confidence on my part that comes with aging, experience, and career success.

Second, I cannot help remarking how opportunistic my work has been. In the vast majority of cases I did the writing in response to invitations from others. It seems surprising that the essays, generated for all sorts of purposes at different times, should have any thematic coherence. It is up to readers and critics to decide on that, but I believe that there is, and if there is such a coherence, it surely testifies to one's ability to capitalize on the greatest diversity of opportunities and say what one wants to say anyway.

References

Adorno, T. W., et al.

1950 *The Authoritarian Personality.* New York: Harper and Row.

Allport, Gordon W.

1937 *Personality: A Psychological Interpretation.* New York: H. Holt.

Benjamin, Jessica

1988 *The Bonds of Love: Psychoanalysis, Feminism, and the Problem of Domination.* New York: Pantheon Books.

Chodorow, Nancy

1978 *The Reproduction of Mothering.* Berkeley and Los Angeles: University of California Press.

Flax, Jane
1990 *Thinking Fragments: Psychoanalysis, Feminism, and Postmodernism in the Contemporary West.* Berkeley and Los Angeles: University of California Press.
1993 *Disputed Subjects: Essays on Psychoanalysis, Politics and Philosophy.* New York: Routledge.
Foucault, Michel
1978 *The History of Sexuality.* Vol. 1. New York: Pantheon.
Freud, Sigmund
1959 [1926] "Inhibitions, Symptoms, and Anxiety." In *The Standard Edition of the Complete Psychological Works of Sigmund Freud,* Vol. 20, edited by James Strachey. London: Hogarth Press. Pp. 73–174.
Habermas, Jürgen
1973 *Theory and Practice.* Translated by M. Viertel. Boston: Beacon Press.
Johnson, Miriam M.
1988 *Strong Mothers, Weak Wives: The Search for Gender Inequality.* Berkeley and Los Angeles: University of California Press.
Lowenthal, Leo
1949 *Prophets of Deceit.* New York: Harper.
Marcuse, Herbert
1955 *Eros and Civilization.* New York: Vintage Books.
Masson, Jeffrey
1983 *The Assault on Truth.* New York: Farrar, Straus and Giroux.
Miller, Alice
1981 *Prisoners of Childhood.* New York: Basic Books.
1983 *For Your Own Good: Hidden Cruelty in Child-Rearing and the Roots of Violence.* New York: Farrar, Straus, Giroux.
1984 *Thou Shalt Not Be Aware: Society's Betrayal of the Child.* New York: Farrar, Straus, Giroux.
Murray, Henry A.
1938 *Explorations in Personality.* New York: Oxford University Press.
Parsons, Talcott, Robert F. Bales, et al.
1955 *Family, Socialization, and Interaction Process.* Glencoe, IL: The Free Press.
Prager, Jeffrey
1998 *Presenting the Past: Psychoanalysis and the Sociology of Misremembering.* Cambridge, MA: Harvard University Press.
Seidman, Steven
1989 "Introduction." In *Jürgen Habermas on Society and Politics,* edited by Steven Seidman. Boston: Beacon Press. Pp. 1–25.
Smelser, Neil J.
1959 *Social Change in the Industrial Revolution.* Chicago: University of Chicago Press.
1962 *Theory of Collective Behavior.* New York: The Free Press.
1963 *The Sociology of Economic Life.* Englewood Cliffs, NJ: Prentice-Hall.
1967 "Sociology and the Other Social Sciences." In *The Uses of Sociology,* edited by Paul F. Lazarsfeld, William H. Sewell, and Harold L. Wilensky. New York: Basic Books. Pp. 3–44.

1969 "The Optimum Scope of Sociology." In *A Design for Sociology: Scope, Objectives and Methods.* Philadelphia: American Academy of Political and Social Science. Pp. 1–22.

1974 "Growth, Structural Change, and Conflict in California Public Higher Education, 1950–1970." In *Public Higher Education in California,* edited by Neil J. Smelser and Gabriel Almond. Berkeley and Los Angeles: University of California Press. Pp. 9–141.

1991 *Social Paralysis and Social Change.* Berkeley and Los Angeles: University of California Press.

1992 "The Rational Choice Perspective: A Theoretical Assessment." *Rationality and Society,* Vol. 4, No. 4, pp. 381–410.

Smelser, Neil J., and Erik H. Erikson (eds.)

1980 *Themes of Work and Love in Adulthood.* Cambridge, MA: Harvard University Press.

Smelser, Neil J., and Robin Content

1980 *The Changing Academic Market.* Berkeley and Los Angeles: University of California Press.

White, Robert W.

1948 *The Abnormal Personality: A Textbook.* New York: Ronald Press.

PART I

Disciplinary Articulations

1

Psychoanalysis and Sociology

Articulations and Applications

In marking its fiftieth volume with a special anniversary issue, *The International Journal of Psycho-Analysis* undertook to assemble an array of contributions under the general title "Psychoanalysis Past and Present," as a way of taking historical note and assessing the present state of the field in its historical perspective. Our contribution is more prospective than retrospective; it marks an essential area of psychoanalytic (and applied psychoanalytic) advance, that our current vigor as an empirical science (of which this anniversary occasion is one of the signs) gives us reason to feel ready to assay. Our starting point is with the simple principle that human life is simultaneously both psychological and social—that both types of forces continuously interpenetrate as they impinge upon human behavior. We shall try to develop the implications of our view that this principle is both a self-evident truth and, at the same time, a source of the most troublesome dilemmas for the student of behavior.

A fundamental feature of organized social life is that it structures the expression of individual biological and psychological needs. This structuring has a positive and a negative aspect. On the positive side, social life provides regular opportunities for the gratification of instinctual demands. The institutions of marriage and prostitution are both contrived, in part, to permit and channel sexual gratifications. Tournaments, athletic contests, ritual rebellions, and even war are contrived, in part, to permit the expression of aggressive impulses. On the negative side, social life structures the occasions for frustration and deprivation. Some impulses—incestuous, murderous, and cannibalistic, for example—are

With Robert S. Wallerstein. Originally published in *The International Journal of Psycho-Analysis* 50 (1969): 693–710.

directly prohibited by normative constraint. More indirectly, but perhaps more important, frustrations and deprivations often arise as by-products of social arrangements that do not have instinctual renunciation as their explicit objective but do lead to that consequence. Political and social stratification systems, for instance, may be established in the name of preserving peace and allocating social rewards, but they may create widespread inequity, disinheritance, and poverty, all of which frustrate and deprive large numbers of people.

Different theorists have stressed the influence of either the psychological or the social side of this process of structuring instinctual needs. Malinowski's functional theory of society, for example, is based on the principle that social institutions are fashioned as a means of accommodating biological needs (Malinowski, 1931). Freud's social writings, by contrast, stress the ways in which civilization demands the renunciation of these urges; he considers especially the more direct forms of prohibition (Freud, 1961 [1930]). Marx (1954 [1848]) also underscores the ways in which society deprives large classes of people, but he treats deprivation as a by-product of social arrangements established for the production of economic commodities, rather than as the intended product of direct prohibitions. Because the empirical structuring of organized social life involves the inseparable intermingling of both psychological and social forces, however, we find no inherent basis for selecting one of these emphases as dominant over the others; all of the invoked processes manifest themselves continuously. Indeed, it seems restrictive (i.e., incomplete) to attempt to develop theories of the instincts and their vicissitudes without simultaneously developing theories of the institutionalization of social values and norms—and vice versa.

The personality's ego-processes mesh with organized social life much as do the drives. With respect to the ego's functions of reality-testing, for example, society provides a great deal of "reality" in ready-made form—reality in the form of institutionalized role expectations as well as authorities, agencies of social control, and agencies of adjudication. At the same time, society's reality is never superimposed in a total way on the individual; every person makes something unique of the social reality he or she experiences. Society also provides structured bases for the operation of the individual's defense mechanisms. Institutionalized stereotypes of the lazy, sexually potent, or vicious minority group member afford a ready-made projective system for persons who have difficulty in coming to terms with these tendencies in themselves (Adorno, et al., 1950). Again, however, each individual tailors such institutionalized projective systems to his or her unique psychological dynamics. Society also provides an array of ready-made ego-ideals and ideologies which form important bases for ego-integration and identity formation; though, again, each individual turns these images to personal use (Erikson, 1959). Finally, society institutionalizes roles whose expectations provide a good "fit" with classical symptomatic behaviors (Fromm, 1949 [1944]). We need only consider the daily round of activities of the postal clerk, the assembly-line worker, and the scholar to recognize that each complements—even encourages and rewards—behavior that is closely linked to the symptoms of the obsessional neurosis. And some of the more bizarre rituals of religious cults and social movements permit, even demand, behavior that could be diagnosed as borderline or psychotic. Whether these roles are absorbed into full systems of pathology, however, depends once again on the psychic dynamics of the individual participants. From these observations it appears that no fully comprehensive theory of the ego is possible without a simultaneous theory of social organization—and vice versa.

A general conclusion emerges from these observations: an adequate psychological theory is not possible unless it is, at the same time, social; and an adequate social theory is not possible unless it is, at the same time, psychological. (In fact, matters are even more complicated than this; a complete and adequate theory would also have to incorporate both biological and cultural variables since these also intrude on psychological and social reality.) Yet man's intellectual reach to this point has been too limited to create manageable theories that simultaneously encompass the full panoply of interacting forces in the empirical world. Man has been caught in a dilemma: where he would try to be realistic in his understanding of the world, he has been overwhelmed by its complexities; where he simplified its complexities, he has perforce been unrealistic. He has steered his way through this dilemma, historically, by creating specialized and narrowed conceptual frameworks for understanding and explaining limited aspects of reality. As we shall see, however, this valuable and even necessary solution also has created a number of new dilemmas and dangers.

The Emergence of Specialized Disciplines

A new and more specialized discipline characteristically arises as a result of scholars' efforts to organize knowledge by selecting a limited range of phenomena for study and by organizing knowledge about these phenomena on the basis of a restricting set of assumptions and assertions. As it evolves, a given discipline will characteristically become narrowed in four ways:

1. It will address itself to particular kinds of problems, or "dependent variables." For example, psychoanalysis has defined as problematic such phenomena as neurotic symptoms, the contents of dreams and parapraxes, and the wide range of behavior dispositions. Sociology has defined as problematic such phenomena as the patterning of behavior via social roles; the formation of groups, organizations, and institutions; and patterns of change in social relations. These phenomena are the "things to be explained" in each discipline.
2. It will address itself to a limited range of *determinants* of the phenomena to be explained, or the "independent variables." For example, psychoanalysis focuses on a variety of drive pressures, of ego and superego operations, as well as of select aspects of the impinging external reality as the main determinants—through their interaction—of adaptive and maladaptive behavior. Sociology selects membership in roles and groups, demographic and social-structural forces, and institutionalized culture patterns as its main explanatory variables. The independent variables are the "things which do the explaining."
3. It will organize these different classes of variables into some kind of logical order to generate hypotheses germane to, and testable within, its theoretical framework. Psychoanalysis, for example, has a number of (metapsychological) points of view—the genetic, the dynamic, the economic, the structural, the adaptive—which organize the basic variables of the discipline into coherent relations with one another. Sociology also has a variety of perspectives on society—the Marxist, the functionalist, and the symbolic interactionist, for example—each of which organizes the major variables of the discipline in its distinctive way; it also has a multiplicity of more specific "models" addressed to more particulate problems, such as that of social mobility or deviance. The operation of logical ordering provides the "theory" for each discipline.
4. It will develop a variety of research methods that are employed as a basis on which to accept or reject explanatory statements about the phenomena under study. In this task psychoanalysis has relied primarily on the clinical case study method—the intensive retro-

> spective analysis of the internal patterning of an individual case—though longitudinal developmental and, to a limited extent, even experimental methods have also been brought to bear on psychoanalytic hypotheses. Sociology is characterized by a wide variety of research methods—experimental, statistical, and comparative, as well as case study. The distinctive research methods chosen are (should be) congruent with the kinds of phenomena under study and the data generated (Smelser, 1967).

By narrowing its focus in these ways, a discipline sets up boundaries that mark off, more or less distinctly, its separate domain of understanding. By this narrowing, to a (relatively) homogeneous and coherent field of phenomena and of organizing principles, behavioral scientists of each discipline have been able to make the study of their chosen sector of human behavior more nearly manageable—through isolating the influence of limited numbers of causal factors upon behavior. One of the fruits of this process of specialization has been an enormous accumulation of systematic knowledge about behaviors in various environments. This detailed knowledge probably could not have arisen without the development of such disciplined and specialized lines of inquiry.

What is concomitantly often not appreciated, because it is a silent additional "given," is that this sharpened focus and (relative) isolation for study has been achieved in each discipline by making a variety of simplifying assumptions about the *other* aspects of the world it has not chosen to study (the content areas of the other behavioral sciences). Speaking broadly, psychoanalysis is centrally an individual and a motivational psychology. The organizing unit of its scientific inquiry is thus the individual, his or her unique history, motivations, intrapsychic conflicts, and behaviors. Though "nothing but" explanations are reductionistic and oversimplifying at best, that offered by Ernst Kris that psychoanalysis is "nothing but" human behavior considered from the point of view of (intrapsychic) conflict is indeed apposite in this context. This overall focus sets psychoanalysis on an analytically different level from sociology—and, for that matter, from all the other social sciences, such as anthropology, political science, economics, etc.—in which the units of analysis are relational qualities between individuals, such as interaction patterns and roles, and organized social structures with behaviors that are oriented to those structures. And—the point here—each discipline has created its focus and its units of analysis by making artificial, indeed "make believe," assumptions about those aspects of behavior which lie outside its domain. Consider the following illustrations.

Most sociological models of social mobility rest on an assumed psychological postulate that individuals within a hierarchical system of stratified positions, opportunities, and rewards are, *other things equal,* more or less uniformly motivated to move upward as far as possible in the hierarchy. This assumption can prove useful in analyzing the behaviors of large numbers of people in the aggregate, though even in this case it must be considered limited and problematical. But in explaining the behavior of any individual within the hierarchical system, other things are never equal. Individuals are always idiosyncratically different in terms of unique developmental histories; they differ radically in what they demand, what they dare, and what they fear with respect to aspiration and position. Oedipal victories and defeats are necessarily differently experienced and differently tolerated. Sometimes whole groups arise to challenge the postulated universal desire for upward movement. The movement embracing the "hippies" or all the present-day "Antinomian personalities" (Adler, 1968) or other species of alienated or dropped-out youth appears to reject the achievement orientation that has been traditional to American society.

On the psychoanalytic side similar simplifying assumptions are made about the social environment. Many theoretical formulations rest on an implicit model of the Western nuclear family and do not consider the varying psychological consequences within multiple or extended family arrangements characteristic of many non-Western societies. Some psychoanalytic formulations are explicitly built on simplified assumptions. Winnicott, for example, employs the concept of "good enough mothering" as a stable parameter necessary for the explication of the two-person, mother–child relationship, and Hartmann has developed the concept of the "average expectable environment" as a stable parameter for the multiperson, individual–society relationship.

Put this way, it becomes obvious that these are indeed only simplifying heuristic assumptions, necessary for the advancement of scientific knowledge within a framework readily manageable by human intelligence, but not at all reflecting the integrated nature of organismic processes. And we must keep just that in mind, that the assumptions at the boundaries of any discipline are arbitrary artifacts erected for heuristic convenience. Social institutions mold role behavior that is processed through the individual participants, each reacting in ways congruent with their own developmental history, abiding character dispositions, and fluctuating expectations, aspirations, and apprehensions. Conversely, every individual uniquely constituted out of his or her own history lives out his or her personality within an impinging and determining social context.

Furthermore, if any of the simplifying assumptions at the boundaries of a given discipline are modified, this will have an impact on the theoretical structure and the specific hypotheses of the discipline itself. Consider the impact on the sociological explanation of social mobility, for example, if the accompanying psychological postulate were that "sons are motivated to follow in their fathers' footsteps." Or consider the impact on an individual's psychodynamics, for example, if the limiting social postulate were changed from that of the "average expectable environment" to that of a "systematically fluctuating or a turbulent environment." In short, the simplifying assumptions, *if treated as variables,* would influence the explanations arrived at in important ways.

What such examples make clear is that an investigator in any one of the behavioral sciences, who necessarily makes some such simplifying assumptions in order to be able properly to encompass his particular inquiry, would profit by awareness of the theory and the research of neighboring disciplines. As Smelser (1967) has said elsewhere,

> insofar as every discipline necessarily restricts its range of inquiry and makes simplifying assumptions about—that is, treats as given—those areas outside this range, each discipline stands to be informed as to the inadequacy of these assumptions by referring to the empirical research and theoretical formulations of neighboring disciplines.

When one then wishes to modify these assumptions for purposes of more exact analysis, clearly they should be modified in accord with the best theory and research available in the neighboring discipline. This process of mutual informing and interactive modification we refer to as the principle of "complementary articulation" between disciplines. In posing the problem of complementary articulation, we ask several questions: How can different branches of knowledge contribute to one another to augment our understanding of behavior as it unfolds empirically? How can the results of one line of disciplined inquiry be brought to bear on the results of another? How can the restrictive assumptions of one discipline be systematically informed by the theory and research of disciplines dealing directly with the subject matter of those assumptions? In short, how can each kind of specialized knowledge be reintegrated with the other branches of knowledge, from which it originally had to split in order to advance and establish its own autonomy?

In addition we believe that the maximization of complementary articulation is more than a luxury or a nice possibility. We believe that it is fast becoming a scientific necessity as various disciplines approach the limits of explanatory power within their customary frameworks. Wallerstein (1964) has elsewhere stressed the importance of prediction—both as a principle and as a tool—as a means to advance validation and theory building within psychoanalysis. At the same time, considered as an independent body of thought, psychoanalysis falls far short in predictive precision, not just because of limiting characteristics of its theoretical structure and inadequacies in its empirical database, but also because of limitations (beyond those internal to its structure) stemming from simplifying assumptions made concerning the realms outside psychoanalysis. These were alluded to (Wallerstein, 1964) in the course of the mention of the

> realm of the long term prediction (in regard to psychoanalytic treatment course and outcome) with all its uncertainties in regard to specific unfolding events and conditions that the future, both in the treatment and in the interacting life situation, will bring. Yet, nonetheless, as analysts we make judgements and have expectations that are often borne out, sometimes are not. We do this on the basis of conceptions that I would like to paraphrase as that of the "*average expectable psychoanalysis* . . . ; and side by side with it, on the basis of a concomitant conception of the "*average expectable environment*" in which likewise relative stability and accountability can be assumed.

The counterpart reasoning could be applied with equal cogency to the other behavioral sciences.

Put more directly, the all too low rate of predictability found in every one of the behavioral sciences is, in considerable measure, a reflection of this limiting phenomenon—that each assumes as givens, or parameters, what are the variables of the other behavioral sciences. And these "givens" do not cease varying just because we assume them to be invariant for specific purposes of analysis. It is in this sense that complementary articulation is not just a utopian luxury but an increasing scientific necessity as we approach the limits (and limitations) of explanatory power within our customary frameworks. Few have individually been able to do this successfully. Most human knowledge is complex enough, and specialized and compartmentalized enough, that few investigators are able to do more than master one primary domain; most are usually secondarily and only casually informed in any other. Characteristically, sophisticated analysts who have ventured sociologically or historically have been relatively naive sociologists and historians, and, of course, the reverse also holds.

Promises, Problems, and Dangers in Complementary Articulation

To make this notion of complementary articulation more tangible, let us follow through one classical empirical issue—that of suicide—in brief detail. This phenomenon poses a problem that is intrinsically interesting and has excited a good deal of curiosity and attempted explanation on the part of both psychoanalysts and sociologists. It constitutes an empirical problem for each discipline because it describes a range of variation in human behavior which we can attempt to explain by reference to a distinctive (and limited) set of interrelated independent variables within the conceptual framework of each discipline.

The classical sociological study of suicide was that of Durkheim (1951 [1897]). One of the central findings he related to his discussion of egoistic suicide had to do with religious grouping; that Protestants persistently display higher rates of suicide than Catholics—a difference which, incidentally, appeared to persist no matter which group was in the minority in a particular national society. Durkheim attributed this difference to distinctive characteristics of the respective religions. Protestantism, he argued, with its traditions of free inquiry and antiauthoritarianism, is a less integrated church community than Catholicism. Because of these features, Protestants are freer than Catholics, less embedded in a cohesive community and thus less protected against tendencies to self-destruction. Consistent with his own methodology, Durkheim argued that the explanation of these different social rates of suicide is to be found at the *social* level—namely, in the variable of social integration.

Durkheim supplemented his social analysis of suicide in a less-known chapter titled "Individual Forms of the Different Types of Suicide." There he did acknowledge individual idiosyncrasies at the outset:

> Each victim of suicide gives his act a personal stamp which expresses his temperament, the special conditions in which he is involved, and which, consequently, cannot be explained by the social and general causes of the phenomenon.

Nevertheless, Durkheim was convinced that these general causes made a "collective mark" on individuals. With reference to egoistic suicide, for example, he argued that the individual expression of the social state of egoism was a "loathness to act" and a "melancholy detachment." He also maintained that egoistic suicides have an "intellectual and meditative nature" because of the "high development of knowledge and reflective intelligence" in egoistic persons. To a psychoanalyst these terms of course suggest the structure of an obsessional neurosis, linked to an exacting superego, perhaps more associated with an individualistic religion like Protestantism.

A troubling question, however, comes to mind as we follow Durkheim's analysis: what about the Protestants who are not moved to suicide? Or, alternatively, what about the Catholics who do commit suicide? A sociologist sympathetic to Durkheim would respond that other social forces—such as the character of an individual's family environment, or the presence or absence of anomic social situations in his or her life—would operate to augment or inhibit the play of the religious influence. There is merit in this answer, but we also suggest that the explanatory power attained by adding and combining social forces reaches a limit, and that it is necessary to supplement the Durkheimian account with a serious attempt to understand the ways in which individuals react to and process these social influences in relation to the play of intrapsychic determining forces. This understanding is surely essential to an understanding of the causes of any individual suicide and is also necessary for refining and extending the explanation of social rates of suicide.

Suicide, as linked to melancholia, has also been the object of classical psychoanalytic study, in the first instance, by Freud (1957 [1917]; 1961 [1923]; 1961 [1924]) and Abraham (1924). Here the basic explanatory principles include object loss, narcissistic regression, the introjection of the ambivalently held lost object, and the turning upon the self of the hostility and destructiveness directed at the once external object. Yet the same difficult question comes to mind in connection with a psychoanalytic formulation: Why is it that all individuals experiencing this particular complex of psychological events and adaptations—all of which are certainly widespread if not universal—do not commit suicide? A psychoanalytically knowledgeable investigator would answer that other psychological factors—such as the resilience and strength of the ego, the particular patterning of defenses against object loss, and the mechanisms available to cope with it—would operate as facilitating or inhibiting factors. We would also stress the necessity, however, of incorporating the consideration of distinctively social factors as well—the availability of a supporting network of meaningful object attachments, the availability of appropriate professional assistance, etc.

An overall fuller explanatory account of the occurrence of suicide, then—whether considered as an individual phenomenon or as a social rate—can be attained by the appropriate encompassing of both psychological and social explanatory variables. As Smelser (1968b) has argued elsewhere,

> whether suicide as a dependent variable is described at the psychological *or* social level . . . the independent variables by means of which we try to account for this behaviour necessarily lie at *both* the social and psychological levels. Suppose suicide is defined in terms of its psychological significance (for example, as the turning of anger upon an object that has been internalized through a process of narcissistic identification); in seeking explanations for suicide, *thus defined*, it is appropriate to inquire what kind of family constellations (a social factor) give rise to this particular complex of self-destructive tendencies. Or suppose suicide is described in terms of its differential incidence between Negroes and whites; in seeking explanations for this social fact, it is appropriate to inquire into the differential distribution of personality traits between the two groups that might account for the different rates.

A complete explanatory accounting, in fact, would call for more than a simple listing of contributing psychological and social factors; it would require the systematic formulation and application of the principles of interaction between both types of determinants over time.

To summarize the conclusions emerging from this example of suicide, the promises of articulating the psychoanalytic and the sociological frameworks in a complementary way appear to be three: (1) One framework can provide an intelligible basis for establishing parameters or limiting assumptions within which another framework generates partial explanations. (2) One framework can be used to supplement the other by accounting for additional variance at those points where the other framework reaches its explanatory limits. (3) The two frameworks, taken together, can provide the conceptual resources for constructing more comprehensive interactive explanatory models.

Yet compelling as these tasks of complementary articulation are, there are clearly conceptual and methodological difficulties in the way of articulating variables that lie at different analytical levels and that reflect the very limitations in the human synthesizing capacity that led initially to the historical separate development of the differing domains of the behavioral sciences—and within which historical traditions particular constellations of scientific problems could be (and were) explained within satisfactorily broad limits. These obstacles to the effective implementation of this goal of complementary articulation are of three sorts: (1) resistances to the process on both the psychological and sociological sides of the boundary; (2) faulty efforts to articulate, linked to unwarranted generalizations or evidences of reductionism; and (3) a tendency and temptation to convert explanatory statements into moral and ideological positions.

On the side of psychoanalysis, there has been for the most part, and with a few spectacular exceptions, an understandable and appropriate modesty against premature forays into the enormous complexity of the social order, against the seductive lure of pronouncements extrapolated carelessly from individual to social dynamic. Psychoanalysts for the most part have followed cautiously the precept, "Shoemaker, stick to your last." Yet caution can also breed a narrow parochialism. As an example, we have in mind the response of a senior and renowned analyst to a question raised for the panel of experts at the International Psychoanalytical Congress in Copenhagen in 1967. The question was, "In what directions can psychoanalysis try to cast light on the phenomenon of so many of our most privileged, most sophisticated, and best educated youth joining the 'hippie' movement, caught in the drug culture, drop outs, and protestors?" The response was that psychoanalysis would be able to study these youth only when and if they should offer themselves for analysis. In disagreement with this position, we do believe that if psychoanalysis has a fair claim to being (or becoming) a general psychology, it would indeed need to (in concert with the other behavioral sciences) have something to say about how one could begin to study and understand (i.e., to construct testable hypotheses within the psychoanalytic frame of reference concerning) this major problem, so dramatic and compelling a part of our current social scene.

But resistance is not limited to psychoanalysts alone. Many social scientists are indifferent or hostile to the incorporation of relevant psychoanalytic variables into their explanations. To choose a somewhat extreme illustration, Herbert Marcuse introduced his remarks to a symposium on violence sponsored by the San Francisco Psychoanalytic Institute in April 1969 by quoting Freud to the effect that the convinced revolutionary, committed to changing society, neither wanted nor needed psychotherapy, the effort to explore, and thereby change, the self. The reason advanced was that the revolutionary was coming to grips with social reality and *its* conflicts and contradictions, rather than with his own internal, neurotic conflicts and contradictions. From this assertion Marcuse went on to develop the theme that it is profitless to study the psychology of revolutionaries (or that of ordinary political leaders, for that matter), the "why" of political behavior, since he declared it not germane to the understanding of political institutions and their change.

The study of political change, Marcuse concluded, must be conducted solely by analyzing political, economic, and social institutions and their contradictions within their own frameworks. From our perspective, the underlying error of assumption here is in the facile equation of psychological influencing and determining causes with neurosis, as if psychic determinism automatically connotes psychopathology.

As we shall develop in our argument, we believe that moral values and political goals are to be determined not by accumulating psychological and sociological insights, but rather in their own right, as moral judgments and philosophical commitments facing people in their capacity as citizens in a political order. But we do not press this viewpoint to the unacceptable position that we cannot shed light on the understanding of political—and other social—processes by reference to the motivational wellsprings of the involved participants. In the first place, there is no reason to suppose that political action has only one determinant. The revolutionary may be simultaneously protesting against a realistically outmoded and unjust social order and struggling to come to terms with neurotic components of his own oedipal history; the defendant of an established order may be simultaneously attempting to safeguard realistically viable institutions and struggling with the pressures of his own unique oedipal configuration. Furthermore, an exploration of the psychological dynamics, especially of the key actors in a time of political moment, surely can add significant understanding to the shaping and powering of their history-making decisions. Robert Tucker, a psychologically informed political scientist, is nearing completion of a full-length biography of Stalin, conceptualized as the psychological portrait of a dictator, in which the attempt is made to relate the psychopathological character formations to those momentous actions that shaped communist and world history. While the task is monumental and calls for the greatest care in interpretation, it seems to us to be a proper kind of task, from both the psychological and sociological points of view.

What is called for here, *within* psychoanalysis, is the particularized psychoanalytic "depth" study of reality, a pursuit to which but few analysts have yet turned their attention. Psychoanalysis has characteristically been only narrowly aware of societal change via its ultimate derivative reflection in the changing character of psychoanalytic practice over time, the different character structures of those who furnish the patient population (character neuroses, borderlines, etc.), the so-called decline of the classical symptom-neuroses, the downward swing of the modal age group (more adolescents and somewhat older still-adolescents, caught without life purpose, beset by identity diffusion), etc. Analysts then say, "We're not seeing the same patients anymore." This of course is many things, including expanding psychoanalytic knowledge of character formation and deformation and concomitant increasing diagnostic sophistication and specification, so that some of Freud's early case studies of presumed hysterics might today well be reconceptualized as borderline states or psychotic characters. But also, this shift in clinical practice is one reflection in the sanctuary of the consulting room of some of the derivative fallout of the processes of change in a rapidly evolving society, seen there only, or primarily, in their impact on therapeutic work rather than in a broader social context.

Sometimes, however, scholars and laymen both show too *little* resistance to crossing the disciplinary line, and the result is a cavalier foray that oversimplifies the empirical world or, even worse, renders it unproblematic through reductionism. We have already pointed to the simplified psychological generalizations that emerged in the work of Durkheim when he argued from explanatory social fact (lack of social cohesion among Protestants) to explained social fact (their higher suicide rate), regarding the individual only as a vessel through which the social forces are processed. The same sort of oversimplification can also operate in reverse, when an investigator argues directly from psychodynamic principles to complex social processes. Erikson (1950), for example, noting the relatively egalitarian structure of the American family, has argued that certain accommodative dispositions regarding conflict and its resolution arise within such a family structure, and has argued further that political processes in the United States Congress recapitulate this familial mode of problem solving. Such a formulation may have merit, but if it is pressed without reference to the complex historical and institutional realities of American political life, it can lead to oversimplified and erroneous explanation (see Smelser, 1968a). Reductionism goes even further and denies the analytical significance of one level by treating it simply as an epiphenomenon of the "true" or "real" processes transpiring at another level. An example would be a "wild psychoanalytic" interpretation of a novel as nothing but the working out of the author's neurotic dilemmas, therefore not seeing its significance as an artistic and as a cultural product to be considered in aesthetic terms and in social context.

Finally, we should like to point to the tendency—both in the investigator and in his or her audience—to turn an apparent effort at complementary articulation to some ulterior or invidious purpose, such as defending or undermining a moral or ideological position. This is the danger of "moralizing" or "ideologizing" of explanations, particularly as they are culled from the complementary framework (since we are more capable of guarding against this within our own framework). It is the conversion of a psychoanalytic explanation into only a species of personal responsibility and therefore of moral culpability, or of a sociological explanation into an indictment of society and its institutions, with the consequent full exculpation of individuals from any personal role responsibility.

Psychoanalysis has been misunderstood and misused in just these ways. In its early years, when its emphasis was on the struggle against the forces of instinctual repression, it was feared by the Victorian "establishment" as a revolutionary and blasphemous threat to the established moral order. Currently, psychoanalysis has become vulnerable to the opposite politically inspired charge that as a science it is against social change, reactionary or status quo oriented, bent only on adjusting those within its purview to the inequities of the existing social and political order. Sometimes, such an attack is invited when the psychoanalytic perspective gets used (wittingly or not) in a skewed and one-sided manner. For example, in looking at the psychology of the revolutionary, an investigator may fail to turn a comparable spotlight either on the psychology of the establishment revolted against, or on the realities of the social and political structure. Such an emphasis may rest on the hidden and prejudicial assumption that the "causes" of the revolutionary movement lie solely in the neurotic conflicts of the revolutionaries, and that, in consequence, the revolt itself will have no adequate reality justification. Lewis Feuer, a psychoanalytically oriented philosopher (and "old leftist"), for example, has recently been taken to task by Crews (1969) for one-sided psychologizing in his hostile interpretations of the New Left in his book attempting to explain the current widespread university student rebellions. Crews stated,

> Feuer, however, detects the politics of the unconscious only in student protesters, never in their antagonists. He tells us of the New Left's "positive advocacy of promiscuity" and "positive advocacy of interracial sexuality," but says nothing about the adult prurience that makes for censorship laws, harassment of non-conforming youth, and fears of miscegenation. Indeed, the opinions of conservative adults seem altogether beyond his criticism.

Sometimes the "ideologizing" of an attempted explanation arises as much if not more in the minds of an ideologically inclined audience as it does in the intentions of the investigator. We have in mind the public controversy stirred by the United States government document *The Negro Family: The Case for National Action,* known unofficially after its principal architect as the Moynihan Report (Moynihan, 1965). In the months after its appearance it was bitterly attacked by militant black leaders and organizations as "psychologizing" the problems of American blacks and implicitly holding them "responsible" for those problems. The document attempted to assess the state of the black family in terms of various sociological indices, each with clear psychological relevance—absent husbands, illegitimacy rates, single-parent families headed by women, fertility rates, family size, unemployment rates, and so on—and addressed itself to the psychological consequences for individuals reared under such circumstances. The report concluded, not unexpectedly, that such individuals grow up with multiple psychological handicaps. Reacting to this analysis—and especially to the perhaps unfortunate phrase, "the tangled web of pathology," that was applied to the blacks' social environment—the critics assailed the document as failing to look at the oppressive racist context of past and contemporary America that directly and indirectly created such a limited, unstable, and deformed family structure. And hence the onus of responsibility has been corruptly displaced from the evil society to the victimized individuals, and one is caught up in the new psychological version of the old racist game. These accusations perhaps do touch some unwitting sources of bias, though it also appears that they go well beyond what can reasonably be read as the intention of the report. The observation that we feel important is that an attempt to diagnose a social ill from a psychoanalytic and/or sociological standpoint can easily be drawn into the arena of political conflict, with the emphasis on the psychological becoming the "conservative" and the emphasis on the social becoming the "radical" pole.

Two alternative approaches, both unacceptable in our minds, may arise from this context of ideologization. The first is the simplistic defensive counterassertion that the only factors necessary to explain—and, by implication, to be held responsible for—the blacks' condition are those implicated in the oppressiveness of a racist society. From the standpoint of understanding and explanation, it is clearly necessary to study the interaction of the whole array of factors, both external and internal to the individuals of the black community. The second approach is to deny that significant psychological trouble exists and to insist that the single-parent, matriarchal black family is only a different kind of family, and that after all there are no really conclusive empirical data that children need a present and stable father, or that they suffer in his absence in ways demonstrably different from or decisively more than those who have fathers, etc.

To summarize, we are convinced that the complementary articulation of the psychoanalytic and sociological frameworks in generating explanations for empirical problems is a necessity, and an overdue necessity, if we are to advance the bounds of predictability and control in the behavioral sciences. It is clearly impressively difficult to attain and must be pursued with due regard for the complexity of both frameworks, with due respect to the independent contribution to explaining and understanding from both analytic levels, and with every effort to protect against the witting or unwitting service of partisan goals ulterior to the scientific enterprise.

The Articulation of Psychoanalytic and Sociological Knowledge in Application to Purposive Action

To this point we have been concerned primarily with the effort to *create* scientifically reliable knowledge and with the problem of achieving a complementary articulation among disciplines in this effort. At this point we shift our perspectives to the effort to *apply* this knowledge to purposive individual or social action. An example on the psychological side would be an individual's application of insights gained in the psychotherapeutic process to his major life decisions. On the social side, an example would be the application of empirical knowledge about the optimal group conditions for human learning to the community's structuring of its educational facilities and resources. Knowledge, in short, is a resource like wealth and authority, and, other things equal, more adequate knowledge leads to more effective purposive action. In this essay we are particularly concerned with the issue of the coordinated application of knowledge generated within different conceptual frameworks to decision-making processes and toward the solutions of contemporary problems that are usually simultaneously psychological and social and economic and political and often also medical in nature. How can principles and data from many specialized disciplines be combined to form the basis for effective purposive action? Can knowledge emanating from different disciplines be combined in such a way as to more properly guide policy and, indeed, to even dictate optimal policy choices?

We here define a "problem" (in a social or psychological sense, as opposed to a scientific sense) as a state of affairs which is perceived as undesirable and which is presumed to be modifiable by appropriate purposive action. Of course the identification of a "problem" is often dependent upon the vantage point, the value position, and the partisan interests of the person doing the identifying. Psychotherapy, for example, is normally conceived of as a process of building knowledge to be applied to effecting more adequate solutions to an individual's personal problems. This view has been challenged (in some contexts) by the assertion that what may *appear* to be predominantly personal problems are often really but aspects of wider social problems. Two black psychiatrists in America, Grier and Cobbs (1968), have addressed themselves to the issue of why blacks are to a certain extent untreatable (or at least, significantly more difficult to treat) within a psychotherapeutic framework in America society. The basic reason for this, they argue, is that the structure of the society imposes repetitive experiences upon its black citizens that are conducive to pathological psychic formations and that, further, continuously reinforce the expectations that derive from the psychopathological perspective. Their argument here is not against psychotherapy per se, but is one of the insufficiency of psychotherapy not just in relation to the larger social problem (of racism in our society) but also (to a varying but significant degree) in relation to the individual psychological problems of those reared under a racist system.

But even when common agreement is achieved on the delimitation of a psychological or a social problem, a number of very important ambiguities and difficulties stand in the way of the effective application of acquired knowledge to its solution. We indicate these ambiguities and difficulties under five headings, and in an ascending order of complexity. They are increasingly complex in the sense that even if the first is solved, the other four remain; if the first two are solved, the other three remain; and so on.

1. Sometimes the "problem" is defined inappropriately as calling primarily for an application of empirical knowledge when it is really a problem calling primarily for the application of a moral or legal principle. A most salient example of this is the famous Supreme Court decision on desegregation in 1954, a decision based at least in part on considerations of the harmful psychological

effects of segregation practices on black people. We are in agreement here with the comment by Judge David Bazelon (quoted in Eisenberg, 1969) on the putative rationale for this decision:

> I would never criticize the courage or the wisdom of the Supreme Court justices who declared in 1954 that public school segregation is unconstitutional. The conclusions of social scientists that separate facilities, however "equal" in tangible factors, engender feelings of inferiority in Negroes were relevant to that decision. But by relying so heavily on these findings, the Court may have misstated the true basis for *Brown vs. Board of Education* and in so doing may have misled the public. In 1896 the court had approved the "separate but equal" doctrine. While the country might then have lacked the sophisticated studies available in 1954, any honest person would have conceded at the time of *Plessy vs. Ferguson* that segregation undoubtedly would have made Negroes feel inferior. The assumption of inferiority was the rationale for the practice; no black man could help but perceive that separate train cars and separate schools kept him in his place.
>
> Since we already know what Kenneth Clark and others told us, the public could justly ask of the Supreme Court in 1954, why the law had changed. The answer of course, was that our values had changed. *Plessy vs. Ferguson* was discarded not because social scientists told us that segregation contributed to feelings of inferiority, but because by 1954 enough people in this country believed what they did not in 1896—that to thus insult and emasculate black people was wrong, and intolerable, and therefore, a denial of the equal protection of the law to blacks.

The point is well taken. It is not that knowledge in the behavioral sciences has advanced sufficiently to have now become an adequate basis for new public policy—though it may be in part that public willingness to accept such knowledge as sufficiently established and sufficiently agreed upon to serve as an appropriate basis for action has changed. But an even more important change is that our consensus on moral values has changed, and that we are now able to take a new moral and legal stand, and to buttress it with the empirical knowledge of the psychological impact and consequences of segregation that had been available in reasonably reliable form all along.

We would, indeed, go even further than Judge Bazelon. It was not so much even the change in values that was decisive. After all, our espoused democratic and egalitarian values are as old as American society itself. It was more the change in power distribution among racial and ethnic groups throughout the society. As blacks have become more powerful politically—with the mass migration from the South, with the widening franchise, etc.—a public shift in practiced attitudes and behaviors has been forced, and American society has had to begin to close the gap between its professed egalitarian ideology and its actual grossly deficient performance.

This is not to say that knowledge is not relevant to these sorts of public policy decisions. Surely it is valuable to know on adequate scientific grounds that "separate but equal" facilities appear to exact social and psychological costs more than they render presumed benefits. It is, however, also valuable to know that integrated educational facilities also exact their social and psychological costs, at least in the short run. For example, Bronfenbrenner (1967) has collated a number of studies that indicate that the integrated school setting exaggerates the handicaps of disadvantaged black children, handicaps bred by prenatal and perinatal damage, father absence, impoverished home environments, and fluctuating repressive and indulgent patterns of child-rearing. He avers further that the integrated school setting also creates problems for white children, who are exposed to much disorganized and antisocial behavior. In the last analysis, however, *neither* type of knowledge can serve as the proper basis for the decision as to whether or not to integrate the schools. Basically, the decision to integrate is founded on the conviction that it is morally reprehensible to deprive any segment of the benefits of society because of imputed (racial) characteristics. What the behavioral sciences can contribute is knowledge of the likely costs and consequences (social and psychological) of integrating rapidly, of integrating slowly, and of not integrating at all.

2. Even if the proper role of knowledge—to assess the probable costs and benefits that may result from purposive social actions—is appreciated, the issue of the adequacy of the existing knowledge still remains. We need not belabor this point beyond a simple statement. Even though considerable research on the psychological and social costs and benefits of racial segregation and integration has been carried out, we are far from possessing conclusive knowledge on the subject. On the side of psychoanalysis, even though decades of treatment and investigation are available, we are still properly dissatisfied with the adequacy of the efforts to apply knowledge of intrapsychic configurations to the understanding of manifest behaviors by way of the psychoanalytic method.

3. A third difficulty confronting the definitive application of knowledge to purposive action—even assuming that knowledge were perfectly adequate—lies in the fact that any purposive action has both costs *and* benefits, and that these cannot be weighed against one another in any simple fashion, even where the problem and the proposed solution are both encompassed within one particulate frame of reference. Take a commonplace example: a public policy decision to clear slums by means of urban renewal and public housing. In order to preserve such public housing for its intended beneficiaries (the displaced slum-dwellers) policymakers have often built in income restrictions, limiting the housing to families below certain stipulated income levels. One consequence of these restrictions has been to force out of the public housing just those families who, by dint of effort, fortune, or appropriate personality dispositions, are in a position to better themselves (and their neighborhood) economically and socially. The effect of this enforced displacement of just these families is to facilitate the creation of a new slum—within the public housing—in the place of the old. And, ironically, migration by the more fortunate or well-off families from the impoverished areas which is volitional and therefore only partial prior to public housing, becomes mandatory and therefore complete after the advent of the public housing. Yet to remove the income restrictions would exact still another type of cost—the subsidization of relatively well-to-do families in low-cost housing with concomitant exclusion of poorer families. There is no simple synthesis of these competing social costs and benefits.

A correspondingly commonplace example from psychoanalytic therapy arises when parents seek psychotherapeutic help for disturbed adolescent youngsters suffering from a variety of symptoms, destructive acting-out behaviors, school failures, and/or severely damaged relationships within the family. Most therapists are aware of the need to be wary of the often unvoiced divergence between the therapeutic goals held by the youngster and those set by his or her family. The parents, who are underwriting the treatment, are often seeking a restoration of the *status quo ante*—the return of their child to the relationship they felt they enjoyed prior to the onset of the pathological behaviors in adolescence. The youngster, who often conceptualizes the difficulties in terms of a struggle for growth and autonomy against restrictive and unsympathetic parents, seeks not restoration but achievement of full independence, experienced from within and acknowledged from without. To focus exclusively on either set of goals precludes a balanced perspective on the whole field of forces and increases the possibility of surprise by unanticipated consequences, like the disruption of the treatment either by the patient or by his or her parents. Yet to strive to balance the two sets of goals is also likely to exact costs—in the form of frustrations—on the part of both patient and parents. Again, no simple or automatic synthesis is available.

4. The issue of conflicting costs and benefits is further complicated by the fact that most purposive social actions ramify on various levels conceptualized within disparate frameworks; they have political and social and psychological as well as other consequences. To weigh these multiple consequences on multiple levels poses even greater difficulties. Let us return to the problem of suicide and its reduction to illustrate the point. One feasible line of policy to reduce the incidence of suicide would be to attack intensively the social conditions of certain high-risk groups, such as the elderly, with the aim of reducing feelings of isolation, desertion, and despair. Suppose a community, with the purpose of reducing suicide rates, then embarked on an ambitious program of establishing Senior Citizen Clubs, as social centers, and making individual helping agencies, such as Suicide Prevention Centers, available to them.

Two sets of questions arise in connection with this kind of social policy. The first concerns the overall effectiveness of these means as an attack on the problem of suicide. Would such a Suicide Prevention Center be catering to a class of persons who would anyway seek help through the already established social welfare, religious, counseling, and psychotherapeutic channels? Would it indeed make any significant difference in the overall incidence of suicide attempts and of successful suicides—or would those same patients have sought out help roughly to the same extent through those other already available helping resources even though they are not specifically designated as targeted on the suicide prevention problem? Contrariwise, could the same money make more overall impact on the degree of emotional turmoil and personal misery (and ultimate degradation and death) if employed in helping and rehabilitative efforts with the youthful drug abuser, the delinquent and the derelict, the chronic alcoholic and the addicted, all caught up in mental disorders that are just as self-destructive, just as "suicidal," albeit chronically rather than acutely? (And can the psychoanalytic perspective that illuminates this *same* self-destructive and suicidal consequence—and underlying motivation—in these disparate populations thus add useful guidance to the formulation of public policy in regard to the wide social problem of disability and death from inwardly turned aggressive and punitive impulses?)

The second set of questions concerns the various programs' side effects, above and beyond the intended impact on the incidence of suicide. To integrate the elderly into more meaningful social communities might perhaps decrease the incidence of suicide, but it might equally well facilitate the formation of conservative political pressure groups among the elderly, pressure groups which are traditionally antipathetic to education programs that call for the passing of school bonds, to community health programs such as fluoridation of drinking water, etc.—to programs, that is, that represent the implementation of other social goals, usually considered to be also very worthy by the very planners who are sponsoring the suicide-control effort. Should this specific suicide-control effort then go forward, even though it is reasonable to expect that it may have as an indirect consequence the possible subversion of other desirable programs? Knowledge of the diversity of consequences of any given program plan is useful in setting public priorities, but the knowledge alone cannot yield the basis for preferring one set of consequences over another.

Such considerations underscore the desirability of an interdisciplinary intelligence for policymakers—bringing a variety of kinds of expertise to bear on public policy questions. We argue for this because an expert in one behavioral science is understandably more knowledgeable in his or her own speciality and will most probably give advice skewed to but a limited range of the possible policy consequences, intended and unintended, desired and undesired. But society's problems, as they develop in concrete situations, do not fit into our academic categories. Our brief illustration in the case of suicide prevention uncovered psychological, social, economic, and political consequences of such a community planning program. Clearly reliable knowledge from many perspectives is more useful to the decision maker than from but a few. Yet public planning and policymaking often operate within a too sharply limited range of considerations. In a series of lectures delivered at the Yale Law School, Anna Freud made the point that lawmakers concerned with family law, with the consequences of marriage and divorce, and with the care of dependent or deprived children, focus almost exclusively upon the proper safeguarding of the legal and financial rights of the involved children. Accordingly, they tend to dictate caretaking and custodial arrangements that make for the maximal husbanding of the child's financial supporting resources. This consideration, however, may be quite at variance with the goal of securing the optimal emotional nurturance from the best available parental surrogates. This latter concern, so central from the psychoanalytic perspective, is characteristically ignored in the public legal process.

5. The greatest difficulties in applying empirical knowledge to purposive action—whether individual or social—arise when there is lack of consensus on what constitutes a cost or a benefit. At this point we reach the question of value differences, which extend beyond differences over policies, strategies, and tactics in applying knowledge.

With regard to some social issues, the problem of value differences usually does not arise, because there is widespread acceptance of the social values in question. Suicide is a good example. In Western civilization there has been no serious question, except in certain extreme, deviant, or bizarre circumstances, that the reduction of the incidence of suicide is an accepted and desired individual and social goal. (If we move outside the West, however, we find some instances of a positive valuation of suicide under particular circumstances. In Japan, for example, suicide has been regarded as a dignifying personal action [hari-kari] and as a symbol of patriotic honor [kamikaze].) When the goal is widely accepted, moreover, the deployment of scientific knowledge for purposive action is seldom thought to be "manipulative" in the invidious sense. Surely the attempt to reduce the incidence of suicide by directly or indirectly influencing the lives of potential victims is an example of manipulation, yet it is not an object of public suspicion because the worthwhileness of the goal is itself unquestioned. It is only when the goals or values are not agreed upon that the specter of a malevolent "manipulation" may be invoked.

Historically, psychoanalysis has attempted to circumscribe this play of values. The cultivation of particular moral values has been regarded as outside the proper bounds of its therapeutic task. Its avowed goal has been only to help the mentally ill achieve the closest possible approximation to a state of ideal (idealized) mental health. As Wallerstein (1963) has delineated at length elsewhere, this task nonetheless involves the analyst, however unwillingly, in value considerations. As pointed out there, even the most ambitious attempts to search out purely empirical indicators for the psychological state of mental health—like that of Jahoda (1958)—could not succeed in taking these criteria of positive mental health out of the field of moral philosophy. Though she postponed it by design to the latter part of her monograph, Jahoda had to finally confront the value issue in mental health assessment. She then attested to it as follows:

> The discussion of the psychological meaning of various criteria could proceed without concern for value premises. Only as one calls these psychological phenomena "mental health" does the problem of values arise in full force. By this label, one asserts that these psychological attributes are "good." And, inevitably, the question is raised: Good for what? Good in terms of middle class ethics? Good for democracy? For the continuation of the social status quo? For the individual's happiness? For mankind? For survival? For the development of the species? For art and creativity? For the encouragement of genius or of mediocrity and conformity? The list could be continued.

Very similar considerations led Hartmann (1939), too, specifically to acknowledge that mental health is, "in part, a very individual matter," and that "the commonly used criteria of health are obviously coloured by *Weltanschauung*, by 'health morality,' by social and political goals"—in short, by values. In a subsequent publication (1960), dealing with the relation of psychoanalysis as a science to the problems of morality and of moral values in general, Hartmann did attempt to distinguish general moral values from specific mental health values.

> It is obvious [he argued] that there are many neurotics who are "highly moral" and many, sometimes the same ones, who are socially useful while there are many "healthy" people who are neither the one nor the other.

He then argued that the proper role of the psychoanalyst was to "concentrate on the realization of the one category of values only: health values. . . ." And while acknowledging that health is a value, Hartmann did not, however, "discuss . . . its position in the hierarchy of values."

The history of sociology has not been correspondingly marked by any like effort to define one set of social goals as central, and then to limit the acquisition and interpretation of knowledge within the constraints created by this set of goals. Some sociologists envisage the goal of social harmony or social equilibrium as the most important; others envisage the goal of generating needed social change through creative conflict as more salient; some accept goals of maximizing personal freedom; while still others stress the goals of maximizing social conformity. As a result, many sociological controversies revolve around the social values advocated by or attributed to various schools of sociological thought, rather than around the appropriate means to realize commonly agreed upon goals. One of the interesting contrasts between sociology and psychoanalysis is that controversies in the former are more likely to revolve around just such questions of proper values and goals, whereas controversies in the latter tend to swirl more around matters of technical implementation, the values and goals of health being taken as given. To the extent that psychoanalysts have disagreements about the moral meanings and dimensions of health, however, value conflicts also enter into their controversies, and this contrast between the two disciplines tends to blur.

The problem of applying knowledge to a social problem becomes, then, most complicated when there is wide disagreement about the goals or values in question. We noted that except for certain extreme, deviant, or bizarre circumstances, the goal of reducing the incidence of suicide would be generally unquestioned in our society. Consider, however, another illustrative case: the hippie phenomenon and the hippie values. We would expect a great disagreement in society as to whether this movement constitutes a desirable or an undesirable presence. Those who look favorably upon the movement might hesitate to refer to it as a "problem" at all. They might argue that, sociologically speaking, the alienated hippie youth are among society's most vital and penetrating social critics, that they are communicating important messages to our established social order, and that only they as a group have generated the courage to do so. On the psychological side, the protagonists would argue that the hippie way of life is a viable alternative psychological style, that the movement has served its member by providing for a release of otherwise intolerable tensions and a basis for structuring and channeling otherwise devastatingly destructive projections. Those who disapprove of the movement might conversely argue that the social protest fails in its essential purpose because it does not offer a viable general social alternative for organizing behavior and operating a complex social and technological order; and that its individual psychological surcease is temporary and illusory, purchased at the cost of a psychological disorganizing process that makes them, the hippies, as a tragic generation, their own chief victims who, in saying the important things that they are saying to us, are paying the price of their own destruction as effectively functioning individuals and members of society.

What is then the proper contribution of psychoanalysis and sociology, both singly and together, to the understanding of controversial movements of this sort, and to the pursuit of effective purposive action in relation to them? Surely the disciplines can elucidate the factual claims made about the effects of such phenomena, and can then assess, as precisely as possible, the costs and the benefits of the phenomena at the individual and social levels. Such knowledge would also be helpful in knowing whether to diagnose the movement as a "problem"—that is, whether its psychological and social costs are significantly greater than its benefits. Yet, as we have argued, the assignment of priorities by which to rank the various costs and benefits—and the decision on what values should underlie these priorities—lies not in the realm of the scientific disciplines but in the moral and political life of the organized community.

Psychoanalysis, Sociology, and Values

We have come then to the limiting conclusion that the moral correctness of a value position can not be derived from the substance of psychoanalysis, of sociology, of the two together, or of the two combined with other existing organization of empirical knowledge. In some measure this is a saddening conclusion. We are, after all, dedicated to the generation and dissemination of scientific knowledge, and we believe such knowledge to be a profoundly important resource for human civilization. We also would wish to believe that from knowledge we should be able to derive guidelines for the proper moral conduct of life. But the reflections and arguments we have adumbrated in this essay convince us that knowledge organized within the framework of a scientific discipline cannot be the basis for the ordering of moral preferences. It is not possible to derive the values of mental health from the data, the concepts, and the theories of psychoanalysis, even though mental health and psychoanalysis have been inextricably linked throughout their history. The value of mental health is an assumed value, within the constraints of which knowledge and derived techniques are organized.

Nor is it possible to derive the value of social harmony, or of democracy as a political system, from the combined insights of sociology and the other social sciences. Nor is it even possible to derive the evil of abhorrent political systems like totalitarian fascism from organized empirical knowledge, for our abhorrence of them rests on our values regarding life, death, and human dignity rather than any scientific insights about the nature of individual and social functioning. Our value preferences must arise from all the exigencies that occur in our struggle to exist together as communities of human beings, rather than from our attempts to understand the basis on which we do so.

We have not covered, however, one special relationship between empirical knowledge and values, and we should like to conclude this discussion by doing so. A major feature shared by psychoanalysis and sociology is that each involves the study of the goals that people pursue in life, and the values that underlie these goals. In particular, both fields have a long history of uncovering goals and values that people are generally *unaware* that they are pursuing. One of the central organizing tenets of psychoanalytic theory is the concept of the unconscious, which, by definition, is constituted of repressed and unknown materials which, nonetheless, form the most imperative motivational wellsprings of human behavior. Sociology does not have a single construct that plays a corresponding central organizing role, but it does have a long succession of scholars who have pointed to the unintended and unanticipated consequences of social actions. A classic example is Karl Marx's famous diagnosis of religion as "the opiate of the masses." The intended consequence of religious beliefs and organizations in this case would be the preparation of the individual for the afterlife through assuring his or her proper conduct in this world. Marx, however, argued that a more fundamental consequence was to buttress the social class arrangements of society by providing the subordinated class with convenient and acceptable rationalizations for its material deprivations, thus rendering it more docile politically. Merton (1968) has formalized this kind of insight in sociology in his distinction between the manifest and the latent functions of social actions, which corresponds very closely to Freud's distinction between the conscious and the unconscious components in the functioning of the human mind.

One aspect of this process of bringing to light knowledge of unconscious or latent springs of individual and social behavior is that such knowledge often acts as an irritant to those who are made to become aware of it. (Let us ignore for the moment those cases of irritation that arise because the knowledge is incorrect or otherwise inadequate.) A major reason for the experienced irritation is that in both cases some fundamental motive or purpose is served by keeping the functions and consequences of the action from consciousness, and this motive is usually in the realm of morals and values. Within the individual personality functioning, the motives for repression are moral in the larger sense, arising from situations of realistic dangers and threatening interactions, or from situations in which the individual's internalized moral sense (superego) is offended. At the social level, the latent functions are similarly unremarked because to focus on them would be to expose aspects of social behavior that are not in keeping with some established and institutionalized value patterns. Both psychoanalysis and sociology are moral sciences, then, in that both take as major objects for study those aspects of individual and social life that are not generally acknowledged openly because to do so would be morally repugnant in some significant sense.

And just because they are irritating in this way, the findings and the theories of psychoanalysis and sociology alike continually generate pressures to redefine moral stances, and perhaps to alter them in fundamental ways. The process of psychoanalytic therapy is aimed at uncovering meanings of behavior that have long been concealed from the individual, and practicing psychoanalysts are aware of the reverberations and pressures to change behaviors that arise in patients as they achieve psychoanalytic insights. In this sense, psychoanalysis is a science of change. Individual treatment, is, of course, dedicated to, and when successful, results in, individual change—including possibly in moral perspectives. But on a larger scale of social consequence, it is the very dissemination of psychoanalytic knowledge throughout the culture, for example the knowledge that sexual repressions play a cardinal role in the genesis of neurotic illness, that has helped bring about significant change in avowed moral positions, the change in sexual mores from Victorian times to our own. It may be less apparent that sociology is in a comparable position in affecting and changing society and its espoused values through the dissemination of its empirical findings. Sociologists, however, are well aware of the touchiness and even the explosiveness of findings and theories that uncover the rationalizations of a ruling regime, a vested interest group, or an idealistic social movement. And, as with psychoanalysis, the broad dissemination of social science findings, for example in regard to race, culture, and human differences, has played a significant part in the current shift in public attitudes and behaviors toward minority group members. Yet neither psychoanalysis nor sociology, in uncovering such irritating, pressing knowledge, is in a position of being able to say exactly what should be done with the knowledge in a moral sense. To claim that would be to revert to the untenable position that one can, in some direct sense, derive moral choices from the generation of knowledge. We have argued that both psychoanalytic and sociological knowledge do have an enormous impact on morality. Yet the responsibility of what moral response to make to this acquired knowledge is, in the end, a moral and not an intellectual one, and calls upon the individual and the society to mobilize the fullest possible resources of character in fashioning a moral stance.

Concluding Note

In this essay we have taken the conceptual framework of a specialized academic discipline (psychoanalysis, sociology) as our starting point, and our considerations have been subsumed under the component parts of the single master question: How does any such framework generate knowledge? We have attempted to respond to this question in four separate and sequential steps: (1) How is knowledge generated within the framework? (2) How is knowledge that is generated within the framework articulated with knowledge generated in other frameworks? (3) How is the combined knowledge, thus generated, related to the knowledge of the correctness of purposive actions? (4) And how is the combined knowledge, thus generated, related to the knowledge of the rightness of moral values? In brief summary, our responses are as follows.

1. Knowledge is generated within a framework by imposing a number of arbitrary and constricting assumptions about the aspects of the empirical world beyond the circumscribed aspect selected for study. Knowledge generated within such a framework can thus be quite definite and certain, because it entails a delimited number of relationships among variables. It is likely, however, to be unrealistic to varying degrees, since it is generated within the context of limiting assumptions, marking off as "givens" or stable parameters the subject matter or the variables set by the frameworks of the other disciplines of the behavior of man.

2. A more realistic and more comprehensive knowledge is generated *between* frameworks by a process that we have described as complementary articulation—i.e., the systematic relaxation of the fixed and constraining assumptions of a framework, and the systematic refinement of those assumptions through infusion of the findings and theories of neighboring frameworks. In many respects such knowledge is more realistic than the first kind, derived from within but one framework, since it is able to account for a larger amount of the overall variation of empirical phenomena than any single framework taken by itself. On the other hand, the difficulties and ambiguities involved in achieving complementary articulations are so great that the behavioral sciences have to this point produced but few successful attempts.
3. Knowledge generated within and between specialized frameworks can inform purposive individual or social action in that it can provide information about the multiple costs and benefits, at differing and interacting levels, of the proposed action. Yet the relative importance (value) of the different costs and benefits cannot be derived from the specialized knowledge, nor can the criteria by which this relative importance is established.
4. Knowledge generated within and between the specialized frameworks of psychoanalysis and sociology does nonetheless have an impact on moral values, because this knowledge intimately concerns the study of morals and the roots of moral judgments and moral behaviors. It often uncovers hidden understandings of behavior, understandings that are often morally disavowed, and when revealed, felt to be morally at fault. Yet while thus generating pressure to redefine and change moral values, empirical knowledge still does not provide a derivative framework for deciding the ultimate moral uses of this knowledge.

And last: all of the above is but a programmatic mapping out of a terrain that we feel to be essential to technical and theoretical advance in our share of the sciences of behavior. The actual realization of complementary articulation in clinical and social practice and research is the task that still lies ahead. We trust to address ourselves to it in our own endeavors.

References

Abraham, K.

1924 "A Short Study of the Development of the Libido, Viewed in the Light of Mental Disorders." In *Selected Papers on Psychoanalysis.* London: Hogarth Press. Pp. 418–501.

Adler, N.

1968 "The Antinomian Personality: The Hippie Character Type." *Psychiatry,* Vol. 31, pp. 325–38.

Adorno, T. W., E. Frenkel-Brunswick, D. J. Levinson, and R. N. Sanford

1950 *The Authoritarian Personality.* New York: Harper.

Bronfenbrenner, U.

1967 "The Psychological Costs of Quality and Equality in Education." *Child Development,* Vol. 38, pp. 909–26.

Crews, F.

1969 "The Radical Students." *New York Review of Books,* Vol. 12, No. 8, pp. 29–34.

Durkheim, É.

1951 [1897] *Suicide.* Translated by John A. Spaulding and George Simpson. New York: The Free Press of Glencoe.

Eisenberg, L.

1969. "Judge David Bazelon." *American Journal of Orthopsychiatry,* Vol. 39, pp. 372–76.

Erikson, E.

1950 *Childhood and Society.* New York: Norton.

1959 "The Problem of Ego Identity." In *Identity and the Life Cycle.* New York: International Universities Press. Pp. 100–166.

Freud, S.

1957 [1917] "Mourning and Melancholia." In *Standard Edition of the Complete Psychological Works of Sigmund Freud,* Vol. 14, edited by James Strachey. London: Hogarth Press. Pp. 243–58.

1961 [1923] "The Ego and the Id." In *Standard Edition of the Complete Psychological Works of Sigmund Freud,* Vol. 19, edited by James Strachey. London: Hogarth Press. Pp. 13–66.

1961 [1924] "The Economic Problem of Masochism." In *Standard Edition of the Complete Psychological Works of Sigmund Freud,* Vol. 19, edited by James Strachey. London: Hogarth Press. Pp. 159–70.

1961 [1930] "Civilization and Its Discontents." *In Standard Edition of the Complete Psychological Works of Sigmund Freud,* Vol. 21, edited by James Strachey. London: Hogarth Press. Pp. 64–145.

Fromm, E.

1949 [1944] "Individual and Social Origins of Neurosis." In *Personality in Nature, Society, and Culture,* edited by C. Kluckhohn and H. H. Murray. New York: Knopf. Pp. 407–13.

Grier, W. H., and P. M. Cobbs

1968 *Black Rage.* New York: Basic Books.

Hartmann, H.
1939 *Ego Psychology and the Problem of Adaptation.* New York: International Universities Press.
1960 *Psychoanalysis and Moral Values.* New York: International Universities Press.

Jahoda, M.
1958 *Current Concepts of Positive Mental Health.* New York: Basic Books.

Malinowski, B.
1931 "Culture." In *Encyclopedia of the Social Sciences,* Vol. 4. New York: Macmillan. Pp. 621–45.

Marx, K.
1954 [1848] *The Communist Manifesto.* Chicago: Henry Regnery.

Merton, R. K
1968 *Social Theory and Social Structure.* New York: The Free Press of Glencoe.

Moynihan, D. P.
1965 *The Negro Family: The Case for National Action.* Washington, D.C.: Office of Policy Planning and Research, United States Department of Labor.

Smelser, N. J.
1967 "Sociology and the Other Social Sciences." In *The Uses of Sociology,* edited by P. F. Lazarsfeld, W. H. Sewell, and J. L. Wilensky. New York: Basic Books. Pp. 3–44.
1968a "Personality and the Explanation of Political Phenomena at the Social-System Level: A Methodological Statement." *Journal of Social Issues,* Vol. 24, pp. 111–25.
1968b "Social and Psychological Dimensions of Collective Behavior." In *Essays in Sociological Explanation.* Englewood Cliffs, NJ: Prentice-Hall. Pp. 92–121.

Wallerstein, R. S.
1963 "The Problem of the Assessment of Change in Psychotherapy." *International Journal of Psycho-Analysis,* Vol. 44, pp. 31–41.
1964 "The Role of Prediction in Theory Building in Psychoanalysis." *Journal of the American Psychoanalytic Association,* Vol. 12, pp. 675–91.

2

Social and Psychological Dimensions of Collective Behavior

The subject of this essay is that class of social phenomena commonly grouped under the label "collective behavior"—including panics, crazes, fads, riots, reform movements, revolutionary movements, and religious cults. My starting point is the commonplace observation that such behavior manifests both social and psychological characteristics. On the one hand, it has a social dimension, since it involves collective or group action by definition, and since many of its causes are rooted in social conditions—conditions such as economic hardship, social disorganization, and political repression. On the other hand, it has a psychological dimension, since the deepest and most powerful human emotions—idealistic fervor, love, and violent rage, for example—are bared in episodes of collective behavior and since persons differ psychologically in their propensity to become involved in such episodes.

Moreover, most theories that attempt to explain why people participate in collective outbursts and collective movements stress either the social or the psychological aspect more or less exclusively, frequently relegating the other, underemphasized aspect to the realm of implicit assumptions. For example, Karl Marx regarded political revolutions as resulting primarily from a particular convergence of economic and social forces at a given stage in the evolution of a society; accordingly, the revolutionaries' psychology was not very important for Marx, since it, like the revolution itself, is a product of overwhelming laws of social development. By contrast, Wilfred Trotter (1922) traced human involvement

This essay was originally published in Neil J. Smelser, *Essays in Sociological Explanation* (Englewood Cliffs, NJ: Prentice-Hall, 1969), pp. 92–121. Reprinted by permission of Prentice-Hall, Inc., Upper Saddle River, NJ.

in crowds and related groupings to the workings of powerful, universal instincts; he touched only incidentally on social determinants of this involvement. Very few if any theorists, however, have attempted to develop an explanatory account that synthesizes the social and psychological causes of collective behavior. In this essay I shall explore the possibility of such a synthesis, emphasizing the psychoanalytic approach on the psychological side.

I shall proceed by the following steps. First, I shall specify the differences between explanations on the social level and explanations on the psychological level. Second, I shall present an example of each type of explanation and attempt to locate the distinctive shortcomings of each. As an instance of explicitly sociological explanation, I shall outline the results of my own research on collective behavior (Smelser, 1962). As an instance of an explicitly psychological explanation, I shall review Freud's essay on group psychology (Freud, 1955 [1922]). Third, I shall specify some of the theoretical and empirical problems that arise when attempting to synthesize these two approaches. Finally, as a more specific illustration, I shall outline the general characteristics of protest movements—first in terms of their typical social aims, then in terms of their probably psychoanalytic significance—and illustrate how social and psychological determinants may interact to give rise to and sustain such movements.

The Psychological and Social Levels of Analysis

The study of psychological systems focuses on individuals as the units of analysis, regarding them as systems of drives, affects, skills, defenses, and so on. In this case the organizing conceptual unit is the person. The study of social systems focuses on certain relations that emerge when two or more persons interact with one another. In this case the organizing conceptual unit is the relation itself.

Ultimately the study of both psychological and social systems is based on inferences from a common body of behavioral data. The investigator of human affairs is confronted with a complex variety of phenomena: verbal and nonverbal communications, expressive movements, physiological states, and interactions of various sorts. To organize these at the *psychological* level, he or she infers or posits that more or less repeated patterns of behavior—e.g., restlessness, searching, eating, quiescence—can be characterized as signifying a "need" or "drive" for the person. It is convenient to use such terms to describe the person's activities, because they organize many discrete items of behavior under one construct. In addition, the investigator may generate constructs about "attitudes," "defense mechanisms," and so on. To facilitate analysis further, he or she may posit certain relations among such constructs, and the result is a "psychological system." Thereafter, any behavioral datum in terms of this system of constructs is significant at the "psychological level."

Similarly, to make sense of behavior at the *social* level, the investigator infers that certain more or less repeated events—performances, interactions, expressions of sentiments, attempts of one person to influence another—can be characterized as signifying a "role." Depending on the environmental context, roles may be subdivided as political, economic, religious, familial, and so on. A general term such as role simplifies the process of describing thousands of discrete events separately. Constructs such as "norm," "sanction," and "clique" may also be developed. Then, when several of these constructs are set in logical relation with one another, the result is a "social system." Thereafter, any datum interpreted in terms of this system of constructs is significant at the "social level."

Any given behavioral datum is inherently neither "psychological" nor "social"; indeed, the same event may be both depending on the body of constructs within which it is interpreted. An outburst of anger on the job, for instance, may be "psychological" in the sense that it gives rise to recriminations of conscience and subsequent adaptations to these recriminations by the individual. The same outburst may also be "social" in the sense that it strains the social relations among employees in the office where it occurs. The status of a behavioral datum, then, is determined by the conceptual system to which it is referred for assessment and explanation.

Conceptually, these frames of reference—the psychological and the social—should be kept distinct. A description of a social system cannot be reduced to the psychological status of persons in that system: a social system must be described in terms of roles, norms, subgroups, and so on. Similarly, a description of a personality system cannot be reduced to the social involvements of the person: it must be described in terms of distinctive psychological units. Empirically, however, these two frames of reference articulate in many ways. A social role may integrate many of an individual's drives, skills, attitudes, and defenses; an individual's motivational predispositions determine in large part whether a system of roles (e.g., a network of friendship) will persist or not; a social role (that of a parent) may be internalized to become part of a child's personality.

In seeking to explain any given type of behavior, both the psychological and social levels of analysis can be used as either dependent or independent variables. A dependent variable, defined briefly, is an identifiable empirical phenomenon or class of phenomena, variations in which we wish to explain. Suppose we wish to explain variations in the incidence of suicide. This behavior may be described either in terms of its psychological motives within the individual victims (Menninger, 1938) or in terms of its aggregated rates among different social groupings—for example, Protestants as compared with Catholics, young persons as compared with old persons—without reference to any personal meaning of suicide (Durkheim, 1951 [1897]). Because these illustrative descriptions of suicide are pitched at two different conceptual levels, it is apparent that the explanatory problems facing the investigator in each case are somewhat different.

Whether suicide as a dependent variable is described at the psychological or social level, however, the independent variables by means of which we try to account for this behavior lie at both the social and psychological levels. Suppose suicide is defined in terms of its psychological significance, for example, as the turning of anger upon an object that has been internalized through a process or narcissistic identification (Freud, 1957 [1917]). In seeking explanations for suicide, thus defined, it is appropriate to inquire into what kind of family constellations (a social factor) give rise to this particular complex of self-destructive tendencies. Or suppose suicide is described in terms of its differential incidence between blacks and whites; in seeking explanations for this social fact, it is appropriate to inquire into the differential distribution of personality traits (for example, intropunitiveness) between the two groups that might account for the different rates. More complicated explanations call for some combination of social and psychological factors (see Henry and Short, 1954; Hendin, 1964). In accounting for the high suicide rates among members of certain Protestant denominations, for example, it might be discovered that the ascetic values of these denominations encourage socialization of children mainly by means of withdrawing love; this in turn would encourage the development of especially repressive superego structures, which would increase the propensity of individuals in this religious group to turn aggression inward. From these observations it becomes apparent that a full explanatory account of any type of behavior must include a systematic combination and formulation of the principles of interaction between both social and psychological determinants.

Applying the two distinctions I have developed—psychological and social levels, and dependent and independent variables—to the subject of collective behavior, we may conclude the following: In describing the phenomena to be explained, it is possible to focus *either* on the psychological significance of, say, riots and reform movements, for the participants; *or* on the differential incidence of these kinds of episodes in various sectors of the social structure. No matter at which level we choose to define the phenomena, it is apparent that a full explanatory account of this behavior will involve a synthesis of *both* social and psychological determinants.

Social Factors in Collective Behavior: An Example

In my own research on collective behavior, I relied on a primarily social definition. Collective behavior is defined as purposive, socially oriented activity by which people attempt to reconstitute their sociocultural environment. Furthermore, people involved in episodes of collective behavior are trying to reconstitute this environment on the basis of a certain type of belief, which I call a generalized belief; in this kind of belief the environment is portrayed in terms of omnipotent forces, conspiracies, and extravagant promises, all of which are immanent. Uninstitutionalized action taken in the name of such a belief constitutes an episode of collective behavior. Even though generalized beliefs are involved, I focused on the social diffusion of these beliefs rather than their psychological significance for the participants. I assumed that no special motive or mentality (such as psychological regression) necessarily characterizes the participants in episodes of collective behavior (Smelser, 1962, chaps. 1, 4, and 5).

Furthermore, the explanatory problem I set for myself was at the social level. I was interested primarily in why various types of collective behavior cluster in time and in certain parts of the social structure—for example, among adolescents, recent migrants, and unemployed people. This general question breaks down into several more specific issues: What distinctive conditions give rise to generalized beliefs? Under what conditions are generalized beliefs translated into collective action? Once collective episodes appear, what conditions govern their spread, duration, and intensity? These questions take the collective episode itself as the primary object of analysis. This focus differs from that of other approaches, which take the behaviors of the individual participant (and his or her psychological state) as the primary phenomena to be explained.

In attempting to generate answers to these questions, I remained mainly at the social level in identifying determinants. Even at this level, a great array of determinants bears on the occurrence of episodes of collective behavior. An intellectual apparatus is required to sort out and arrange these determinants, if one is to advance beyond eclectic identification of determinants from one case to another. The intellectual apparatus I chose to employ is the "value-added" approach. Applying this approach to the social determination of collective behavior provides a way of ordering its determinants on a scale from general to specific. Each determinant is seen as operating within the scope established by the prior, more general determinant. Each determinant is viewed as a necessary but not a sufficient condition for the occurrence of an episode of collective behavior; taken together, the necessary conditions constitute the sufficient condition for its occurrence. Let me illustrate the several determinants of the value-added scheme with reference to the occurrence of financial panic.

The first necessary condition for the occurrence of panic is *structural conduciveness*. An example of structural conduciveness is the ability of actors to dispose of their resources rapidly at will. If property is closely tied to kinship and can be disposed of only on the death of the father, panic is ruled out as structurally impossible; the property is locked into the social structure and cannot be moved unless the institutional framework is altered. If, on the other hand, free and rapid disposal is permitted—as it is in the stock exchange—panic becomes possible. The word "possible" must be stressed; structural conduciveness alone does not cause panics; it merely establishes a range of situations within which panic can occur and rules out other situations in which it cannot. As a determinant, therefore, structural conduciveness is not very specific.

The second determinant is some kind of *strain*. The most obvious kind of strain in the determination of financial panic is the threat of financial loss. The threat of financial loss alone, however, can give rise to many other kinds of behavior than panic (scapegoating, reform movements, etc.); consequently, this strain must be seen as operating within the context of conduciveness. It is now possible to see the logic by which the several determinants are organized: each time a new determinant is introduced, it is seen as operating within the scope of the previous determinant, and an increasingly great number of alternative behaviors are ruled out. The process of determination becomes progressively more specific.

The third necessary condition involves the growth of a *generalized belief*, in which the threat is exaggerated and seen to be imminent. The result, in the case of panic, is a hysterical belief—cognitive structuring of an uncertain threat into a definite prognostication of disaster. Various precipitating events (such as the closing of a bank) give focus to this belief and provide "evidence" that the terrible threat is at work.

The fourth necessary condition is *mobilization* of people for action in the name of a generalized belief. In the case of the panic this may be realized by a single dramatic event, such as rumor of a "panic sell" by a single leading holder of securities. In more complicated social movements, leadership may be more deliberate and highly organized.

Finally, it is necessary to mention *social control* as a determinant. In its more general sense, social control refers to the activation of counterdeterminants for the conditions just listed. It is helpful, however, to distinguish between counterdeterminants of a preventive sort (dealing with conduciveness and strain) and counterdeterminants which appear only when the collective episode has made its appearance. In the case of panic, social control is effected, for instance, by spiking scare rumors or by actually preventing potential sellers from selling. This last measure is sometimes employed by governments attempting to stop an international flight of capital.

The value-added approach, in sum, is a logical patterning of social determinants, each contributing its "value" to the explanation of the episode. To round out the exposition of this approach, let me illustrate how three of these determinants—strain, conduciveness, and social control—operate with reference to quite a different kind of collective behavior: social movements that turn into violent revolutions.

The types of strain that can potentially give rise to revolutionary sentiment are so varied as to be bewildering—economic hardship, migrations of populations, defeat in war, religious persecution, value differences among different groups in the population, and many others (Smelser, 1962, pp. 338–47). If an investigator is interested in establishing a relation between a specific type of strain (e.g., economic depressions) and revolutionary movements, he or she will be able to illustrate the case extensively in the historical record but will also find that economic depressions give rise to many other kinds of behavior, and that endless other types of social strain give rise to revolutionary movements. To determine whether social strains will work their way into a revolutionary ideology or some other kind of behavior, it is necessary to turn to the variable of structural conduciveness.

The rise of many potentially revolutionary ideologies in the colonial countries during the first half of the twentieth century was preceded by a period in which the colonial powers "closed the door" on various kinds of protest against colonial domination. The colonial powers were relatively successful in "pacifying" the colonies—that is, ruling out hostile outbursts—and they were relatively unresponsive to modest demands for institutional reform by the colonials. (The British provide an exception to this generalization in some of their colonies, for example, Ceylon.) The history of many colonies before the appearance of aggressive nationalism is one of the colonial powers "reminding" the colonials, sometimes with force, that the colonial powers were both effective in imposing their will and inflexible in the face of demands for reform. It was in this context of closing off other alternatives—combined with a multiplicity of strains—that various nativistic and other ideological forerunners of revolutionary nationalism made their appearance in the colonies.

The appearance of a potentially revolutionary ideology, however, does not necessarily lead to an aggressive revolutionary outburst. Indeed, some of the ideological movements in the colonies experienced a long existence either as underground groups harried by colonial authorities or as cults of withdrawal. (The growth of the peyote religion among the permanently repressed American Indians is perhaps the most striking example of the latter.) The subsequent career of these potentially revolutionary ideologies depends above all on the behavior of agencies of social control. If authorities continue to be effective in crushing opposition, unresponsive to demands, and repressive of expressions of revolutionary sentiment, the movement tends to drift toward the cult form. If, however, the agencies of control suddenly lose their effectiveness, the movement turns in an overtly revolutionary direction. It is not so much the nature of the ideology of the movement as the behavior of the authorities that determines this change of direct. The ineffectiveness of the authorities may take many forms—division among the ruling classes themselves, weakening through military defeat (the British and the Dutch defeats in Southeast Asia at the hands of the Japanese in World War II are examples), or the fraternization or defection of the rulers' military forces. In sum, then, we call upon separate combinations of determinants to account for the rise of a revolutionary ideology and its expression in revolutionary form. The rise of the ideology is accounted for mainly by a specific combination of strain and conduciveness, whereas its translation into action depends above all on the behavior of the agencies of social control.

Some Shortcomings of the Sociological Explanation

By examining different combinations of the several social determinants, it is possible to throw some light on why collective episodes cluster in time and in certain parts of the social structure. But this approach can be criticized as incomplete or erroneous, or both, on two grounds—first, that it offers an inadequate account of the social determinants themselves; and second, that it ignores, oversimplifies, distorts, or otherwise treats inadequately a number of psychological variables that must be taken into account to give a full explanation of episodes of collective behavior. Leaving aside the first line of criticism for the moment, I shall attempt to identify some of the implicit and perhaps questionable psychological assumptions upon which the social account is based.

First, the account rests on the unspoken assumption that the various social factors exert their influence on the individual human mind, indeed that they must be combined in the minds of participants in order to cause an episode of collective panic. The simultaneous existence of a stock market in New York City (structural conduciveness), the fear of economic loss on the part of the French peasants (strain), and the rumor of panicky selling of suburban real estate in Sydney, Australia (a precipitating event around which a hysterical belief crystallizes), surely will not cause a panic. These conditions must operate in the same place, and in fact must influence the same individuals, if panicky behavior is to occur (see Brown, 1965). So, at the very minimum, the apparently social account assumes that the external social conditions impinge on and are combined in individual minds.

Once this assumption is granted, a torrent of objections to the sociological account is unleashed. How can it be imagined, for example, that the social condition of being unemployed (strain) has the same impact on all individuals it affects? One person may experience unemployment as a minor crisis to be weathered until an opportunity for reemployment arises, another may experience it as a blow to his identity as a male, and another may experience it as an occasion for rage at the economic system. If we ignore this diversity of psychological meanings of the same event for different individuals, we are guilty of presenting an unwarranted psychological generalization about human reactions to economic deprivation. Furthermore, if we hold to the implicit assertion that unemployment affects all equally, we discover ourselves in the questionable position of accepting the proposition that all unemployed people are predisposed to enter some episode of collective behavior if other social conditions are present. In short, the simple presentation of social factors, accompanied by the assumption that they affect everyone they touch equally, without independent psychological processing of these factors, yields little power to explain why some, not all, of those affected become participants. The social account alone is not very discriminating.

Even if a listing of social conditions could provide a degree of discrimination between participants and nonparticipants, it would do little to explain the different *types* of participation. Some participants become involved as leaders, others as activist followers, others as passive followers, others as sympathizers who do not actually engage in any overt behavior, and so on. Reference to internal psychic structures and processes is necessary if we are to discriminate among individuals in terms of their threshold for different kinds of involvement.

In some cases participation in an episode of collective behavior would appear to have little to do with social conditions at all. Certainly some of the generalized beliefs that enter collective outbursts—fear of entrapment as an ingredient of panic or a sense of religious mission as an ingredient of a religious cult, for example—exist as enduring psychological predispositions with little reference to the particular social environment of individuals. Indeed, it might be said that some individuals are more or less completely "programmed" psychologically to "act out" in collective episodes—certain types of phobic individuals in panics and certain types of borderline psychotic cases in bizarre religious cults, for example—and that what the social environment provides is an opportunity. A small religious cult in San Francisco, made up of several individuals from various parts of the country who have drifted into the metropolis and each of whom had a long experience of involvement in religious causes (see Lofland, 1966), could scarcely be said to be the product of social conditions in San Francisco. Its most important determinants are to be found in the psychological life histories of the individual members.

In sum, any account of the recruitment into, or the internal composition of participation in, a collective episode must rest on a consideration of the psychological dynamics of the individual person. Furthermore, recruitment, composition, and quality of participation determine in part the content, timing, and social direction of the episode. It follows that any purely sociological account of collective behavior can offer only a limited explanation.

Psychological Factors in Collective Behavior: An Example

Freud's ambition in writing "Group Psychology and the Analysis of the Ego" was not to create a full-scale theory of collective behavior, but rather to raise "a few questions with which the depth-psychology of psycho-analysis is specially concerned" (1955 [1922], p. 71). His essay is sufficiently comprehensive, however, to merit treating it as a relatively coherent, distinctively psychological account of some aspects of collective behavior.

Freud distinguished between individual and social or group psychology, even though he found the distinction to be an imprecise one. "Individual psychology," he wrote, "is concerned with the individual man and explores the paths by which he seeks to find satisfaction for his instinctual impulses" (ibid., p. 69). Invariably, however, the search for gratification involves social objects—parents, siblings, loved ones, and so on. But, Freud added, in speaking of social or group psychology proper, it is usual to set these intimate relations aside and treat group psychology as "concerned with the individual man as a member of a race, of a nation, of a caste, or a profession, or an institution, or as a component part of a crowd of people who have been organized into a group at some particular time for some definite purpose" (ibid., p. 70). Within group psychology, he felt it important to distinguish between short-lived groups on the one hand and "stable groups or associations in which mankind pass their lives, and which are embodied in the institutions of society" on the other (ibid., p. 83). Yet in his own illustrations he did not adhere consistently to the distinction. His two most striking empirical illustrations came from highly stabilized groups—the church and the army—whereas his major theoretical formulations concerned "primary groups" that "have a leader and . . . not . . . much 'organization'" (ibid., p. 116). The latter types of groups— primary or uninstitutionalized—are those that usually form during episodes of collective behavior.

So much for Freud's definitions and scope of interest in social groupings. What aspects of the behavior of these collectivities did he wish to explain? In reading his essay it is possible to discern four distinct preoccupations. First and most generally, he was preoccupied with the reasons why people enter such groups and engage in such behavior at all. Second, he was interested in accounting for the resemblance between the mentality and action of these groups and that of children and primitives. Here he took as his starting point Gustave Le Bon's classic description of the crowd mentality—the crowd as impulsive, changeable, and irritable; incapable of sustained attention, criticism, or perseverance; and governed by a sense of omnipotence, exaggerated feelings, magical formulas, and illusions (Le Bon, 1960 [1895]). Third, he was interested in why participants in primary groups display such adulation and submission to leaders. Finally, he was interested in explaining why these participants experience such a sense of equality and solidarity—even identity—with their fellow participants.

Before outlining his own contribution to these issues, Freud criticized several authors who had previously attempted to account for the mentality of groups. In particular, he attacked several theories of suggestion, involving the claim that the group renders people susceptible to suggestion, and thus leads them to take leave of their critical faculties and give vent to their primitive emotions. Freud found this theory—presented by Le Bon and several others—to be a shallow one, since it gives "no explanation of the nature of suggestion, that is of the conditions under which influence without logical foundation takes place" (Freud, 1955 [1922], p. 90). In addition, he discarded as circular Le Bon's emphasis on the force of the leader's "prestige" in causing crowd behavior, since "prestige . . . is only recognizable in its capacity for evoking suggestion" (ibid., p. 88). Finally, and more indirectly, he criticized McDougall's views on the conditions that prevent involvement in crowd behavior. McDougall had argued that if individuals are integrated into social organizations that possess a division of labor, definite traditions and customs regulating the interaction among members, and some continuity of existence, they will be less likely to be drawn into primary groups governed by emotionalism and an uncritical mentality (McDougall, 1920). Freud, however, changed the import of McDougall's insight. Instead of viewing it as an attempt to outline a set of social conditions, Freud redefined the question in more psychological terms. "[McDougall's] problem consists in how to procure for the group precisely those features [of organized participation in a structured collectivity] which were characteristic of the individual and which are extinguished in him by the formation of the [primary] group" (Freud, 1955 [1922], p. 86).

While launching these criticisms, Freud was also changing the nature of the question he was addressing. Instead of asking, "What characteristics of groups bring out primitive mental characteristics in the individual?" Freud now wondered, "What psychological forces induce people to form and stay together in groups?" By focusing on the second question he hoped to reach an explanation of the mental qualities of group life that were not, in his opinion, well accounted for by the theorists he criticized.

Freud found the answer to his question in the concept of libido, or Eros. Indeed, his whole theory of group participation rests on a peculiar combination of instinct-object relationships in the individual. These relationships involve not object-cathexes so much as identifications with objects. Freud outlined three types of identification: first, the original form of emotional life with the father as an ideal in the early history of the Oedipus complex; second, a regressive form, in which the object is introjected in the Oedipal crisis; and third, identification with other persons on the basis of some commonly quality—for example, the identification of members of a ship's crew with one another on the basis of their common subordination to the captain's authority.

Using this classification of identifications, Freud characterized the essence of involvement of a primary group. First and foremost, a group's members are identified with the leader in the second sense of the term; they "have put one and the same object in the place of their ego ideal" (ibid., p. 116). They have regressed from the condition of having definite object-relations with the leader to the condition of introjecting the leader as their ego ideal. In addition, the group's members are identified with one another in the third sense of the term; they "have . . . identified with one another in their ego" because they share in common subordination to the introjected leader (ibid.). This phenomenon accounts in part for their experience of solidarity and equality in the group. But the collective spirit of equality is fostered by still another mechanism. All members of the group are desirous of the leader's love and envious of one another for his love. Since all cannot possibly gain his exclusive love, however, they renounce their selfish desires and believe that the leader does and should love all of them equally. "No one must want to put himself forward, everyone must be the same and have the same" (ibid., p. 120). This attitude explains the growth of primitive social justice in groups. The total result of this combination of instinctual forces and objects is that everyone in a group is equal except the leader, and the leader is superior in equal degree to all the others.

By now Freud had supplied an account of the last two of his preoccupations—the relations between leaders and followers, and the relations among followers. But how to explain the primitive emotionalism and the loss of critical faculties of the group? To shed light on this question, Freud turned to his theory of the primal horde and treated all primary groups as instances of psychological and presumably historical regression:

> The uncanny and coercive characteristics of group formations, which are shown in the phenomena of suggestion that accompany them, may . . . be traced back to the fact of their origin from the primal horde. The leader of the group is still the dreaded primal father; the group still wishes to be governed by unrestricted force; it has an extreme passion for authority; . . . it has a thirst for obedience. The primal father is the group ideal, which governs the ego in place of the ego ideal. (Ibid., p. 127)

These features—as well as the loss of consciousness, the dominance of the mind by affects, the impatience, and the impulsiveness of crowds—"correspond to a state of regression to a primitive mental activity" (ibid., p. 122). Unlike those he criticized, Freud did not view these characteristics as products of the group's social influence over the individual, but rather as products that emerge as a concomitant of the same psychological tendencies to regressive identification that lead people to form groups in the first place.

Some Shortcomings of the Psychological Explanation

In criticizing Le Bon, Freud found his characterization of the crowd mentality inadequate because it rested on a rather mystical notion that the group influences people in such a way as to bring out new and unusual mental characteristics and types of behavior. In criticizing the sociological approach, I noted that it involved a number of questionable generalizations about the effect of social situations on beliefs and behavior. In both instances the explanation regarded the individual person as a kind of passive vessel through which the social forces work; or to put it another way, the individual is not seen as processing or modifying, much less initiating these social forces. Freud's account avoids this difficulty by specifying psychological dynamics which lead people to enter social groups and behave in certain ways.

Despite this singular advantage, Freud's theory suffers from a number of shortcomings, some of which suggest the need for a systematic synthesis with those approaches that emphasize social factors. The following problems seem most important:

1. Freud's account is incomplete on psychological grounds alone. The weakest link of his argument appears to be the appeal to the logic of regression to the primal horde to account for the various psychological characteristics described so vividly by Le Bon—the impulsiveness, irritability, credulousness, emotionality, and so on. Reliance on this type of explanation can be criticized on the grounds that it involves some mystical notions about man's capacity to regress through the centuries to a primitive historical past. Leaving this line of criticism aside, however, and reading the idea of the primal horde in its metaphorical rather than its literal historical meaning, Freud's concept of regression is still subject to criticism. Basically his theory amounts to a process of regression to a pre-Oedipal state of identification with an authority figure. But two features of this kind of regression—features treated elsewhere in Freud's writing—appear to be underplayed in this account of group psychology.

   First, Freud tended to overemphasize the positive side of the identification of the followers with the leader and with one another—loving the leader equally, being loved by him equally, and loving one another equally. This emphasis appears both in his empirical characterization of the church and the army, and in his more general theoretical formulation (ibid., chaps. 5 and 10). He gave much less attention to the negative side of the ambivalent feelings toward authority figures. He did refer to the hostile attitude of members of religious groups toward outsiders who do not believe in the leader, and he did speak of the envy and hostility of followers toward one another because each of them desires the exclusive love of the leader, but he did not deal with the phenomenon of hostility toward the leader himself.

   Second, in characterizing the process of regressive identification, Freud tended to overemphasize impulse expression and to underemphasize the ego's defensive operations. Le Bon's description, which Freud accepted, deals almost exclusively with the expression of id impulses normally forbidden by the ego in deference to superego imperatives. The view taken by Freud is that the superego, being replaced by the object of the leader, relinquishes its controlling function. Freud's other accounts of identification, however, are more complex than this, in that they bring into play a number of other defenses—repression, projection, denial, and displacement, for example (Freud, 1955 [1909], 1961 [1923]). If Freud's theory of regressive identification has general validity, we should be able to account for the content of the group mentality by reference to these mechanisms as well as those of identification and regression. Freud did not explore these additional mechanisms in his essay on group psychology.

2. Because much of Freud's explanation is carried by the single mechanism of regressive identification with a leader, his account suffers from being unable to account for several aspects of group behavior. It is true that reliance on this mechanism provides a specific explanation for the relations between leader and followers and among followers. But without further elaboration, this explanation shares with the sociological explanation an inability to discriminate among differential degrees of involvement in collective behavior—involvement as leader, as active follower, as sympathizer, as spectator, and so on. Presumably this would depend on the differential propensity of individuals to regress to a level of identification, but without specification of further psychological conditions under which this is likely to occur, such a statement is not very helpful. Furthermore, the mechanism of regressive identification is nonspecific with respect to the *form* of collective behavior—violent rioting, reform movement, religious cult, and so on—that may appear. All these forms manifest the general regressive relations among leaders and followers, but nothing in Freud's psychological account explains why one rather than another of these types of episodes would arise. In sum, Freud's explanatory variable of regressive identification is too general to account for more than a few broad contours of collective behavior; it says little about the questions of differential recruitment into an episode of collective behavior or the directions of group behavior.

3. Finally—and related to the second line of criticism—Freud's theory, with few exceptions, leaves out of consideration the social factors that influence people to enter into group activity. It strikes me that more might be made of McDougall's insights than Freud made of them. By noting that involvement in a group with definite organization, specialization of tasks, traditions and customs, and so on inhibits involvement in outbursts of collective behavior,

McDougall was asserting also that the absence of these social-structural factors constitutes an occasion for people to be drawn into such episodes. To translate McDougall's point into psychoanalytic language, involvement in a structured social organization provides the individual with opportunities for stable object-attachments of various sorts, and this diminishes the probability of regressive identification. Correspondingly, if the social organization itself undergoes some sort of disintegration, this increases the probability that the individual will be placed under strain and, as a consequence, will reconstitute his object-world in a regressive direction. Freud declined to accept this implication of McDougall's reasoning, which identifies a typical social occasion—loosening of social attachments—that encourages individuals to enter into episodes of collective behavior. To make this point in more general terms: If Freud's theory is to offer an adequate account of the content and timing of collective episodes, it cannot rest solely on the type of psychological mechanism he specified; there must also be a systematic account of the social conditions that facilitate the activation of these mechanisms.

Ingredients of a Synthetic Approach

In this section I shall spell out the requirements of a synthetic explanation for episodes of collective behavior which I hope can minimize the shortcomings associated with the sociological and the psychological approaches, each considered singly. In the final section I shall illustrate some of these requirements with reference to a typical protest movement.

The first requirement of any explanation of collective behavior is to specify the aspects of this behavior that demand explanation (dependent variables). At various points in the exposition I have identified explicitly or implicitly the following kinds of variation: (1) Variation in the *type* of collective behavior—panic, craze, hostile outburst, reform movement, revolutionary movement, religious cult, and so on. Why, in general terms, do these types of behavior erupt, and under what conditions should we expect one rather than another type? (2) Variations in *timing of occurrence.* Why do these types of behavior occur at one time rather than another? (3) Variations in *content,* in terms of the beliefs that accompany these types of behavior. Under what conditions do hysterical beliefs, beliefs in personal and social regeneration, etc., arise? (4) Variation in *recruitment and differential participation*. Why are some people more attracted to episodes of collective behavior than others, and why do they differ in their degree of involvement? (5) Variations in the *relations among participants*. How can we account for the particular types of authority relations, division of roles, etc., in groups that form during episodes of collective behavior? (6) Variations in the character of the episode *over time*. Does a collective outburst have different characteristics during its period of incipient development, its period of explosiveness, and its period of decline? If so, how do we account for these differences? Not every explanation of collective behavior need address itself to all these questions, but it is essential that the precise scope of the problems to be addressed is made explicit.

The second requirement of an explanation synthesizing the social and psychological approaches is that the dependent variables be described in two languages—one at the conceptual level of the social system, and one at the conceptual level of the psychological system. The range of *social* meanings of a movement for equal feminine rights, for example, would include its significance for the traditional organization of sex roles, its significance for a political party that may wish to capitalize on such a movement to gain support in its bid for electoral success, its significance for the structure of domestic law, and so on. The range of *psychological* meanings of the same movement would include its significance for the types of sexual identification of participants with maternal figures, its significance from the standpoint of feminine envy of the male's superior advantages, and so on. A major *social* meaning of a religious cult such as the Black Muslims may lie in its challenge to traditional racial and political arrangements; a major *psychological* meaning may lie in a rebirth of personal identity for blacks who have experienced a life of poverty and rootlessness. Any episode of collective behavior should be described, therefore, in terms of what it is for the social system and what it is for the individual.

This double description yields the following advantages for the investigator of collective behavior. First, it enables him or her to translate social and psychological determinants, respectively, directly to the dependent variable at parallel conceptual levels, and thus to avoid reductionist or simplistic causal statements. For example, if the social significance of the feminist movement—the reconstitution of traditional sex roles—is appreciated, the investigator is less likely to attribute the impetus of the movement exclusively to considerations of conflict over sex identification, even though the involvement of some participants may be explained in these terms. Second, it enables the investigator to avoid characterizing psychological states of individuals by reference to data at the social level, and vice versa. For example, in the literature on collective behavior it is common to assume that all the participants in a race riot are motivated by racial hostility, since conflict between the races is the dominant social characteristic of the episode. But more careful study of the participants shows that while some do appear to be motivated by racial antagonisms, others are drawn into the disorder only after social controls have broken down, their defiance being directed more toward the police and other public authorities; still others appear to seek economic advantage through looting (Smelser, 1962, pp. 257–61). The motivations of the participants, then, have to be ascertained by direct psychological measures, not the gross social features of the episode. Furthermore, the social aims of an episode of collective behavior cannot be characterized by reference to the motivational states of individuals. It is erroneous, for example, to characterize social movement exclusively in power-oriented terms on the basis of the political motivations of selected participants.

The third requirement of a synthetic explanation is to specify and show the interaction among the various social and psychological determinants of collective behavior. These determinants can be classified conveniently under four headings: structural setting, deprivation, mobilization for action in the name of a belief, and the operation of social and personal controls.

1. The structural setting—both social and psychological—for involvement in collective behavior. At the *social* level this setting has two aspects—the opportunity for alternative lines of behavior other than the collective outburst, and the social moorings of potential participants that might inhibit their involvement. With respect to the first, the events leading up to the outburst of riots in American prisons in 1952 and 1953 provide an example. Prior to this time many prisons had evolved a system of informal inmate self-government, whereby leaders among the prisoners dispensed favors among other inmates and received their various complaints about prison conditions. The informal leaders also maintained close communication with guards and wardens. During a period of penal reform in the years before the early 1950s, however, "the

inmate clerks and assistants were shorn of their power, and replaced by paid, Civil Service personnel" (Hartung and Floch, 1956, pp. 54–55). Administration became more formal, more distant, and less receptive to the expression of prisoner grievances than it had been under the preceding informal system. Partly as a result of such reforms, "there appears to have occurred a marked disturbance and disruption of the channels normally established for the airing of grievances and distribution of rewards. The general resentment resulting from this condition was directed, mobilized, and heightened by inmate leaders" (Ohlin, 1956, pp. 24–25) In this case the disappearance of alternative channels of protest increased the probability of uncontrolled hostile outbursts.

One of the common background features of episodes of collective behavior is that the stable social linkages of individuals are "loosened" in various ways. Riots, for example, tend to break out on hot summer Sundays at beaches, recreational resorts, taverns, and public dance halls—in short, in those corners of the social structure where people are most likely to be away from their familial and occupational role attachments (Lohman, 1947). Students and adolescents generally have a high rate of participation in various types of collective outbursts; one reason for this is that they are in the age-grade "gap" between the relatively well-defined role of being a child and the relatively well-defined cluster of occupational, marital, religious, and other adult roles. As youths enter these adult roles, their predilection for involvement in both frivolous and serious episodes generally diminishes. Recent migrants to large cities, who are generally relatively unattached to trade union, voluntary association, or neighborhood groups, tend to be drawn disproportionately into bizarre religious cults (Holt, 1940; Fauset, 1944). These kinds of facts lend weight to McDougall's assertion that involvement in a social organization with definite and specialized roles, traditions, and continuity operates as a counterinfluence to involvement in collective outbursts.

To view this point from the *psychological* side, if an individual is involved in a number of relatively stable role structures, this may mean a relatively stable distribution of libidinal energy. But this is not necessarily the case. The stability of an individual's psychic world of object-representations and identifications is in part independent of the stability of his or her actual, contemporary object-world. The reason for this is that the stability or instability of psychological structure is only in part a function of an individual's current reality involvement; it is also a function of his or her personal history, including the resolution of crises at various stages of development.

In explaining the differential recruitment and participation in a collective outburst, then, it is necessary to refer to the degree of structural permissiveness at both the social and psychological levels. In the case of the prison riots of 1952 and 1953, for example, a partial explanation of why the riots occurred in some prisons rather than others can be given in terms of the recent structural "reforms" that had cut off alternative opportunities for expression of grievances and hostility. The riots clustered in the reformed prisons. But within these prisons, not every inmate rioted, even though all were presumably affected in some degree by the reforms. To account for this differential involvement, recourse must be made to psychological determinants. According to some accounts, the rioters were composed mainly of psychopathic and homosexual inmate leaders, and more passive individuals who feared reprisal or loss of favor in the eyes of the riot leaders (MacCormick, 1954). But, again, in those prisons that had not recently experienced penal reform, even these types of individuals did not often initiate and participate in hostile outbursts. This illustration reveals how the incorporation of both social and psychological factors magnifies the power of the explanation of the differential incidence and recruitment into the riots.

2. The deprivation—defined both in social and psychological terms—that operates as an impetus to collective behavior. Up to this point I have considered only the structural opportunities for involvement in collective outbursts. These opportunities alone, however, do not guarantee that behavior will occur. There has to be some sort of more active "push" to behavior, and this normally takes the form of some real or imagined deprivation. For example, in the prisons, the inmates' grievances centered around conditions such as "poor, insufficient, or contaminated food; inadequate, unsanitary, or dirty housing; sadistic brutality by prison officials," or some combination of these (Hartung and Floch, 1956, p. 51). These reality conditions, combined with the exaggeratedly suspicious attitudes toward authority on the part of the selected prison population, made for a high level of hostility. When these

conditions of deprivation are combined with the structural conditions described above, the probability of overt violence is augmented.

Another example will show how social and psychological factors interact to determine the exact level of threat or deprivation. A common background condition for collective panic is the presence of some uncontrollable danger of unknown proportions, such as an approaching army or an air raid alert. When this kind of threat is combined with a structural setting of limited and closing exits, collective panic is very likely to occur (Smelser, 1962, pp. 135–43). But in addition to the presence of realistic danger, an individual's sense of guilt, anxiety, hostility, and especially his or her tendency to project these outward are important determinants of his or her susceptibility to possibly dangerous situations. During the air raid drills in New York City in World War II, for instance, most people remained calm, but a small number of citizens—both adults and children—experienced seizures of acute anxiety. Clinical analysis of persons who showed this reaction revealed that they

> were individuals who in their family relations experienced intense hostility together with great fear of retaliation if they expressed it. They felt that they would be precipitated into great danger if the hostility which they inhibited precariously and with great effort were to break through. This, then, was the explosion which they dreaded, the image of which became projected on the outer world. The danger of bombs exploding thus seemed imminent to them although it did not to others in the same external circumstances. (Wolfenstein, 1957, pp. 7–8)

An analysis of situations leading to panic would uncover some situations in which the realistic threat is so overwhelming that almost all affected individuals would be driven to panic, other situations in which individuals "bring" diffuse anxieties to circumstances that are not realistically very threatening, and still other situations—presumably most—in which the threatening agent is a function of both the external environment of the persons affected and the psychological predispositions they bring to this environment.

3. Mobilization for action on the basis of a belief. On the *social* side this determinant refers above all to the appearance of a leader or leaders who have the capacity to create or assemble a rumor of ideology that defines the situation as one calling for collective ac-

tion, to disseminate the belief, to elicit and focus the affects of followers, to stimulate them to action, and perhaps to coordinate this action. If these key elements of leadership and coordination are not present, the impetus to an episode of collective behavior will be manifested in other forms of behavior.

On the *psychological* side many individuals may be "readied" for action insofar as they are appropriately motivated, hold appropriate beliefs, and are receptive to direction from a demagogic leader. The most famous studies attempting to isolate this kind of individual are the University of California studies of authoritarianism, in which anti-Semitic and other sociopolitical attitudes were traced to typical family experiences and typical personality constellations (Adorno, et al., 1950). Though the investigators in these studies limited themselves to the study of family and personality determinants of attitudes, presumably those individuals designated as "authoritarian" would be more likely to be drawn into episodes of collective behavior directed against Jews and other minority groups.

I shall discuss the question of ideology and leadership in greater detail in the final section of this essay.

4. The operation of social and personal controls. Once a collective outburst has begun to develop, its course, direction, and intensity are dependent in large part on the social and personal controls operating on the participants. I have already indicated a number of ways in which social controls influence collective behavior. Probably the type of response on the part of authorities that most aggravates and intensifies an episode of collective protest is harshness and rigidity that alternate with evidence of weakness. Harshness and rigidity provide the participants with "evidence" of the vicious character of the authority, and thus justify extreme and militant tactics; weakness or collapse in the face of threats provides "evidence" that these extreme tactics are in fact ineffective, and encourages participants in protest movements to give credence to their own fantasies of omnipotence. On the other hand, an agent of control who is firm but patient, consistently prohibiting certain types of protest but consistently permitting and giving serious consideration to others, provides neither kind of evidence to participants in collective protest movements and thus tends to contain the protest.

Many who have written about collective behavior have stressed the uncontrolled and impulsive behavior of participants. It should not be forgotten that such behavior is continuously conditioned by the operation of personal controls. At one moment in the history of the Free Speech Movement at the University of California, for example, hundreds of individuals were mobilized to engage in illegal action in the name of free speech, when the question concerned the political rights of students; at another moment only a handful were mobilized for a day or two of mischief in the name of free speech, when the question amounted to the right to be obscene in public. Of course, many different conditions affected the two episodes, but one key difference is that in one case the moral sensitivities of many were aroused to the point where they would forgo certain personal controls, whereas in the other their moral sensitivities were offended to the point where they would not even sympathize with the protest, even though the leaders of both episodes justified their protest in the language of free speech.

One of the many dilemmas facing the militants within any social movement arises from the tension between their desire for extremist tactics and their fear that the moral sensitivities of the moderates will be offended by such tactics. Later I shall enumerate some reasons why protest movements attempt to provoke authorities into repressive actions. Certainly one reason for such behavior on the part of militants is to generate "evidence" for the moderates that the authority is arbitrary and cruel—evidence which, accepted by the moderates, would justify their participation in extreme and otherwise reprehensible actions.

In this section I have discussed four sets of variables separately, considering each at the social and psychological levels as they bear on the determination of episodes of collective behavior. In closing this section, it is essential to note that in any empirical case the several sets of variables combine and interact with one another in very complicated ways. It seems to me that one of the highest theoretical priorities for the field of collective behavior is not so much to search for new variables as to generate explanatory models that incorporate the interaction and feedback relations among the several sets of known influences on collective behavior.

Social and Psychological Significance of Protest Movements

In the final section of the essay I shall probe a little deeper in describing the social and psychological characteristics of collective behavior. I shall take the protest movement as a type case. Rather than focus on a single example, however (such as a pacifist movement or the Townsend Movement), I shall describe a number of characteristics that are common to many protest movements. First I shall describe those characteristics at the social level. Then I shall outline what I consider to be a common—though by no means universal—psychodynamic significance of these characteristics. The object of this exercise is to provide the reader with more circumstantial and detailed suggestions than it was possible to give in the preceding section.

COMMON ELEMENTS OF SOCIAL PROTEST MOVEMENTS

Protest movements—whether reform or revolutionary in spirit—develop remarkably similar ideologies. These ideologies have both negative and positive components. On the negative side there is a sense of foreboding, of great anxiety about threats to social life, and the specification of agents in society who are responsible for these threats. In the prohibition movement which culminated in the Eighteenth Amendment, liquor became a symbol for a variety of forces—the city, the "foreign element," Catholics, and so on—which were felt to be undermining traditional values of American Protestantism. These forces were, in a rather mysterious combination with liquor, causing "disease, destitution and depravity," and were, as "the Great Destroyer of the Temple of the Soul," working against organized religion (Odegard, 1928, pp. 29–34). Supporters of the Townsend Plan in the 1930s found generalized economic threats in a social system which left the aged isolated and poor, and generalized moral threats in tobacco, liquor, petting, and the laziness of the young. Adherents of the movement also singled out political authorities (especially Roosevelt and the Supreme Court) whom they viewed as obstacles to the realization of their design to eradicate these evils (Neuberger and Loe, 1936). The negative components of the ideology, then, are great anxiety, which focuses on the decay of social and moral life, and great hostility, which focuses on some individuals or groups in society. If the movement is of the reform variety, opposition tends to be directed toward "vested interests" in the society who resist reform; if the movement is revolutionary, protest tends to be directed against the ruling authorities themselves as the source of evil.

On the positive side, those who adhere to protest movements often endow themselves and the envisioned reconstitution of society with enormous power, conceived as the ability to overcome that array of threats and obstacles which constitute the negative side of the adherents' world-picture. The proposed reform or social change will render opponents helpless and will be effective immediately. Because of this exaggerated potency, adherents often see unlimited happiness in the future if only the basis for threat, frustration, and discomfort will disappear. Consider the symbolism of the Townsend Plan. Meetings of adherents often produced the following chant:

> Two hundred dollars a month.
> Youth for work, age for leisure,
> Two hundred for the oldsters
> To be spent in ceaseless pleasure.
> (Whiteman and Lewis, 1936, p. 75)

The Townsend planners planned not only to save capitalism but also to engulf competing plans: the movement would "swallow the EPICS and Utopians . . . would gather the Technates and Continentals under its wings. Humanity marches on" (ibid., pp. 101–2). Symbols of omnipotence also appeared:

> Nothing can stop us! (cheers and more cheers). Not even President Roosevelt and the Supreme Court can stop us (tremendous cheers—no one is afraid of that big bad wolf, the Supreme Court). The speaker can hardly go on. Higher and higher he lifts his voice in exultation—"No, not even Almighty God can stop us!" (Ibid.)

Thus normative movements frequently display a worldview of conflicting forces of good and evil which characterize many types of generalized beliefs—two omnipotent forces locked in combat.

Protest movements also display those characteristics noted by Freud—an exceptional solidarity between leader and followers; a tendency for the leader to be endowed with supernatural, superhuman, or exceptional powers; a corresponding tendency for followers to subordinate themselves to the decisions of the leader because of those powers; an exceptional solidarity among adherents of the movement; and a correspondingly great antagonism to opponents of the movement and other outsiders.

On closer examination, the relations between those inside the movement and those outside are more complex. While outsiders are commonly treated as enemies, it is also important to note that protest movements often depend on public support for their success and continuously engage in efforts to win it. The support required for success need not be universal; it may only be the support of some critical constituency. For example, the degree of faculty support for the students and corresponding faculty opposition to the university administration was of crucial significance for the fortunes of the Free Speech Movement during 1964–65 at the University of California. Necessarily, then, the relations between adherents and outsiders have a double aspect. On the one hand, outsiders are viewed as unenlightened, untrustworthy, or heterodox; but on the other hand, they are viewed as possible supporters if won over to the cause.

One final feature of protest movements deserves mention. Once the major aim of the movement is realized—for example, when some offensive statute is removed from the books, when some desired social reforms are affected—one might normally expect the movement to dissolve. Frequently this happens, but there are other tendencies that lead many movements to endure beyond their "natural" life. Some movements persist in a "watchdog" capacity to protect and consolidate gains. Others turn to issues and reforms related to their original purpose. Still others attempt to provoke authorities into hostile actions which presumably will breathe new life into the movement. One striking feature of the Free Speech Movement during the spring of 1965—the months after its days of brilliant success in gaining various political rights during the period from September through December, 1964—was not so much its fragmentation and decline as the efforts of its fragmented sectors to bring the movement alive once again over new issues. Among these efforts were the challenge to the universities over the control of student government, the short-lived effort to set up a "free university" in opposition to the University of California, various efforts to defy minor university regulations in order to provoke the university into repressive action, and the attempt to push the free speech issue to a new level by insisting on the right to utter obscenities in public. It was as though the days of December had provided a particular sort of gratification for many participants, and the subsequent history of the movement witnessed a number of attempts to re-create those days, even though the particular historical circumstances were no longer the same as in that period.

PSYCHODYNAMIC MEANINGS OF THE COMMON ELEMENTS OF PROTEST MOVEMENTS

As indicated in the last section, many features of protest movements are explicable by reference to social situations in which they arise. To increase the power of our explanation of them, however, reference must be made to their psychodynamic significance. I shall conclude this essay by suggesting a number of these deeper psychological meanings. In any given situation, of course, participants may either "bring" these meanings to a protest movement or have them "evoked" by the circumstances of the movement; most situations would show a continuous interplay between internal psychic determination and external stimulation.

Let me begin by reviewing the psychic ingredients of two common childhood situations—the Oedipal situation of the child, in which he or she enters into competition with the parent of the same sex for the love of the parent of the opposite sex; and situations in which the child competes with siblings for the attention and affection of the parents. Needless to say, these situations resemble one another in many respects and may be fused in various ways in the child's psychological development, but they are distinguishable conceptually.

The Oedipal situation is marked by several types of ambivalence. Toward the father, the boy experiences feelings of love, affection, and direct identification (Freud, 1955 [1922], p. 105); yet at the same time he is filled with feelings of competition and rage toward the father because he stands in the way of the boy's sexual desires for his mother. Simultaneously the boy is afflicted with the related feelings of castration anxiety and homosexual anxiety. Toward the mother, the ambivalence is between positive sexual attraction, on the one hand, and his frustration and anger because she refuses to be seduced away from the father, on the other.

Typically the Oedipal conflict is resolved mainly by a process of repression and identification—repression of the anxiety-provoking elements, and identification with the same-sex parent. Most conspicuously, the repressed elements are the hostile and erotic impulses toward both the father and the mother. What remains is the internalized superego, which becomes the seat of moral anxiety, and feelings of de-eroticized affection for the mother.

With respect to the relations among siblings, similar ambivalences, both toward the sibling and toward the parents whose affection is desired, are in evidence. In addition, the mechanisms of resolving the ambivalences are similar, though not quite so dramatic or phase-specific as in the Oedipal situation. The "preferred" solution is to repress the hostile and erotic elements of the ambivalences toward the siblings; to retain the gentler feelings of brotherhood, affection, and loyalty; and to identify with them. As Freud indicated, however, the identification in this case does not involve regarding them as superordinate, but rather regarding them as equally subordinated, loved—or whatever—by the parents.

Viewing these common psychodynamic processes with reference to the common features of protest movements, it seems to me that the protest movement is typically an occasion which permits the repressed elements of these crises to emerge and be gratified, though certain other defenses continue to operate.

This formulation applies most dramatically to the ambivalent attitudes toward authority figures manifested in protest movements. On the one hand there is the unqualified love, worship, and submission to the leader of the movement, who articulates and symbolizes "the cause." On the other hand there is the unqualified suspicion, denigration, and desire to destroy the agent felt responsible for the moral decay of social life and standing in the way of reform, whether that be a vested interest or a political authority. There is one important difference, however. In the Oedipal crisis the ambivalence is directed toward a single individual, the father; in the protest movement the ambivalence is split between two types of object. This splitting appears to serve a number of defensive purposes. It permits the gratification of feelings of love and passivity as well as the feelings of hostility toward the authority figure, but by a combination of projection and denial it also avoids the anxiety that is created when these ambivalent feelings are focused on the same object. In addition, these defenses—when combined with rationalization—permit certain kinds of behavior that might otherwise be reprehensible to the individual participants: passive dependency, now justified because of the sheer power and wonder of the leader; and destructive or even violent behavior, now justified because of the fundamental evil of the enemy. The same mechanisms of splitting, projection, denial, and rationalization all seem to operate when the hated object is not so much an authority figure as a sibling figure—such as a minority group that is perceived as gaining too many social advantages or "forgetting its proper place."

An ambivalence characterizes the relations of adherents to the movement to potential sources of outside support, but it is a different sort of ambivalence. This traces more to the child's Oedipal wish to seduce the opposite-sex parent into joining in the destruction of the same-sex parent; or, in the sibling situation, the wish to seduce the parent into joining in the destruction of the sibling. It seems to me that one of the common meanings of a movement's desire for solidarity and support is a manifestation of this kind of wish. This would account for the extraordinarily solid, eroticized ties among "converts" who have become "committed" to the cause. At the same time, these feelings are tinged with ambivalence: At the positive extreme is the joy of gratification if the seduction is accepted; at the negative extreme is the pain of bitter frustration if it is refused. Adherents to a movement must always be prepared to be disappointed with supporters who are less than totally committed. Perhaps this ambivalence lies behind the cynical disdain with which core members of a movement sometimes regard their less committed followers. Perhaps it also lies behind the attitude frequently expressed by adherents that "those who are not with us are against us," an attitude which suggests that the ambivalence toward outsiders is also subject to splitting and the associated defenses.

This kind of logic also throws some light on the future state of social bliss, peace, and harmony that is frequently envisioned by adherents to a cause. These visions tap very vivid Oedipal and sibling-destruction fantasies of what the world would be like if only the hated objects were obliterated and the child could have the loved object to himself or herself. This fantasy, usually subjected to severe repression, comes closer to the surface, albeit in disguised form, in the ideologies of social protest.

Finally, the tendency for adherents of protest movements to create conditions that might reactivate the movement is also highlighted by these psychological considerations. The striking feature of the protest movement is what Freud observed: It permits the expression of impulses that are normally repressed. But the participant continues to defend against the impulses involved—especially the hostile and erotic ones by mechanisms such as projection, denial, rationalization, and splitting. The efforts—sometimes conscious and sometimes unconscious—of leaders and adherents of movements to create issues, to provoke authorities, and even to be martyred by these authorities would seem to be in part efforts to "arrange" reality so as to "justify" the expression of normally forbidden impulses in a setting which makes them appear less reprehensible to the participants.

Concluding Remark

By describing a protest movement at both the social and psychological levels, it is more nearly possible to see in detail how the various determinants—structural setting, deprivation, mobilization, and controls—feed into such movements from both levels. In concluding, I express the hope that I have avoided two biases in this essay—first, the bias that episodes of collective behavior arise as "natural" consequences of disequilibrating social conditions, and that under these conditions any "normal" human being would be drawn into such episodes; and second, the bias that episodes of collective behavior are no more than seizures of "acting out" of impulses and conflicts that are irrelevant to existing social conditions. Some statements, lifted from context, may appear to reveal one or the other of these biases. The entire spirit of the essay, however, is to avoid the conceptual and empirical distortions that arise from either bias, and to work toward a synthetic approach.

References

Adorno, T. W., et al.
1950 *The Authoritarian Personality.* New York: Harper and Row.
Brown, Roger
1965 *Social Psychology.* New York: The Free Press of Glencoe.
Durkheim, Émile
1951 [1897] *Suicide.* Translated by John A. Spaulding and George Simpson. New York: The Free Press of Glencoe.
Fauset, A. H.
1944 *Black Gods of the Metropolis.* Philadelphia: Publications of the Philadelphia Anthropological Society.
Freud, Sigmund
1955 [1909] "Analysis of a Phobia in a Five-Year-Old Boy." In *Standard Edition of the Complete Psychological Works of Sigmund Freud,* Vol. 10, edited by James Strachey. London: Hogarth Press. Pp. 3–149.
1955 [1922] "Group Psychology and the Analysis of the Ego." In *Standard Edition of the Complete Psychological Works of Sigmund Freud,* Vol. 18, edited by James Strachey. London: Hogarth Press. Pp. 65–143.
1957 [1917] "Mourning and Melancholia." In *Standard Edition of the Complete Psychological Works of Sigmund Freud,* Vol. 14, edited by James Strachey. London: Hogarth Press. Pp. 243–58.

1961 [1923] "The Ego and the Id." In *Standard Edition of the Complete Psychological Works of Sigmund Freud,* Vol. 19, edited by James Strachey. London: Hogarth Press. Pp. 12–59.

Hartung, Frank E., and Maurice Floch
1956 "A Social-Psychological Analysis of Prison Riots: An Hypothesis." *The Journal of Criminal Law, Criminology and Police Science,* Vol. 48, pp. 51–57.

Hendin, Herbert
1964 *Suicide and Scandinavia.* New York: Grune and Stratton.

Henry, Andrew F., and James F. Short
1954 *Suicide and Homicide.* New York: The Free Press of Glencoe.

Holt, J. B.
1940 "Holiness Religion: Cultural Shock and Social Reorganization." *American Sociological Review,* Vol. 5, pp. 740–47.

Le Bon, Gustave
1960 [1895] *The Crowd.* New York: Viking Press.

Lofland, John
1966 *Doomsday Cult.* Englewood Cliffs, NJ: Prentice-Hall.

Lohman, Joseph D.
1947 *The Police and Minority Groups.* Chicago: Chicago Park District.

MacCormick, Austin H.
1954 "Behind the Prison Riots." *Annals of the American Academy of Political and Social Science,* Vol. 293, pp. 18–20.

McDougall, William
1920 *The Group Mind.* New York: G. P. Putnam's Sons.

Menninger, Karl A.
1938 *Man Against Himself.* New York: Harcourt, Brace, and World.

Neuberger, Richard L., and K. Loe
1936 "The Old People's Crusade." *Harper's Magazine,* Vol. 172, pp. 426–38.

Odegard, Peter
1928 *Pressure Politics: The Story of the Anti-Saloon League.* New York: Columbia University Press.

Ohlin, Lloyd E.
1956 *Sociology and the Field of Correction.* New York: Russell Sage Foundation.

Smelser, Neil J.
1962 *Theory of Collective Behavior.* New York: The Free Press of Glencoe.

Trotter, Wilfred
1922 *Instincts of the Herd in Peace and War.* London: T. Fisher Unwin.

Whiteman, L., and S. L. Lewis
1936 *Glory Roads: The Psychological State of California.* New York: Thomas Y. Crowell.

Wolfenstein, Martha
1957 *Disaster: A Psychological Essay.* New York: The Free Press and the Falcon Wing's Press.

3

Erik Erikson as Social Scientist

My objective in this essay is to throw light on two questions. First, *was* Erik Erikson a social scientist? Second, what *kind* of social scientist was he? My short answer to the first question is "yes"; my short answer to the second question is "a very good one." I will organize my elaboration of that assessment under four headings:

- Erikson the quintessential interdisciplinarian
- Some unresolved methodological issues in his interdisciplinary program
- Erikson's diagnosis of and verdict on Western, especially American, society
- Erikson's sociological idealism, which contains elements of positive utopianism

Erikson the Quintessential Interdisciplinarian

Erikson was, above all, a psychoanalyst, and it can be argued plausibly that his most enduring contributions are to psychoanalysis, in the form of his profound recasting of the psycho-sexual-social development of the individual person. But one cannot think of his contributions to knowledge without acknowledging immediately that he

Originally published in *Psychoanalysis and Contemporary Thought*, from the special issue entitled *Ideas and Identities: The Life and Work of Erik Erikson*, ed. Robert Wallerstein, 19, no. 2 (1996): 207–24. Reprinted by permission of International Universities Press, Inc.

had many other intellectual identities, and, more important, he brought these identities continuously into creative synthesis with one another.

His most notable interdisciplinary adventures were in anthropology and history. In *Childhood and Society* (Erikson, 1978 [1950]), arguably his most influential work, he developed his revised scheme of psychosocial development in the full comparative context of the Sioux, the Yurok, Hitler's Germany, and Gorki's Russia. It is no exaggeration, either, to state that he can be regarded as the inventor of modern psychohistory, embodied principally in his works on Luther (Erikson, 1962 [1958]) and Gandhi (Erikson, 1968a), but also in other work on Shaw, Jefferson, Christ, Einstein, and others. In these works Erikson was as much historian as psychoanalyst, and as much an integrator of the two as a practitioner of each—virtues which lend enormous credibility to this work.

Yet I find other disciplinary incarnations of Erikson as well. He was a lifelong artist—in his prepsychoanalytic avocation, as a student of the aesthetics of children's play, and as a consistently "seeing" or "visual" type of person in his human observations. He was an economic historian. If one reads the several-page account of the industrial history of Ahmedebad (Gandhi's city) and forgets it was Erikson writing, one would find an economic historian plying his craft—from the standpoint of archival data cited, descriptive variables employed, causes invoked, and interpretive schemes used (Erikson, 1968a, pp. 262–63). As a sociologist myself, I easily identified that dimension in Erikson as well. He was sensitive to the power of social stereotypes, as is clear from his comparison of the comparative social stereotyping of Ahmedebad and Pittsburgh (Erikson, 1968a, p. 29). He was sensitive to the sociological significance of caste in India, race in America, occupational niche in Reformation Germany, and gender and sexism in Victorian Vienna. Finally, as I hope to demonstrate, Erikson had at least a schematic sociological diagnosis of modern Western society.

Not only was Erikson many disciplinary persons; those persons were always conversing productively with one another in his work, as the following statements reveal:

- On his characterization of the volume *Childhood and Society:* "a psychoanalytic book on the *relation* of the ego to society" (1978 [1950], p. 16, emphasis added).
- On development: "The cogwheeling stages of childhood and adulthood are . . . truly a system of *generation* and *regeneration*—

for into this system flow, and from this system emerge, those social attitudes to which the institutions and traditions of society attempt to give unity and permanence" (Erikson, 1964b, p. 152).

- On the identity process: It is located "*in the core of the individual* and yet also *in the core of his communal culture,* a process which establishes, in fact, the identity of those two identities" (Erikson, 1968b, pp. 265–66).
- On the meshing of individual neurosis and social history: "Luther . . . was an endangered young man, beset with a syndrome of conflicts. . . . He found a spiritual solution. . . . His solution roughly bridged a political and psychological vacuum which history had created in a significant portion of Western Christendom. Such coincidence, if further coinciding with the deployment of highly specific personal gifts, makes for historical 'greatness'" (Erikson, 1962 [1958], p. 15).
- On psychohistory: "[It] is the study of individual and collective life with the combined methods of psychoanalysis and history" (Erikson, 1974, p. 13).
- On interdisciplinarity itself: "Only psychoanalysis and social science together can eventually chart the life cycle interwoven throughout with the history of the community" (Erikson, 1959a, p. 18).

In my estimation, this creative blending of perspectives to generate new insights and truth through integration is one of the keys to the understanding of Erikson's creativity.

Now, when a psychoanalyst—or any other kind of discipline-oriented scholar—makes such commitments to become more comparative, more historical, more developmental, and more incorporative of different analytic levels in his work, this necessarily generates a tension—a kind of disciplinary unease or discomfort. That tension arises from an inevitable pressure to relativize the universals of one's discipline. A simple example demonstrates this principle: in his theory of dreams, Freud posited a universal psychosexual meaning to certain symbols, such as water, snakes, and ovens with bread in them. As one moves through different cultural contexts and different eras of history, however, it becomes progressively more difficult to hold to this universal formulation, and more essential to qualify it through relativization or historicization.

Erikson did not escape this tension. In fact, he celebrated it by pointing out the necessity of making the concession to relativity and historicity. Some examples follow:

- On national character: "It will not do to call one nation psychiatric names. Every nation has *particular* regressive syndromes to which it is apt to revert to when safety and identity are threatened" (Erikson, 1945, p. 369).
- On the universalism of neurosis: "It is not enough . . . to reduce [Gandhi's crisis with his father] to the 'Oedipus Complex' reconstructed in thousands of case histories as the primal complex. The oedipal crisis . . . must be evaluated as a part of man's over-all development. [It] may be called the *generational complex*" (Erikson, 1968a, pp. 131–132).
- In a similar vein, Erikson reported a sympathy for the approach of an old shaman woman in Northern California, pointing to the value of her outlook and therapeutic methods *in the context of her society* (Erikson, 1964c).

In his biography of Erikson, Robert Coles noted this tendency. Erikson, he said, was suspicious of "wild" psychoanalyzing—that is, the indiscriminate application of invariant psychoanalytic categories to persons, artistic productions, and historical events. "Erikson had literally tried to complicate things, and stop the wholesale transfer of psychoanalytic concepts to Indian tribes or German politicians or Russian novelists" (Coles, 1970, p. 165). Coles went on to suggest that one of Erikson's motives in selecting *identity* as a core integrating concept was to get away from culture-bound, less inclusive psychoanalytic categories in his studies of history, biography, and anthropology. Be that as it may, Erikson did make the move toward relativization and historicization, and in the process became less wild and less orthodox. While this move no doubt both charmed and disarmed many potential skeptics, it also involved him in some unresolved methodological problems, to which we now turn.

Methodological Problems in Erikson's Interdisciplinarity

One can speak only in positive terms about Erikson's effort to cross the bridges among disciplinary frameworks and between different levels of analysis. It must be recognized, however, that this is an exceptionally difficult kind of intellectual operation—and for that reason rarely undertaken. Furthermore, those who attempt these syntheses and face the difficulties are often drawn into intellectual resolutions that leave much to be desired.

What are the difficulties? They lie in the very nature of disciplinary—indeed, disciplined—thought. In order to be disciplined, the investigator has to narrow the focus of inquiry to manageable proportions. The main way of doing this is to make two orders of assumptions about the world: (1) what order of reality is central and problematical, and (2) what order of reality is peripheral and nonproblematical. For example, in the first case the psychoanalyst typically has taken the inner psychological reality of impulse representation, conflict, defense, adaptation, and psychopathology as problematic; the economist typically has taken the realities of market interchange among individuals and organizations as the primary analytic focus. By contrast, for example, the psychoanalyst, as a rule, does not raise central, disciplined questions about the structure and functions of institutions or cataclysmic social changes, but, at best, takes them into account as features of the patient's psychic environment, thus preserving the analytic focus on the individual; the economist, as a rule, takes individual tastes and social institutions as "given," thus permitting him or her to proceed with a certain degree of analytic neatness and simplicity.

It should be evident from this brief characterization that this analytic simplification is both necessary and theoretically powerful, but at the same time oversimplifying and distortive of the totality of reality. Furthermore, what one disciplinary specialist takes as peripheral the other takes as central, and vice versa. To ask that one take the other's as *also* and *simultaneously* central is to invite a disciplined thinker to desert his or her creative simplifications and enter into the messy, multivariable, more realistic world but at the same time sacrifice the analytic power associated with his or her own discipline.

Despite the difficulties of venturing outside the disciplinary boundaries, scholars sometimes undertake to do so. It is not an overstatement to say that, in most cases, they do so badly. Typically they employ one of two closely related strategies, each of which soon becomes unproductive and illegitimate. The first is to argue by *analogy;* simply stated, this is to assert that processes at one level are like those at another—the person or society is a machine, the society is an organism, the group has a mind, the institution of marriage functions like any economic market, and so on. The second is to argue by *reduction;* simply stated, this is an attempt to translate, without loss, all statements at one analytic level into statements regarding the operations of variables at another level. Examples of reductionism are explaining mental phenomena in exclusively physiological terms, thus reducing the former to the latter, or, with Marx and Engels, explaining the state exclusively as the servant of the dominant ruling class, thus robbing it of independent analytic significance.

I will dismiss the questionable strategies of analogy and reduction, largely because Erikson himself rejected them as antithetical to his whole intellectual mission. There is a third strategy that, to my mind, offers most promise. It goes as follows: to preserve the analytic gains of disciplinary simplification by retaining distinctive levels of analysis, but to relax systematically the parameters (the "givens") and to trace the ramifications of that relaxation—for example, to have the economists envision motivational givens other than economic maximization, and trace the ramifications of these variations for economic behavior and the functioning of markets. (For a development of this strategy for psychoanalysis and the other social sciences, see Wallerstein and Smelser, 1969.)

I mention this analytic strategy partly as a way of highlighting what Erikson did *not* do as a social scientist. Erikson was certainly cognizant of and interested in theoretical issues, both in psychoanalysis and in the social sciences, but I would submit that he was not interested in the systematic theoretical formulation of those issues, with an accompanying attention to the logical structure of theory, the production of systematic hypotheses, rigorous testing of those hypotheses under controlled conditions, and all the rest. Rather, I would also submit, he was predisposed—through his own aesthetic predilections and through his thoroughgoing clinical training—to take an alternative approach, an approach that was individually and historically specific. As is well known, Erikson focused on the innovative, creative, generation-shaping, historically transforming individual—Luther, Gandhi, Jefferson, Martin Luther King (in passing), and others—and treated them in terms of the intersection of their biographies with their historical eras. These historical eras also were specific: the Reformation, colonial India, the transition from late colonial to early republican America, and the civil rights revolution. So, in the end, Erikson stayed with the mode of the "life history" and the "case history," though he regarded these as "no longer manners of speaking" (Erikson, 1974), in that individual biography and historical reality were always in interaction with one another. In a word, Erikson's approach, even to interdisciplinarity, was consistently and always in the clinical mode.

The inevitable shortfall of this mode, of course, lies in its lack of generalizability. It remains forever rooted in the specific individual and the specific historical era. As far as general formulations are concerned, they are just that—*general.* For example, momentous historical transitions occur under conditions when there is a decisive meshing among individual neurosis, a political and psychological vacuum generated by previous social change, and "highly specific personal gifts." These conditions are quite nonspecific, and Erikson never went further in attempting to identify them in generic terms that would be identifiable in a variety of historical settings—that is, as principles.

The same methodological problem appears elsewhere in Erikson's work, though in different garb. This has to do with the generalizability of his "stages of life" scheme beyond the Western historical context. On the one hand, Erikson formulated the scheme in very general if not universal terms—basic trust, initiative, guilt, intimacy, generativity, despair, and so on. On the other hand, in illustrating the *social* side of some of the stages, he linked that side to institutions that are distinctively Western, if not American, in reference. For example, in *Childhood and Society,* Erikson (1978 [1950]) remarked that in the industry versus inferiority phase, "the inner stage seems all set for 'entrance into life,' except that life must first be school life"; schools, of course, are not found in all societies. And in the identity versus role confusion stage in adolescence, he spoke of the power of "cliques and crowds," and of "falling in love," which are, evidently, like adolescence itself, somewhat modern and Western-looking. Once again, the tension between universal reference and cultural specificity appears.

Erikson experienced this issue directly in his seminar in Ahmedebad. He found there what he diplomatically described as Indians' nonacceptance of his developmental scheme on account of its evident inapplicability to Indian religious, historical, and contemporary conceptions of development. He himself made a heroic effort to reconcile the evident cultural differences. But in the end he found only a general point of comparability:

> It would be fruitless to compare these [Western and Indian] schemes point for point. What is more important is the principle which makes them comparable at all—that is, the epigenetic principle according to which in each stage of life a given strength is added on to a widening ensemble and re-integrated at each later stage in order to play its part in a full cycle—if and where fate and society permit. (Erikson, 1968a, p. 38)

But we must pause here and ask what is being done. Faced with obvious cross-cultural noncomparability, the temptation is—and Erikson gave into it—to move in a *general* direction, so that what was noncomparable becomes comparable through inclusion. But in that operation the whole scheme loses applicability through its very generalization. What we witness is the tension between comparability and specificity of formulation. Erikson struggled with but did not resolve that tension, but if it will help matters any, it is also true to say that none of us ever has.

A Diagnosis of Western, Especially American, Society

The preceding material has demonstrated that Erikson was a keen observer of society, as well as an original thinker with respect to the multiple linkages between individual and society. In addition, it is possible to extricate from Erikson's writings a recurrent set of ideas about the contemporary Western world. I will emphasize here the tension between alienation and admiration on the one hand, and between negative and positive utopian elements in his thought. Needless to say, we will also find a mixture of both description and evaluation, of both neutrality and ideological commitment.

There are evident reasons to suspect that, in his own development, Erikson had tendencies to distance himself from his own society, to be correspondingly alienated, and to search continuously for his own identity. He says as much. Writing in 1964, he described himself as a young man: "an artist . . . which can be a European euphemism for a young man with some talent, but nowhere to go" (Erikson, 1964a, p. 20; see also Erikson, 1972 [1970]). Elsewhere he referred to "my generation of alienated youth in Europe" (1968b, pp. 10–11), without actually confessing—but strongly suggesting—that he belonged to that generation. Furthermore, there was a certain consistency in his alienation. Not only did he exhibit that general distance from society in his youth, but he also refrained from unalienating himself by joining groups of alienated German youths—groups that sometimes had sinister overtones (Coles, 1970, p. 16).

The second circumstance contributing to Erikson's sense of alienation and preoccupation with identity was his experience as an immigrant to America, a discontinuity that fed into already ambiguous identities—German or Danish, Jewish or non-Jewish. Again there are no secrets here; Erikson tells us that his status as an immigrant focused him on the problem of identity (Erikson, cited in Evans, 1967, p. 29), and he added that his migration from East to West in the United States accentuated this preoccupation.

Be all that as it may, one discovers in Erikson's writings a certain idealization of the simplicity and complexity of the West's (and America's) past and corresponding disenchantment with the present, modern world. At one moment he contrasted primitive tribes with modern civilizations. In the former, people "have a direct relation to the sources and means of production . . . to [children], body and environment, childhood and culture [and] . . . are all one world." In our times, however, "[the] expansiveness of civilization, together with its stratification and specialization, force children to base their ego models on shifting, sectional, and contradictory prototypes" (Erikson, 1959b, p. 22). On another occasion he noted that while the agricultural and mercantile stages of development generated their own distinctive forms of alienation, under conditions of contemporary industrialization, "man turns other men and himself into tools, and the machines he runs into machinery which runs him . . . the *technological* world of today is about to create kinds of alienations too strange to be imagined" (1964c, pp. 104–5). For America, Erikson had an evident nostalgia for its early years: "the first self-made nation, creating itself out of immigrants who came from all the pseudospecies of the world and converged here" (K. Erikson, 1973, p. 121). But America, like the rest of the modern world, seemed to have gone haywire in its pace of change. It had fallen victim to a kind of "quantitative overreach" (K. Erikson, 1973, p. 121):

> How can we really grasp, in one lifetime—to speak only of what America has wrought—Hiroshima, the moon landings, or, for that matter, our moral malaise at the height of our mechanized power of destruction? And . . . how few of us can feel sufficiently in touch with a sufficiently significant number of human beings to be activated by and to activate them, insulated as many of us are in compartments within the gigantic networks of long-range mobility, of industrial complexes, and telecommunication. (Erikson, 1974, pp. 80–81)

To move to specifics, what were the precise features of modern, industrial, technological civilization that Erikson regarded as alienating? The following appear in his commentaries:

- *Mechanization:* "Industrial man's attempt to identify with the machine as if it were a new totem animal leads him into a self-perpetuating race for robot-like efficiency, and yet also the question as to what, when all adjustments are made, is left of a human 'identity'" (Erikson, 1964c, p. 105).

- *Technological overdevelopment:* After mentioning Hiroshima and the landing on the moon, Erikson (1966) concluded that "[America] overreached its own comprehension of itself." He went on to express the hope that change "could yet become part of a planned world fit for a wider identity and a new adulthood on earth, but not by way of the cosmic coercion of gadgetry . . ." (p. 501).
- *Institutional decay:* Erikson speaks of "*anxieties* aggravated by the decay of existing institutions which have provided the historical anchor of an elite's identity" (Erikson, 1964c, p. 104).
- *The danger of totalitarianism:* "Technological centralization today can give small groups of . . . fanatic ideologists the concrete power of totalitarian state machines . . ." (Erikson, 1959c, p. 159).
- *Pseudospeciation and the possibility of world-destruction:* "[Is man] destined to remain divided into . . . 'pseudo-species' forever playing out one (necessarily incomplete) version of mankind against all the others until, in the glory of the nuclear age, one version will have the power and the luck to destroy all others just moments before it perishes itself?" (Erikson, 1972 [1970], p. 24).

It was this last possibility that held out the greatest dread for Erikson. It was a version of the "cultural lag" theory of social change: the human cultural tendency to bond into mutually antagonistic groups has failed to evolve into a recognition that man is one species, and because of the development of technology, that tendency now threatens the very existence of the human race. "[Man] may not only blow himself up with an atom bomb, but he may . . . poison his woods and water at home now, and outer space in the future. He may also create a way of life for himself which personality and organism cannot bear (even if specialized organisms and personalities survive) and which the generational process cannot bear" (Erikson, cited in Evans, 1967, p. 109).

Such is the negative portrait that Erikson painted of our technological, complex, and divided society. In connection with that portrait, the following paradox has come to my mind: If one examines the content of the portrait, it is remarkably similar to the composite portrait painted by the mass society theorists of the 1940s and 1950s—Emil Lederer, Hannah Arendt, Erich Fromm—who stressed the depersonalization and institutional erosion of modern society—and the theorists of the critical school or Frankfurt school—Adorno, Horkheimer, Herbert Marcuse, and later Jürgen Habermas—who stressed the oppressive and humanly destructive effects of technology, bureaucracy, and mass communication. I cannot find any significant particulars of difference between these schools of thought and Erikson's diagnosis.

The paradox is this: why was Erikson never really assimilated to these schools, especially to the radical, neo-Marxist left represented by the critical school? It is clear that he was not. But why? I venture the following three hypotheses for consideration.

1. Erikson made a different use of psychoanalysis than did the mass society and critical schools. Erikson remained a psychoanalyst as such, though he modified that field fundamentally in a social direction. The critical theorists in particular *relied* on psychoanalysis, but they regarded it as a liberating, indeed critical, mode of thought, which could, much as Marxist thought did, unmask the contradictions of the modern West. The critical theorists, especially Marcuse, actively *rejected* psychoanalysis on the grounds of its individualist bias—that is, they claimed that psychoanalysis located social problems on the individual and thus excused society, whereas, in their reality, the sickness of society lay with the society itself.

2. Social class—the central preoccupation of the Marxist tradition—scarcely figured in Erikson's theoretical formulations. He was sensitive to class in society, as we have seen. But he left it out of his diagnosis of society. In his characterization of pseudospeciation, he argued that "in all his past man has based much of his identity on mutually exclusive group identities in the form of tribes, nations, castes, religions, and so on" (Erikson, 1972 [1970], p. 24). But there is no mention of class or class warfare—the central proposition of his like-minded, left-minded contemporaries.

3. Most important, in my mind, is the fact that the phenomenon of oppression, the hallmark of all Marxist and neo-Marxist derivatives, did not figure centrally in Erikson's characterization of modern industrial society. He would notice it; for example, he pointed out that systems based on "suppression, exclusion and exploitation" generate evil self-images on the part of those dominated—a version of the phenomenon of identification with the aggressor (Erikson, 1959a, p. 31). But there was no systematic incorporation of oppression in Erikson's characterization of modern life, and this, I would argue, placed him in a different arena from other social critics who shared so much of his negative view of that life.

Utopian Elements in Erikson's Thought

I have just laid out the essentials of Erikson's negative utopia, as these appeared in his diagnosis of contemporary society. These ingredients are a materialistic fetishism, worship of technique, bureaucracy, and social complexity; an instrumentalization and depersonalization of human relations; alienation and despair; directionlessness; loss of identity; and an irrational pseudospeciation—irrational because it is likely to become the instrument of the destruction of humanity, when combined with the nuclear technology at hand.

At the same time, we also discover vivid elements of a positive utopia recurring in Erikson's writings—elements that also help explain his wide appeal as a thinker in the twentieth century. This utopia was not systematically laid out; he took some of it from earlier periods in history, some from other societies, and some from the future. A number of themes touch on the idea of harmony:

- *The psychological harmony provided by proper identity:* "The key problem of identity . . . is . . . the capacity of the ego to sustain sameness and continuity in the face of changing fate. But fate always combines changes in inner conditions, which are the result of ongoing life stages, and changes in the milieu, the historical situation. Identity connotes the resiliency of maintaining essential patterns in the processes of change" (Erikson, 1964c, pp. 95–96).
- *The harmony of the social and the psychological:* "only by maintaining, in its institutionalized values, meaningful correspondences to the main crises of ego development, does the society manage to have at the disposal of its particular group identity a maximum of the conflict-free energy accrued from the childhood crises of a majority of its young members" (Erikson, 1959c, p. 155). Elsewhere he noted desirability of "fit' between institutions and phases of psychosocial development—for example, between religion and basic trust, and between legality ("law and order") and autonomy (Erikson, 1959b, pp. 64–65, 73–74).
- *On the harmony between maleness and femaleness:* Erikson held excessive masculinity to be responsible in part for some of the ills of our time. The dominant male identity is, he said, "based on a fondness for 'what works' and for what man can make, whether it helps to build or to destroy" (Erikson, 1968b, p. 262). He saw women's

identity as a counterforce: "Maybe if women would only gain the determination to represent publicly what they have always stood for . . . they might well add an ethically restraining, because truly supranational, power to politics in the widest sense" (Erikson, 1968b, p. 262). In another context he regarded Gandhi's rejection of British colonialism as a kind of rejection of Western masculinity, and he wrote, with evident admiration, of Gandhi's mix of maleness and femaleness, as well as the "basic bisexuality" of Indian civilization (Erikson, 1968a, p. 44).

- *On the harmony among generations:* "The utopia of today . . . is based on a reduction in the number of births *and* a new ethic based on a greater awareness of what each generation owes to the next . . . All over the world today there is more of a sense . . . that whatever is going to happen to the next generation is our problem today" (Erikson, cited in Evans, 1967, pp. 109–10).

But Erikson's greatest preoccupation, I believe, was with the evils of pseudospeciation and the potential of that warped system of identity for world destruction. His antidote was for a transformation of identity in a universal direction. He saw in Freud's writings on eros "the implication that [the future] demands an all-human adulthood" (Erikson, 1982, p. 95). For Erikson, the realization of this means a true utopia. It would give "[man] a chance to act as an adult *and* as a knowing participant in one human specieshood . . . this would overcome pseudo- (or quasi-) speciation; that is, the splitting into imaginary species that has provided adult rejectivity with a most moralistic rationalization of the hate of otherness" (Erikson, 1982, p. 95). Thus, in the end, Erikson emerges as kind of panhumanist, an advocate of the universalization of human identity, which alone can provide the basis for realization of maturity and an ethic of mutual acceptance and love.

Conclusion

I have used the world "utopian" to characterize both the negative and positive elements of Erikson's diagnosis of society. That use is deliberate, and for two reasons. The term both reflects his outlook and possesses elements of unrealism. Erikson's diagnosis of the contemporary West is certainly selective, one-sided, and short on specifies; his view is the subject of continuous debate between cultural pessimists and cultural optimists; that debate, moreover, has not been and will not be finally resolved. His hopes for a harmonious, universally inclusive, and ethical world seem likewise simple and unrealizable, given the apparently irreducible evidence of the potential for human conflict and destruction.

Yet, in the very last analysis, to leave the judgment at that would be wrong. In the end we have to respect, admire, envy, and love Erikson for his ideals. Like the world leaders who fascinated him and commanded his attention, Erikson led the way in elevating us to levels of thought and hope that we, on our mundane own, are almost never capable of attaining. He will live in future generations not only for the brilliance of his thought but also for his spiritual elevation. For both of those we owe him eternal gratitude.

References

Coles, R.

1970 *Erik H. Erikson: The Growth of His Work.* Boston: Little, Brown.

Erikson, E. H.

1945 "A Memorandum to the Joint Committee on Post War Planning." In *A Way of Looking at Things: Selected Papers from 1930 to 1980*, edited by S. Schlein. New York: Norton. Pp. 366–74.

1959a "Ego Development and Historical Change." In *Identity and the Life Cycle,* Vol. 1. New York: International Universities Press. Pp. 18–49.

1959b "The Problem of Ego Identity." In *Identity and the Life Cycle,* Vol. 1. New York: International Universities Press. Pp. 18–171.

1959c "The Problem of Ego Identity." In *Identity and the Life Cycle, Psychological Issues.* New York: International Universities Press. Pp. 101–166.

1962 [1958] *Young Man Luther: A Study in Psychoanalysis and History.* New York: Norton.

1964a "The First Psychoanalyst." In *Insight and Responsibility.* New York: Norton. Pp. 17–46.

1964b "Human Strength and the Cycle of Generations." In *Insight and Responsibility.* New York: Norton. Pp. 110–57.

1964c "Identity and Uprootedness in Our Time." In *Insight and Responsibility.* New York: Norton. Pp. 83–107.

1966 "Remarks on the 'Wider Identity'." In *A Way of Looking at Things: Selected Papers from 1930 to 1980*, edited by S. Schlein. New York: Norton. Pp. 497–502.

1968a *Gandhi's Truth: On the Origins of Militant Nonviolence.* New York: Norton.

1968b *Identity: Youth and Crisis.* New York: Norton.

1972 [1970] "Autobiographic Notes on the Identity Crisis." In *The Twentieth Century Sciences: Studies in the Biography of Ideas,* edited by G. Holton. New York: Norton. Pp. 3–32.

1974 *Dimensions of a New Identity: The 1973 Jefferson Lectures in the Humanities.* New York: Norton.

1978 [1950] *Childhood and Society.* 2d ed. New York: Norton.

1982 *The Life Cycle Completed: A Review.* New York: Norton.

Erikson, K. T. (ed.)

1973 *In Search of Common Ground: Conversations with Erik H. Erikson and Huey P. Newton.* New York: Norton.

Evans, R. I.

1967 *Dialogue with Erik Erikson.* New York: Harper and Row.

Wallerstein, R. S., and N. J. Smelser

1969 "Psychoanalysis and Sociology: Articulations and Applications." *International Journal of Psycho-Analysis,* Vol. 50, pp. 693–710.

PART II

Psychoanalytic Sociology

4

Some Determinants of Destructive Behavior

The problem of evil is so ancient, so intractable, and so complex that it is scarcely possible to utter the phrase without evoking dozens of connotations—connotations which are simultaneously biological, psychological, social, moral, and theological. For this reason, discourse on the subject is likely to run afoul; because the term *evil* taps so many meanings, we stand a good chance of talking past one another at all times. In this chapter I address the problems of why and by what mechanisms evil becomes socially acceptable and therefore likely to be perpetrated. But because the term *evil* is such an ambiguous one, I begin by setting forth a few definitions and distinctions that are intended to frame the universe of discourse within which I operate here.

Initially it is essential to draw a distinction between evil on the one hand and force and violence on the other. In some situations the exercise of force and violence are universally agreed not to be evil, even though these situations may be regarded as regrettable necessities of the human condition. As an illustrative situation I have in mind the right—even the duty—of a parent forcibly to restrain a child from walking into traffic, even though this act may do some physical and psychological violence to the child. As another I have in mind the right—even the duty—of a police officer to exercise force and violence to prevent one citizen from forcibly abducting another. It seems ill advised to regard such situations as perpetrations of evil.

What meaning, then, ought we to reserve for evil, considered in its social context? I think the term is most appropriately applied to situa-

Originally published in *Sanctions for Evil,* ed. Nevitt Sanford and Craig Comstock (San Francisco: Jossey-Bass, 1971), pp. 15–24. Reprinted by permission.

tions when force, violence, and other forms of coercion exceed institutional or moral limits. By this definition the following kinds of situations qualify: (1) When individuals or groups not empowered by a legitimately accepted order to exercise coercion do so—for example, in armed robbery or wanton mob destruction. (2) When individuals or groups legally and institutionally empowered to exercise coercion exceed the legitimate limits of that exercise—for example, a parent who tortures his or her child, a policeman who brutally beats a citizen, a military unit which massacres civilians. However, because the goodness of the institutionalized order cannot always be assumed, a third situation must be added: (3) When the institutionalization of the exercise of coercion offends some higher standards of humanity or morality that we feel ought to be observed—for example, the police state, which is solidly institutionalized, to be sure, but which may be regarded as evil because it assaults the freedom, dignity, and civil liberties of its subjects.

I am interested in the causes of these kinds of evil. I concentrate here especially on the cultural and social determinants. In particular, I ask four related but distinguishable questions: (1) How is evil legitimized? What kinds of shared values or beliefs or sentiments are appealed to in order to render the prosecution of evil permissible or desirable? (2) How is evil authorized? The question of legitimization refers mainly to cultural values or standards. The question of authorization refers to the social context of the behavior. What persons or agencies authorize evil? Who gives it the green light? These questions suggest the importance of identifying the roles people in authority play in the genesis and prosecution of evil. (3) How are people mobilized for evil actions? The question of authorization refers to the degree to which organized social arrangements permit or encourage evil. In addition to gaining permission, however, people must often be positively stimulated, organized, and led to perpetrate evil. The question of mobilization concerns especially the role of leadership. Sometimes those who authorize destructive actions are also instrumental as leaders, but not always. For this reason, it is important to distinguish between authorization and mobilization as separate social determinants of evil actions. (4) How is evil rationalized? This question arises by virtue of the fundamental fact that even if evil actions are legitimized and authorized, they invariably occur in the context of other, competing values and standards that define them as illegitimate and, indeed, evil. Evil invariably occurs, that is, in a context not only of its own legitimization but also of a contrary set of values that label it illegitimate. A tension is thus created between two standards of conduct. Rationalization refers to the shared cognitive processes by which people attempt to smooth over and otherwise come to terms with that tension.

In the remainder of the essay I identify some of the processes that are involved in legitimizing, authorizing, mobilizing for, and rationalizing evil. I consider these processes both in relatively spontaneous, unstructured situations and in institutionalized, structured situations.

One of the most profound aspects of evil is that the one who does the evil is typically convinced that evil is about to be done to him or her. He or she regards the world or at least part of it as dangerous or bent on destruction and therefore something justifiably to be destroyed. Sometimes this belief appears fleetingly in a moment of crisis. I have in mind the inexperienced National Guardsmen, called in periodically to quell ghetto disturbances in 1967, who, upon hearing or thinking they heard shots, literally panicked and began shooting in various directions. This reaction seems to have happened also in the Kent State tragedy. I also have in mind the rumors of atrocities—sometimes justified and sometimes unjustified—that typically run through the ranks of both rioting citizens and those who are attempting to put the rioters down. These fleeting beliefs and rumors identify an enemy and pave the way for destruction.

Sometimes these beliefs develop over long periods of time. During the winter of 1968 I did some consulting work for the staff of the National Advisory Commission on Civil Disorders. As part of this work I examined some fairly detailed data on the racial disturbances in Plainfield, New Jersey, in July 1967. It was both instructive and saddening to see the sequence of incidents—the unmet demands, the miscommunication between racial leaders and town leaders, the death of a policeman—that led to the buildup of two inflexible sets of beliefs, one held by blacks and one by the police. Both sets were identical in structure: they portrayed the other side as vastly more deliberate, organized, cunning, premeditated, and malicious than the other side actually was. These sets of beliefs had several consequences. They provided for each side a cognitive framework within which almost any kind of behavior could be regarded as evidence of malevolence. For example, black demands for a public meeting were interpreted by the police as evidence of the blacks' intention to mobilize for attack; if they did not demand a public meeting, the police suspected that they were meeting secretly to mobilize for an attack. And the blacks interpreted police behavior in similar ways. Furthermore, these beliefs justified preventive attacks on the part of both sides, attacks which further confirmed and consolidated the beliefs themselves. And, finally, as these beliefs became more and more rigid and stereotyped, the behavioral options left to either side—other than lashing out in rage at the other—were progressively diminished. Such social-psychological dynamics often lead to destructive behavior; the external world, or some part of it, is regarded as an incarnation of evil, and this perception leads to the perpetration of evil.

In still other cases the belief in the enemy becomes part of a developed ideology and may become institutionalized in the sense that it legitimizes continuous destructiveness. The rumors that often preceded lynchings in the post-Restoration South were that a black man had assaulted a white man or raped a white woman—thus confirming the general belief that the black person was a dangerous, uncontrolled animal and thus making that person's destruction, in the minds of the whites, both legitimate and imperative. The stereotype of the Jew in Nazi ideology and the stereotype of the Japanese in America in World War II, although differing in content, legitimized destructive behavior which would have been regarded as evil under other circumstances.

One legitimizing ingredient of destructiveness, then, is to hold a belief that some enemy is simultaneously evil, intelligent, and omnipotent. Furthermore, because these beliefs have such a strong component of anxiety, they are likely to be very volatile, generalizing and switching from object to object, particularly in times of danger or crisis.

The instances I have just cited constitute the negative side of the belief system that legitimizes evil. But they are only half the story. In addition, the perpetrator of evil typically holds fast to a corresponding belief in his own omnipotence and moral superiority. To believe that one is an indestructible saint or crusader makes it easy to spread destruction in the world. Indeed, that belief often demands that one stamp out evil.

In those unstructured situations I mentioned, these beliefs often appear only in embryo. They may be as simple as the brief but exhilarating sensation of omnipotence that the soldier experiences when plunging a bayonet or shooting a bullet into a hated enemy. Or they may emerge as that momentary surge of magical thinking that runs through a crowd when it stones a hated political leader who has been publicly executed. These fleeting moments of omnipotence that accompany destructive actions make these actions both easy and attractive.

The legitimizing function of these beliefs is seen clearly in religious and political ideologies. Consider, for example, the righteous and crusading spirit of the church militant with its Christian soldiers—a spirit which has infused the Christian tradition in various ways and which has been employed on numerous occasions to legitimize excesses of violence. Or consider the other side of the coin—Nazi anti-Semitism: a firm belief in the racial and moral purity and superiority of the Aryan race, by virtue of which the evils of the world were to be overcome. Or, to bring the illustrations perhaps closer to home, consider one strand of the traditional cultural myth of American masculinity, particularly as it is manifested repeatedly in folk heroes such as Superman, the Lone Ranger, and Batman. Here is the one-man vigilante, who, by sheer dint of his hypermasculine qualities, his cleverness, and, above all, his moral superiority, brings the evil forces at least to justice and perhaps to their destruction. (This myth reveals the moral ambivalence often concealed by beliefs in moral righteousness. The mythical superman must be above the law. Usually, moreover, the official representative of the law—the sheriff or the police commissioner—must sit on the sidelines, helpless, and be rescued by the extralegal but superhuman and supermoral stranger who takes the law into his own hands and saves the day.)

I do not mean to equate all these illustrations in every way or to assert that they all have an equal potential for erupting into destructive behavior. And although arguing that these cultural myths help to bring people to the threshold of destructive behavior, I do not assert that the beliefs automatically manifest themselves in such behavior. Indeed, such cultural myths enjoy a more or less universal and permanent existence and tend to be activated only under certain historical conditions. Some of these historical conditions come into existence, moreover, when destructive behavior is authorized and rationalized. I turn now to a few brief illustrations of these other conditions.

Above and beyond the cultural beliefs that predispose people to perpetrate the kinds of actions we have been considering lies the separate question of the social milieu. The literature on collective behavior is replete with theories of the group mind, the anonymity that the crowd provides, and the magic of the demagogue. Rather than review these theories—most of which are rather too general to be helpful—I focus specifically on a few examples in which authority and leadership are likely to facilitate or impede destructive behavior.

Let me begin with a simple and hypothetical, but, I am certain, typical example. The coach of a college or high school football team is, in one respect, supposed to be a model of discipline and self-control for the athletes on his team. After all, the maximization of these qualities presumably contributes much to winning games. Traditionally, too, coaches have taken an interest in the general conduct of the players—their grades, their dietary habits, their general moral conduct. Yet this authority is often exercised with a mock severity or, indeed, permissiveness. An example is the coach's remark, made with a grin and a wink, to his players on a road trip, "O.K., boys, remember, no whoring around before the game tomorrow." A prohibition on the face of it, the remark is actually an informal authorization of a visit to the brothel and an indication that no sanctions will be invoked. And although the mock prohibition does not mobilize the boys for the adventure, it increases the probability that they will mobilize themselves.

Consider the role of authorization now in relation to destructive behavior and in situations other than the informal, unstructured illustration I have given. The likelihood of rampages of destructiveness is greatly heightened when some person or agency in authority condones or at least permits these rampages. The most naked form of authorization is that in a totalitarian state which establishes mass destruction, concentration camps, or slave labor camps as a matter of official policy. But this form is not the only one. Consider the military policies in Vietnam of search and destroy, free-fire zones, and using whatever means are necessary to destroy the enemy. These policies say, in effect, that anything goes and, although not ordering civilian massacres, set the normative climate that encourages military units to exceed whatever limits on destructiveness may otherwise be observed. Or, finally, consider the political or military authority that simply remains silent, thus establishing an atmosphere that does not oblige troops to destroy but does not oblige them not to either. Furthermore, if effective counterauthorizing agencies—for example, courts capable of handing down severe penalties for brutality—do not exist or are feeble, the probabilities are increased that evil may be authorized or quasiauthorized with impunity.

In some cases those who authorize evil also mobilize people and resources into a destructive apparatus. A totalitarian government bent on mass extermination and an army girded for total war are instances of simultaneous authorization and mobilization. In other cases, however, authorization involves a posture of permissiveness or ambiguity on the part of authorities, a posture that does not openly and positively sanction—and thereby guarantee the perpetration of—destructiveness. In these cases the mobilization for evil develops through independent social mechanisms.

Consider again my hypothetical example of the athletes away from their home institution for a road game. After the mock admonition from the coach, which sets the stage for a sexual adventure, a number of athletes, rooming in the same motel, are sitting around, bored and waiting. One of the athletes suggests that they go out and find prostitutes. The idea is discussed, and after a while the informal leader of the group says he is not in the mood; the project dies. Or, after the suggestion is made and discussed, the informal leader says he thinks it is a good idea. One of the others protests, saying he is not interested. One of his buddies says, "What's the matter, are you a fairy or something?" He gives in, and they all leave.

The latter situation illustrates how the several determinants I have outlined combine to produce an episode of behavior. The action—going to a brothel—is legitimized by the appeal to some ideal of masculinity. The ideal invoked is that it is important to be a man (and not to be its obverse, a homosexual). The action is given authorization by the mock admonition by the coach. And it is mobilized by invoking norms and personal influence in the small group. None of the determinants alone is sufficient to produce the episode, but when all combine, it is very likely to occur.

Although one hesitates to generalize too much from this situation, some of the lynchings, massacres, and rapes of history must be written according to this script. A military unit, fatigued after battle, perhaps demoralized and angry after its own partial decimation, finds itself in an isolated situation, away from many usual social controls. The sport of killing a few "goons" arises as a collective assertion of some vague but strongly held ideal of masculinity (and possibly a collective denial of in-group rivalry and homosexuality). The event may be triggered, moreover, by the critical initiative taken by a formal or informal group leader.

As I indicated, the rationalization of evil is similar to but distinct from its legitimization. By rationalization I mean the ways in which the perpetrators of evil come to terms with their own consciences and with the value systems that condemn their behavior as illegitimate. Much can be learned about rationalization by studying the familiar psychological mechanisms of defense—projection, denial, displacement, intellectualization, and rationalization itself. The study of individual reactions to the My Lai massacre is striking confirmation of the defensive lengths to which people go to protect themselves from their consciences, even when they have not been directly involved in the evil act itself.

As though individuals were not good enough at making rationalizations on their own, society and its language provide us with dozens of ready-made homilies and proverbs by which we may build bridges between our consciences and our reprehensible behavior. Consider the following: "All's fair in love and war." "Done in the line of duty." "It was either them or us." These utterances are simple reassurances that the actor need not bear all the guilt for the deed because special circumstances justify it. Insofar as these reassurances are readily available and commonly accepted, deeds of evil are rendered easier to execute.

Much of what I have written in this essay strikes a somewhat pessimistic note with respect to the prevention and control of evil. After all, humans are very ingenious and prolific at legitimizing, authorizing, and rationalizing almost anything, evil included. Furthermore, many of the forces that go into the legitimization and rationalization of evil are very firmly rooted in the depths of impulse life, in social and political conflicts, in ideological and religious traditions, and in situational vicissitudes. As a result, they are likely to be very impervious to modification by deliberate social policy.

However, it does seem possible and plausible to dedicate social energies to the reform of systems of authorization. I have in mind new legislation at all levels restricting the excesses that military and police personnel perpetrate. I have in mind the widespread institutionalization of civilian review boards for checking police and military conduct. I have in mind new policies that honor people by public citation for the exercise of restraint and control in explosive and violent situations—medals for refusing to kill instead of medals for killing. I have in mind programs for the mass media that portray bravery and courage as the capacity to refrain from destructiveness when the opportunity allows. I expect that none of these measures or even a combination of all of them will bring an end to evil and destructiveness. As I indicated, evil is an intractable problem and to attack it is like attempting to assault a granite boulder with one's bare hands. However, the most promising line of attack is on those very structures that are institutionalized around the issues of violence and destructiveness. What is required is an attempt to shape them as institutional structures that are vitally necessary for social existence, to be sure, but at the same time to regard them as necessary evils rather than as holy instruments designed to stamp out evil. To tailor legislation, policy, and procedures in line with this rationale seems to me the most feasible means to break into and deflect those cumulative and seemingly irreversible sequences of behavior that end in destructive excesses.

5

Vicissitudes of Work and Love in Anglo-American Society

In this speculative essay I shall explore the ways work and love have been valued and institutionalized in recent Anglo-American history and then briefly consider their future. First, a few definitions and distinctions are in order. Two modes of human action frequently distinguished in this essay are the instrumental and the affective. The instrumental mode refers to the disciplined organization of activities toward the accomplishment of designated tasks; the affective mode refers to expressive or gratificatory attachments to both human and nonhuman objects. This distinction has appeared in diverse guises in the history of philosophy and has constituted a central basis for much contemporary thinking in social theory (Parsons, 1960; Parsons and Shils, 1951). More specifically, these two modes of human action are reflected in the distinction between work and love: work is one variety of instrumental activity, and love can be regarded as one organization of affective attachments.

Analytically the distinction between the instrumental and the affective may be considered at several levels—the personality, the culture, and the social structure. At the personality level we clearly observe people at work and people in love, recognize these orientations in ourselves, and distinguish between the two easily enough. Yet I would argue that the distinction, to be useful at this level, should be regarded as identifying aspects of human action but not discrete orientations, because in fact the two orientations are often so inextricably meshed that it becomes difficult to distinguish between them. For example, one can love one's

Originally published in Neil J. Smelser and Erik H. Erikson (eds.), *Themes of Work and Love in Adulthood* (Cambridge, MA: Harvard University Press, 1980), pp. 105–18.

work, and one can—indeed, is well advised to—work at love. What we call "work" invariably has some kind of expressive dimension, and what we call "love" is never without an instrumental component, though they may be repressed or denied in various ways.

At the other two levels, however, the distinction can be made more clearly. Cultures and worldviews may value or devalue either the instrumental or the expressive mode, or both; may ignore one or the other; and may regard the two as complementary, mutually exclusive, or antipathetic. At the social-structural level, each of the two orientations may be compartmentalized in various ways. This is most clearly seen in the pervasive tendency to institutionalize the "instrumental" or "work" orientation into discrete occupational roles, governed by an array of norms in relative isolation from other arenas of life. And while the normative regulation of affective expression is perhaps less self-evident, institutionalized norms of love, marriage, kinship, and friendship clearly define the times, places, and situations in which impulses are and are not to be gratified, and feelings are and are not to be experienced (Durkheim, 1951 [1897]; Davis, 1936).

Separation and Mutual Exclusion

At the cultural level, modern British and American history have been characterized—in different ways, as we shall see—by the increasing instrumentalization and rationalization of life, with a corresponding split between the instrumental and expressive modes. With respect to the cultural origins of this split, I would join Weber in pointing initially to the ever-increasing rationalization of life that was symbolized but not exhausted by the ascetic wings of the Protestant Reformation (Weber, 1930). With respect to the social-structural manifestation of the split, I would point primarily to the rise of depersonalized occupational roles, especially in business and professional life, as the models for dedicated work and as the institutional realization of middle-class values. Weber stressed the religious discipline of Protestantism, but he also saw the advent of Protestantism as part of a larger movement toward the rationalization of the universe. This rationalizing impulse invaded many spheres of life other than the religious—the legal, the economic, the academic—everywhere heralding the virtues of discipline, calculation, instrumentalism, labor, and self-control. In many instances, however, the rationalizing impulse has not been explicitly religious, as it was in the case of Protestantism. In modern times, the world has witnessed efforts to transform and rationalize society under the aegis of diverse values and ideologies, including communist and socialist ideologies of progress, and including—especially in developing countries—ideologies that envision simultaneously the restoration of traditional cultures and the revolutionary transformation of society.

Certainly in the West the commitment to the virtues of instrumentalism and rationality has meant a corresponding downplaying of expressive gratification. The Puritan strand of Protestantism was openly hostile, attempting actively to repress the sexual, aesthetic, playful, and other expressive realms of life as foreign and irrational. Relaxation and play were accepted as a part of rebuilding for the serious business of a methodically conducted life. Even when the expressive mode of action has not been the subject of direct or comprehensive attack, it has often been regarded as in the realm of "pleasure" or "entertainment," to be enjoyed only after it has been earned by the devotion of energies to the rational, workaday world.

A number of ideological trends in the nineteenth century simultaneously reflected and deepened this cultural tendency to dichotomize the instrumental and the expressive. The ideology of Victorian prudery marked the high point of the conquest of discipline, rationality, and self-control, as well as the most extreme negation of impulse gratification. That ideology involved a near-total denial of sexuality for women and defined sexuality and its related affects as a lack of control and discipline on the part of the male—a kind of regrettable pathology. Consider also some parts of the corpus of the discipline of economics as it developed in the nineteenth century. I have in mind the fundamental distinction between production on the one hand, which involves the systematic "building up" of value by the rational organization of skills and other resources, and consumption on the other hand, which involves the "use" or "running down" of products in the gratification of individual "tastes." That distinction, however useful for analytic purposes, clearly parallels the distinction between instrumentality and expressiveness. Also, that which went into production—labor—was widely regarded as having nothing to do with enjoyment or positive affect; it was measured in units of "disutility" which had to be extracted by rewards (wages) extrinsic to the work activity itself. Consider, finally, the ideological adaptations that occurred when psychoanalysis became more or less widely accepted in the West. Without regard to the qualifications that Freud himself placed on that theory, the public came to regard sexuality and impulses generally (libido) as constituting the irrational side of man, opposed in all respects to discipline and rational control. The "irrational" aspect of the theory of psychoanalysis—as well as of the work of Schopenhauer, Nietzsche, and other "irrationalist" thinkers—tended to be exaggerated largely because these theories were judged in terms of the values of instrumental rationalism, the dominant perspective of the time. The fundamental cultural dichotomy, in short, broke through and manifested itself in ideological and intellectual developments of very diverse kinds.

Especially in his writings on bureaucracy, Weber emphasized the depersonalizing and dehumanizing effects of the trend toward the greater rationalization of life, and he regarded certain modern charismatic trends as a "reassertion" of the irrational (Weber, 1948). When efforts are made to resist rationality and its associated values, those values are discovered to be so powerful that they can be attacked only by completely denying them and asserting the overwhelming importance of their negations—that is, pure and unadulterated affect, irrationality, indiscipline, and the like. In other words, because of the strength of the values of instrumental rationality, suggested solutions for the dilemmas of the human condition have tended to assume an extremist either-or character. It has proved difficult to generate belief systems that are a genuine synthesis of rational or irrational—or, if you will, instrumental and expressive, or work and love—ingredients. Rather, the relationship has tended to be a dialectic one. Critics of the rationalist tendencies are driven into constructing denials and negations, which take the form of romanticism, irrationalism, expressionism, and hedonism. Consequently, the cultural dynamics of the modern West have tended to put work and related instrumental activities into one joyless category and love and related affects into a separate category, and then to represent them as mutually exclusive. This cultural opposition has dominated the structure of Western thought for several centuries and has limited the number of moral and psychological solutions for the dilemmas of human existence.

A number of recent cultural phenomena have involved a rejection of the instrumentalist work ethic and a glorification of expression. Many of the movements of the aesthetic left, including bohemianism, the hippie movement, and others, involve sharp critical reactions against the dominant values of instrumentalism, whether these be characterized as "bourgeois," "decadent," or "square." Yet such protest movements have found it difficult to develop substantive and positive ideologies of their own. Similarly, the hedonistic ethic as manifested in the "sensuous life" ideology of *Playboy* magazine and related publications involves a rejection of discipline and work. (Indeed, the word "playboy" has historically referred to a man who does not work but spends his life playing; by and large the term has had negative connotations.) Yet that movement, like the broader pornographic revolution of which it may be considered a part, has also failed to develop an ideological position that goes beyond the negation of discipline and the positive stress on sensuality, which is considered to be the opposite of discipline.

These intellectual and ideological trends illustrate the fundamental opposition between instrumentalism and affect that is so deeply rooted in the modern Western tradition. They also suggest that even when individuals and groups try to break out of what Weber called the "iron cage" of rationality, they find themselves still caged, because they are again constricted by the narrowness of the alternatives they envision.

Moving back to the individual, this extreme split between the instrumental and affective can be regarded as cultural encouragement for two types of adaptation that are commonly described as neurotic. Each adaptation involves an effort to deny the individual's connection with some aspect of psychic reality that is intrinsically associated with the human condition. On the one side there is a temptation to repress the affective, emotional, loving side of life altogether. This is the classic solution of the methodical rationalist as depicted by Weber. This temptation is probably the dominant one, even today. It is an invitation to clothe oneself in the garments of the obsessive-compulsive and to push down, as obsessive-compulsives do, the expressive side of life. For the minority, protesting segment, the temptation is to act out the negation of the dominant values. By fostering the notion that affect and the actions associated with it constitute the whole of human existence, proponents of this position encourage people to live out their lives without reference even to the instrumental, disciplined dimensions that are part of affective attachments and expression. Insofar as both adaptations deny a proper mix of the instrumental and affective modes, the living of social life becomes correspondingly impoverished and alienating.

Some Social-Structural Complications and Variations

The account just given of the two trends in Western cultures is overly simple for two reasons. First, it ignores variations in the ways in which instrumental rationality is valued and ignores the contrapuntal interplay between this mode of action and other cultural forces. Second, this simplistic account suggests that the relation of the two to the societies they have influenced has been one of simple conquest. That is clearly not the case. Any cultural trend, however powerful, takes root in the historical context of the societies it affects and is modified accordingly. This two-way influence may be illustrated by tracing the different courses taken by these two cultural trends in Great Britain and America during the nineteenth century and examining the way those trends have affected the social structuring of work and love relationships in the two countries.

The chief difference in historical context between Great Britain and America is that in Great Britain the values of instrumental rationality were carried by a religious tradition (Nonconformism) that was from the beginning subordinate in power to the established Church of England, and by a group (the middle class) that was subordinate in status to the landed aristocracy. America lacked both a formally established church—though Puritanism and its variants were dominant culturally—and, especially after the Jacksonian era, anything approaching a landed aristocracy. In England, furthermore, the aristocracy had developed according to a "gentlemanly" ethic in which one of the positive virtues was *not* to work, either in a formal occupation or at home, where personal servants did the work and symbolized the status of the family. America lacked both the tradition of aristocratic disdain for work and the corresponding division of society into a small "leisured" and a large "working" class. Thus, when the middle classes came to consolidate themselves in both societies, they did so in a very different class context.

Matthew Arnold, England's sensitive mid-nineteenth-century sociological observer of many nations, undertook to characterize British and American society in his *Culture and Anarchy* (1869). In a somewhat whimsical moment, he announced that it was "awkward and tiresome" to refer always to "the aristocratic class, the middle-class, and the working-class" in Great Britain. Instead, he wished to call the aristocracy the "Barbarians," a class which had descended from that stock and which stressed, in its contemporary manifestation, personal liberty, honors and consideration, field-sports, and pleasure. To the middle classes he attached the label "Philistine," suggesting business, money lending, religion, propriety, and sobriety (and the values of instrumental rationality, I might add). The working class he described as "Populace," which "raw and half-developed, has long lain half-hidden amidst its poverty and squallor, and is now issuing from its hiding-place to assert an Englishman's heaven-born privilege of doing what it likes." English life, he maintained, could not be understood without continuous reference to these three great orders. He went on to say, "America is just like ourselves, with the Barbarians quite left out, and the Populace nearly. This leaves the Philistines for the great bulk of the nation;—a livelier sort of Philistine than ours . . . but left all the more to himself and to have his whole swing. And as we have found that the strongest and most vital part of English Philistinism was the Puritan . . . middle-class . . . so it is notorious that the people of the United States issues from this class, and reproduces its tendencies" (Arnold, 1869, pp. xxx–xxxi). Arnold's observation is not entirely original; other observers (notably Tocqueville) had noted the absence of a feudal tradition in America, and still others (notably Marx) had noted the weakness of a genuine working class. His observation also appears to be exaggerated. Nevertheless, following through some of its implications leads to insights on the social structuring of work and love in the two societies.

BRITISH MIDDLE CLASSES

By "the middle classes" I refer to that wide band of families in Great Britain sustained by a husband-father in professional (law, medicine, clergy, and civil service) occupations, business and mercantile positions, and—toward the lower end—roles such as schoolteacher and clerk, which began to appear in greater numbers in the latter part of the nineteenth century. Insofar as this class propounded the values assigned to them by Arnold, they deviated from the aristocratic ideal by stressing the value of rationality, work, and discipline. As these classes consolidated their gains in the early part of the nineteenth century, there developed simultaneously a powerful ideological movement that split the world of work from the world of sentiment, giving the former to men and the latter to women. This movement, associated with the early Victorian family, extolled the womanly virtues of gentleness, kindness, softness, radiance, purity, and devotion—virtues to sustain a happy home and family. Since the worlds of business, politics, and community were foreign to women's nature, women ought to remain as the spiritual and emotional center of the home and not partake of the workaday world. In fact, the participation of middle-class women in the labor force in the first half of the nineteenth century was negligible. As a result of these ideological and economic developments, British middle-class society effected a split between the rational, instrumental world and the sentimental, affective world strictly along sexual lines.

Though deviating from the aristocratic ideal with respect to attitudes toward work, the middle classes nevertheless accepted certain values of gentility and respectability and incorporated many status symbols from the aristocratic model. In particular, the increasingly prosperous middle classes in the middle and late nineteenth century began to adopt a lifestyle that included an education for one's children in an appropriate private school, a respectable material position, frequent social entertainment, and above all personal household servants for cleaning, cooking, serving, and caring for and educating one's children. This lifestyle represented respectability and gentility throughout the middle-class ranks and was adopted to the degree that the family income would permit. From the standpoint of the role of women, however, the main implication of the inherited tradition was that it was neither respectable nor genteel to work in a paid occupation. Virtually no women in the middle classes nor any women aspiring to middle-class respectability participated in the labor force until new occupations, such as schoolteaching and clerical work, began to open to women later in the nineteenth century.

One of the fascinating ramifications of the lifestyle of the middle classes was that the traditional obligations associated with the role of women—relating to work and, to some extent, love as well—began to "empty out," with little emerging to take their place. Because of the taboo on working, women were excluded from the paid labor force. By hiring paid servants, women were progressively relieved of domestic labor as well. And, particularly in the wealthier reaches of the middle classes, the hiring of nurses and governesses meant that the middle-class woman was losing some of her child-rearing responsibilities. What remained was the actual bearing of the children, the (sometimes difficult) managerial responsibility for a number of servants, and the status-maintaining functions of visiting and entertaining in a proper style.

Another feature of the role of the middle-class woman in the mid-nineteenth century was that virtually the only career positively sanctioned and designed for her was marriage and family. Girls participated minimally in the secondary educational system of the day—the middle-class schools and great public schools—and were oriented to no particular occupational role. What education they received was either from parents or from governesses, and stress was laid on genteel but impractical subjects such as singing, dancing, and modern European languages. Virtually no preparation for the world of occupational work was available.

Despite the fact that marriage was virtually the only career available to women, many of them were unable to find eligible men to marry. This unfortunate circumstance came about because so many men emigrated from Great Britain during this era, and because in the middle classes it was not respectable for a man to marry before he was earning an income sufficient to support a family according to an appropriate middle-class standard. Thus many women faced the prospect of entering late—or perhaps not at all—the only viable adult role that society had designed for them.

This complicated confluence of forces—changing middle-class attitudes toward work, the exclusion of women from the world of work and from preparation for it, the reliance on personal servants as a mark of gentility and respectability, and demographic developments—can hardly be regarded as a deliberate creation of British society at the time. Taken together, nevertheless, they tended to exclude women from virtually all instrumental and many expressive activities and to create an unviable personal situation for many. It was from this confluence, moreover, that the first significant stirrings of feminism arose in the mid-nineteenth century. By and large, women appeared to accept the assignment to the predominantly domestic realm. Except for a modest protest against the asymmetrical divorce laws, few voices were heard complaining about the position of women *within* the middle-class family. It was, rather, on behalf of the women who were excluded from that family—the unmarried and the widowed—that feminist protests first were heard. There was a minor movement to encourage single women to emigrate, primarily to become wives of men who had already emigrated. The more significant stirrings, however, were on the part of groups of women concerned mainly with generating opportunities for unmarried women. It was from this source that the early agitation for improving women's secondary education and providing colleges for women arose in the mid-nineteenth century, and from which philanthropic and reformist activity also developed (Banks and Banks, 1964; Banks, 1954).

British Working Classes

Generally speaking, before the onset of industrial production, the working family itself constituted an economically productive unit—the peasant family and the household craft family are prototypes.

This social structure permitted a fusion between the instrumental and affective facets of family relationships because the family members worked together. Industrialization, with the economic efficiencies that arose from its rational organization, put these families out of business as productive units and generated the system of wage labor. Under this system, a member of the family—usually the husband-father but sometimes others as well—left the premises of the household and worked for a large portion of the day for wages which were brought home to cover expenditures that maintained the family as a social unit. The working-class family became more specialized, focusing on the emotional and child-rearing side and giving up its role as an economically productive social unit and as the organizing base for many of the instrumental activities of its members.

Of course individual families often deviated considerably from this general model. The family's adoption of this wage-earning organization was gradual in Great Britain; in many cases the family as a whole retained its instrumental involvement in the economy. For example, early in the Industrial Revolution the family as a production unit in the home survived in some industries, particularly in textiles, and even in the factory, workers were permitted to hire wives and children to help tend machines and perform ancillary tasks (Smelser, 1959).

But beyond the limited practice of family hiring, the distinctive feature of the British experience during the industrial transition—in contrast with the American experience—was that a very high proportion of the working-class women and children continued to be active wage earners in the labor force. The continued involvement of women is partly explained by the fact that the British industrial revolution was dominated by the cotton and woolen textile industries, where the work was light enough for women to be efficiently employed. This was not the entire story, however, for large numbers of women were employed in arduous jobs as well—in mining, for instance—which suggests that manufacturers were motivated to utilize female labor wherever they could, because of the relatively lower wages it commanded. Another distinctively British feature contributing to the high utilization of female labor lay in the importance of personal servants (maids, cooks, ladies-in-waiting, and so on) as an ingredient in the upper-class genteel lifestyle. The great majority of these servants were drawn from agricultural and working-class families.

At the same time, the expectation that women would continue to maintain primary expressive responsibilities as wife and mother in the family did not diminish. Fertility remained high among the working classes until very late in the nineteenth century. Their families were large, and workers, many of whom remained near the poverty line, could seldom afford paid domestic labor to care for children. For the woman who chose to stop working during the period when her children were young, there was a decline in family earnings at a phase in the life cycle when material demands were heaviest. This period of deprivation was likely to continue until the older children were able to augment family earnings by taking employment—at about age twelve or thirteen—or until the mother could resume working, relying on the older children to care for the younger.

The children of the working classes contributed to the family's economic welfare from a very early age. Various parliamentary inquiries into popular education in the first three-quarters of the nineteenth century produced consistent evidence that, by and large, when children were able to contribute anything, however small, to the family income, they were put to work. The age at which children began to work varied from industry to industry, but it ranged from seven to eleven. Child labor constituted one of the principal barriers to the spread of popular education in Great Britain, as families would terminate or interrupt their children's education when they could begin to earn. The children's wages were generally turned over to the parents, with bits returned to the children as pocket money; in later years they retained their wages and paid for their keep.

This "instrumentalization" of the British working-class family clearly overloaded the wife-mother's role with both work and affective responsibilities and taxed the family's capacity as a viable affective unit. One response was to diffuse affective responsibility by relying on extended kinspeople, especially grandmothers, and older children, especially daughters, to care for the younger children when the mother worked outside the home. Sometimes, too, the child's principal affective ties were with peers, and the large numbers of children in street gangs became a menacing problem in the eyes of reformers.

THE AMERICAN FAMILY IN THE EARLY INDUSTRIAL PERIOD

During the early years of America's industrial revolution, the split between the world of work and the family was generally sharper and more widespread than in Great Britain, and the instrumental–affective split along sex-role lines was correspondingly more extreme.

The circumstances accounting for this difference are rooted in economic, religious, and class differences. The first important industrial developments in the United States occurred mainly in the 1820s and 1830s—though there were some small stirrings earlier—in the textile industry in New England and in a number of other industries in the Middle Atlantic states. In contrast with the British experience, however, this industrial development did not involve a massive incorporation of working-class women into the ranks of factory labor. Women were employed, to be sure, but in smaller proportions. Furthermore, those women employed in the mills increasingly tended to be immigrants rather than women of Anglo-Saxon stock. Finally, demand for domestic servants was generally low, partly because service was not so conspicuous a feature of American middle-class life. Thus, American working-class women were less involved than British in the world of work—occupationally defined—though they were heavily involved in the instrumental side of maintaining a household and family.

At the same time, in the 1820s and 1830s, there developed a vigorous ideological movement that rationalized women's nonparticipation in economic life and glorified a more or less exclusively domestic role for the wife and mother. This movement has been termed the "cult of true womanhood" and resembles in large measure the dominant early Victorian attitude toward middle-class women in Great Britain. The same domestic virtues were extolled, and the same consignment to the hearth and home was made, but in certain respects the American experience offers contrasts with the British. In both early industrial America and early Victorian England, ideologists extolled the sanctity and the purity of women and called for their protection from the ruder aspects of the profane world. But in England the admonition against work for pay was based not only on this Puritan theme but also on the class-related theme that it was not *respectable* to do so; this value of respectability was rooted in the traditional aristocratic emphasis on leisure as an essential part of a lifestyle appropriate to the higher ranks. By contrast, the American ideologists of true womanhood did not denigrate work as such. Rather, they rationalized woman's domesticity in a more typically Puritan style. Women represented the highest and most spiritual emotions, and these should be protected from harsh reality, and above all from sexuality. Accompanying the focus on true womanhood was a second ideological strand, which has come to be known as the "prudery" movement. This movement portrayed men as base, sensual, and depraved, and women as pure and without low passion. Its mission was to protect women from the menace of sex, and even to stamp it out altogether, except for narrowly reproductive purposes. So while the dominant British ideology on women was rooted in both class and sexual symbolism, the American ideology was more nearly exclusively Puritan in character.

The experience of women in America did not show the same discontinuity between the middle and working classes as existed in Great Britain. In England, the values of respectability and gentility tended to filter down from the upper through the middle classes, stopping only at the working class, for whom respectability did not include an extreme split between the instrumental and the expressive modes of behavior along sex lines. By contrast, the American deification of the purity of women was a Puritan, middle-class movement that tended to diffuse more generally throughout the community, including the working class, as might be expected in a young society in which class lines were relatively indistinct.

I have stressed the different historical routes taken by British and American society in the period of their early industrialization, and indeed one should not lose sight of those differences. But it should also be emphasized that both countries succeeded in accomplishing a radical split between the sexes—in America perhaps more generally so than in Great Britain, since in the British working classes the split between the family (female domain) and workplace (male domain) was never so clear. The period of early industrialization, moreover, generated and consolidated the division of roles between the sexes in both countries that has constituted the basis for all feminist protest, right up to the contemporary "women's liberation" movement. Feminism has defined its mission as opposing the historical heritage of a structural division between the instrumental and the affective along sex lines and its attendant inequalities.

A Glimpse into the Future

There is reason to believe that the process of isolating the affective dimension of life is not complete, though the future will not bring a simple extension of the assignment of the expressive realm to women. The increasing isolation of affectivity, rather, will occur as the result of a new set of arrangements in the family which are now developing. These new arrangements involve the increasing structural separation of the marital relationship from the parental relationship. This separation might be regarded as building on and extending the earlier process of differentiation that tended to remove much of the instrumental mode from the family, leaving it primarily responsible only for the affective relations between and among parents and children. In the United States and to some extent more generally in the developed societies, a number of trends are resulting in the progressive removal of the child-bearing and child-rearing functions from the affective relations between the adult man and woman. These trends include an increasing rate of illegitimacy, which means a large proportion of single-parent homes; an increasing divorce rate, also resulting in a greater proportion of single-parent homes; the growing participation of women in the labor force, which separates them from their children, even at an early age; and an increasing growth of nursery schools, prenursery schools, playgroups, and the like, which augments the separation from the parent or parents at early ages.

Such trends—all of which probably will continue into the future—suggest that the relationship between adults and children is becoming more specialized, more formally organized, and more instrumental. Furthermore, affective attachments between adults are moving away from simultaneous responsibility for the rearing of children. Put another way, the affective relations between adults—whether married or unmarried—are in the process of becoming more isolated and less intertwined with other dimensions of social life. I would observe that the very recent trend toward greater toleration of "alternative" marital forms—for example, communal marriages, gay marriages, and sexual liaisons without marriage—rests at least in part on the fact that the marital relationship has become relatively isolated from the rest of social life; accordingly, experimenting with marriage forms affects much less of the rest of life than it has in the past. There is also reason to believe that in the future more and more people will question the necessity of the legal marital bond as the dominant institutional basis for adult affective relationships, largely because the social realities that once necessitated and shored up that legal bond will have so weakened. Insofar as that occurs, we will likely witness the simultaneous emergence of a vast range of new experiments in personal intimacy that will make the experiments of the 1960s and 1970s appear modest by comparison.

References

Arnold, Matthew

1869 *Culture and Anarchy: An Essay in Political and Social Criticism.* London: Smith, Elder.

Banks, J. A.

1954 *Prosperity and Parenthood: A Study of Family Planning among the Victorian Middle Classes.* London: Routledge and Kegan Paul.

Banks, J. A., and Olive Banks

1964 *Feminism and Family Planning in Victorian England.* Liverpool: Liverpool University Press.

Davis, Kingsley

1936 "Jealousy and Sexual Property." *Social Forces,* Vol. 14, pp. 395–405.

Durkheim, Émile

1951 [1897] *Suicide.* Glencoe, IL: The Free Press.

Parsons, Talcott

1960 "Pattern Variables Revisited." *American Sociological Review,* Vol. 25, pp. 467–83.

Parsons, Talcott, and Edward A. Shils

1951 "Values, Motives, and Systems of Action." In *Toward a General Theory of Action,* edited by Talcott Parsons and Edward A. Shils. Cambridge, MA: Harvard University Press. Pp. 45–243.

Smelser, Neil J.

1959 *Social Change in the Industrial Revolution.* Chicago: University of Chicago Press.

Weber, Max

1930 *The Protestant Ethic and the Spirit of Capitalism.* Translated by Talcott Parsons. London: George Allen and Unwin.

1948 *From Max Weber.* Edited by H. H. Gerth and C. Wright Mills. London: Routledge and Kegan Paul.

PART III

Ambivalence

6

Collective Myths and Fantasies: The Myth of the Good Life in California

In entering the study of collective myths and fantasies, I note first that I am aware of—and humbled by—the really noble tradition of studies in the fields of psychoanalysis and anthropology. In the former, the heritage includes the names of Freud himself, Rank, Jung, Roheim, and Erikson; in the latter we find Westermarck, Fraser, Malinowski, Levi-Strauss, and Eliade. While these scholars have relied more or less on the special assumptions of their own disciplines, in both cases they have acknowledged that collective myths and fantasies provide an important link between the psychological and social sides of life. Freud regarded the formation of neuroses, the dynamics of fantasies and dreams, and "the creations of the popular mind in religion, myths, and fairy tales as manifesting the same forces in mental life" (Freud, 1959 [1910], p. 252). In one place he referred to myths as "distorted vestiges of the wishful phantasies of whole nations" (1959 [1908], p. 152). In a perhaps overenthusiastic moment, he characterized mythology as *"nothing but psychology projected into the external world"* (1960 [1901], p. 258), but his writings consistently stressed the infusion of collective myths into the religious, legal, and other institutions of humankind. On the other side of the disciplinary boundary, Malinowski stressed the social functions of the myth—"it expresses, enhances, and codifies belief; it safeguards and enforces morality; it vouches for the efficiency of ritual and contains practical rules for the guidance of man" (1971, p. 19). At the same time, and consistent with Freud's psychological emphasis, he noted that the telling of myths is "in satisfaction of deep religious

Originally published in the *Humboldt Journal of Social Relations* 2, no. 1 (Fall/Winter 1983–84): 1–15.

wants, moral cravings, social submissions, assertions, even practical requirements" (1971, p. 19).

In this essay I want to continue the stress on both the psychological and the social significances of collective myths and fantasies. I hope to open up a few new avenues of exploration of these phenomena, and unlike many past traditions of emphasizing classical, primitive, and folk myths far from our own civilization in time and place, I am going to concentrate—for illustrative purposes—on a myth which is close at hand: the myth of the good life in California.

Definition of Myth

Early in my explorations, I decided to consult the *Oxford English Dictionary,* which told me that a myth is "a purely fictitious narrative usually involving supernatural persons, actions, or events, and embodying some popular idea concerning natural or historical phenomena." Upon reflection, I found this definition a letdown. It is a mistake to regard myths as "purely fictitious." I also found the stress on the supernatural to be constricting. So I turned elsewhere and sought the assistance of a competitor, *Webster's Unabridged.* Among its six or seven meanings for myth, one especially caught my eye: "a belief or concept that embodies a visionary ideal (as of some future utopian state or condition), for example, the Marxian fostered myth of a classless society." I liked this one better, partly because of its reference to fantasy, and partly because the myth of California seemed to be a clear instance of this meaning. In the end, however, and on the basis of my explorations, I came to regard this meaning as only half correct; my reasons for so regarding it will constitute a large part of my analysis.

The Structure of Myth: First Approximation

To begin, let us consider two simple classical myths, both dealing with gold and greed, which will prove to be important California themes: the myth of King Midas and the myth of the goose and the golden eggs. In the first, Midas had showed generous hospitality to Silenus, and Bacchus permitted him to ask any recompense he wished. Midas asked that whatever he touched would turn to gold. The very wish proved his undoing, however, since even the food he touched turned to gold, and he could not eat. So he had to ask Bacchus to revoke the favor. The second, equally familiar, involves a man who owned the goose that laid one golden egg a day. Not satisfied with the riches being accumulated, the man killed and cut open the goose, thus stopping the supply. In both myths there is desire and punishment, wish and renunciation. In both cases, moreover, there is a certain correspondence between the punishment and the crime—greed ends in the threat of starvation, and insatiability ends in deprivation. Even these simple fables offer a *number* of possibilities for identification and affective reactions on the part of the hearer. In the Midas myth, the hearer may identify with the generous Midas, the greedy Midas, the starving Midas, the penitent Midas, the generous Bacchus, or the mischievous Bacchus and may take a positive or negative posture toward any or all of these representations. Incidentally, these simple myths also reveal a social use made of them: social control. In this process *one* facet or ingredient is highlighted and made a mandate. In my daughter's literature book, where I turned to refresh my memory on the goose and the golden eggs, the story was followed up by the moral: "Beware of being greedy. It doesn't pay to be impatient." But the rest of the ingredients—the greedy wish, for example—are there to be heard as well.

As a first approximation, then, we may say that a myth has a structure that is ambivalent in at least two senses: it contains a wish and its appropriate negation; on the part of the hearer, it permits an ambivalent orientation to each of those two elements. A myth, like a dream, is full of opportunities for psychodynamic play. It is a playground for reversals, condensations, undoing, and the rest of the possibilities. A myth might be regarded as lying on a continuum of mental productions. At one end is the dream, next the daydream, next the myth, next the ideology, and, finally, formal theoretical-empirical thought. The related dimensions running along this continuum are the relative dominance of primary or secondary process, the degree of formal structure, and the self-conscious application of rules, logic, and inference to the mental production itself.

The Historical Elaboration of Myth in Cultural Context: The California Myth

From its inception, the name "California" has brought to mind a kind of utopia. Appearing in Spanish fiction in the late fifteenth century, it was an invented word, referring to a mythical island, and was one of a family of visions—including the Seven Cities of Cibola and El Dorado—of "an early paradise, with unbounded productiveness without labor, with beautiful women, gold and pearls" (Gudde, 1969, p. 48). From the beginning, the myth made reference to "productiveness without labor," and to gold and women. The land of California was thought to be located "at the right end of the Indes" and inhabited by "handsome black women like Amazons." Apparently these fantasies were closely associated with the hopes of the Spanish explorers of the time. When explorers did reach the western shores of what is now the North American continent, they applied the name of "California" to the coastland. Some time later, Sir Francis Drake named the same area "New Albion." For almost a century, there was a kind of linguistic war between the Spanish and the British over the correct name, a war symbolically representing the prior discovery and claim to the land (Gudde, 1969, p. 49). The Spanish finally won this verbal battle; ultimately, the British acknowledged that victory. In fact, in the 1850s, London's "fast young men" adopted the name "California" as a slangy synonym for "money," no doubt in response to the recent drama of the California Gold Rush. I am, personally, pleased that "California" won out, since "New Albion" seems a drearier name (try to think of San Francisco, New Albion). It has fewer of the fantastic and utopian connotations of the original version of "California" and would not fit so neatly into my analysis.

Be it noted, then, that "California" as a vision predated the establishment of the American nation by several centuries. It connoted plenty, ease, and, we might say, the good life. But in the nineteenth century, when that myth was revived and supercharged by the discovery of gold and the frantic migrations of the mid-century, its *cultural context* was very different from that of the Spanish context in which it was invented. What were the main features of that cultural context? I turn first to Max Weber's famous thesis concerning the religious origins of the capitalist economic spirit in the seventeenth and eighteenth centuries. Weber especially stressed the psychological tensions in ascetic Calvinism, a dominant force in colonial America, as well as in northwest Europe. The religion of Calvin was, in the first instance, one of complete predestination of human affairs by God. Weber summarized the implications in the following way:

> We know only that a part of humanity is saved, the rest damned. To assume that human merit or guilt play a part in determining this destiny would be to think of God's absolutely free decrees, which have been settled from eternity, as subject to change by human influence, an im-

> possible contradiction. The [human and understanding] God of the New Testament [has been replaced] by a transcendental being, beyond the reach of human understanding, who with His quite incomprehensible decrees has decided the fate of every individual and regulated the tiniest details of the cosmos from eternity. (Weber, 1958, pp. 103–4)

Weber regarded this doctrine as one of "extreme inhumanity." He argued that it "must above all have had one consequence for its adherents: a feeling of unprecedented inner loneliness of the single individual." The doctrine also generated a haunting sense of uncertainty. "The question, Am I one of the elect? must sooner or later have arisen from every believer and have forced all other interests into the background" (Weber, 1958, p. 110). It was in the context of this intense religious anxiety that the Calvinistic emphasis on worldly activity arose as the most suitable means of "counteracting feelings of religious anxiety" (Weber, 1958, p. 112) and the surest sign of salvation. In Calvinism, this worldly activity took the form of sober self-denial and systematic self-control. Predictably then, the Calvinistic ethic contained the following elements:

- "the avoidance of all erotic pleasure . . ."
- "the elimination of all ideal and exploitative enjoyment of unearned wealth and income . . ."
- "the avoidance of all feudalistic, sensuous ostentation of wealth . . ."
- "the avoidance of all surrender to the beauty of the world, to art, or to one's own moods and emotions . . ." (Weber, 1968, p. 556).

The ethic is renunciatory, ascetic, and joyless in the extreme and calls for a rationally controlled pattern of life; and "when success crowns rational, sober, purposive behavior, . . . such success is construed as a sign that God's blessing rests upon such behavior" (1968, p. 556).

What concrete form did this rationally controlled pattern of life take? To illustrate this Weber turned to the homilies of Benjamin Franklin, who, more than anyone, symbolizes the secular American manifestation of Puritanism in the eighteenth century. It was Franklin's assault on idleness of any kind—of time, of hands, of money—and his exaltation of the values of prudence, industry, frugality, punctuality, and honesty that caught Weber's attention (Weber, 1958). These attributes, he argued, were the very ones that were so important in building the rational organization of economic activity that contributed to the institutional success of capitalism.

The paradox, of course, in this analysis is that those very qualities, bred of anti-materialism, end in the accumulation of tremendous material rewards. In the end, Weber saw this as undermining asceticism. He encapsulated the problem in a famous quotation from John Wesley, the founder of Methodism:

> I fear, wherever riches have increased, the essence of religion has decreased in the same proportion. Therefore I do not see how it is possible in the nature of things, for any revival of the true religion to continue long. . . . For the Methodists in every place grow diligent and frugal; consequently they increase in goods. Hence they proportionately increase in pride, in anger, in the desire of the flesh, the desire of the eyes, and the pride of life. (Weber, 1958, p. 175)

Catholic writers and other scholars such as Pitirim Sorokin (1937) have challenged Weber's interpretations by claiming that from the beginning the driving force behind Protestantism was not asceticism but, rather, material desire. This line of criticism is consistent with their belief that Protestantism was essentially a secular development. It is not necessary, however, to take a stand here on first causes. Ascetic Protestantism contained the themes of renunciation, asceticism, and labor on one side and worldly success, impulse gratification, and happiness on the other. It portrayed these as locked in powerful tension with one another. This worldview contained the ingredients *and* the structure of a myth and permitted the possibility of psychological ambivalence toward any one or all of these ingredients.

The Puritan background is one important element of the cultural context in which the myth of California must be assessed. A second and closely related part of that context is the complex of myths created over a series of decades in the late nineteenth century by that master maker of myths, Horatio Alger, Jr. Beginning with the publication of *Ragged Dick* in 1867, Alger supplied America's booming, high capitalist period with some of its principal myths. As Franklin had taken a step away from the joylessness and asceticism of Calvin—especially in his own personal life—so Alger took another worldly step, for it was the wealth that counted, and there was luck as well as hard work involved. Or, in John Seelye's words:

> It was for Alger's boys to work hard, honor your parents (excepting wicked stepparents), save your money, aim high, don't smoke, gamble, or drink hard liquor, and some day you will stop a runaway horse, behind which will be a carriage containing a rich man's daughter whose father will reward you with a good job and a chance to get ahead in the world, all of which will have been sent to you by God for having worked hard,

> honored your parents, saved your money, aimed high, and not smoked, gambled, or drunk hard liquor. (Seelye, 1965, p. ix)

With this preoccupation with wealth, it seemed inevitable that Alger would turn to California; indeed, six California novels appeared between 1878 and 1891. All were on the "get rich" theme, but Alger made some concessions to discipline and renunciation; his boys stayed away from the saloons and gambling halls, and they worked hard. Lest the readers suspect Alger had strayed too far from the ghost of Calvin, he explained his recipe for success in the preface to *The Young Miner: Or, Tom Nelson in California:*

> Though [Tom's] prosperity was chiefly due to his own energy and industry, it is also true that he was exceptionally lucky. Yet his good fortune has been far succeeded by that of numerous spirits in Colorado, within the past twelve months. Some measure of prosperity generally awaits the patient and energetic worker and seldom comes to those who idly wait for something to turn up. (Alger, 1879)

The California myth, itself, locked inextricably with the mythology of gold in general, went the rest of the way. Wealth was for the finding, women were loose, whiskey was plenty, and public disorder prevailed. The California myth in the context of nineteenth-century culture was one of a *family* of myths, all struggling with the same tension between renunciation and reward. The California myth is the negation of Calvin—or its natural culmination, if you follow the Catholics and Sorokin—for it renounces work and discipline and revels in worldly pleasures.

The theme of gold-for-the-finding was only one phase in the development of the California myth. In the past century it has been elaborated along a variety of different lines. The content became more diverse. The myth of mastery and conquest of the West, which had predated even the Gold Rush with James Polk's mission of "manifest destiny," continued to be prominent throughout the frontier period. Toward the later part of the century, the themes of natural beauty joined those of abundance as the rhapsodies of John Muir caught the public imagination. Oil, automobiles, and other industries "took off," and the myth of opportunity and plenty was renewed again and again. Perhaps the most dramatic elaboration was that of the Hollywood myth, which added the element of instant exhibitionism to that of instant narcissism—the magical rise to stardom with the world at one's feet. The magic includes also the notion of being "discovered" and plucked from obscurity by a powerful director—much like the Alger boys' sponsors and Little Orphan Annie's Daddy Warbucks. A later phase was that of the good life, as symbolized in the pages of *Sunset Magazine,* with the outdoor architecture, the barbecue, the sun, the green, and the ease. As if driven by some repetitive compulsion, Californians have endowed Marin County and some aspects of life in Silicon Valley with the principal ingredients of the California myth. Whatever variations, the theme remained the same—what Mark Jurgensmeyer has described as "a blending of grace and works that would have pleased John Calvin." He hastened to add that while it had the ingredients of Calvinism, those ingredients were surely rearranged: "the work for Californians was fairly easy and the rewards of grace were bountifully immediate" (1980).

Jurgensmeyer went even further. He saw in the myth of California a kind of religion, which he defined as a "symbolic gesture toward ultimate restoration and transformation" (1980). What were the ingredients of this religion? Jurgensmeyer mentioned three:

- "Freedom from guilt." If one starts over again, one is free from the burdens of the past, ghosts, and former actions.
- "Freedom from obligations." For those who migrated to California this meant to sever ties with the past, friends, and community. California connoted a vague, happy association of the free, an anonymous congregation of souls, united by their commitment not to intrude on one another.
- "The purifying powers of change." This is the counterpart of redemption and rebirth, not in the future, as many ideologies have it, but in the present.

Religion perhaps, but to the fundamentalist churches, the easy life in California has proved to be anti-religion, voiced first from the pulpit, and more recently, from television evangelists, who in their messages restore what the myth of California has denied—guilt, responsibility, and certainty.

The antagonism between California's religion and evangelistic, often Calvinistic, churches suggests that, upon reflection, we could not seriously believe that the California myth could remain in isolation from these elements in the American tradition and that to embrace that myth means sooner or later and in some way, we must pay a price for it. As we explore further what the myth of California connotes, we find a seamier aspect, which exists side by side with utopia and permits us, in our inner psychological dialogues, to pay that price. One part of the price is that which accompanies *any* utopia sired by discontent with one's circumstances: disillusionment and depression. Those who experienced the guilt, the obligations, and the staleness in their home communities and sought liberation by migrating to California were bound later to discover a fundamental truth: an irreducible amount of an apparent alienation from one's external environment is *internal* in character; to pin one's hopes for happiness on a change of circumstances is to invite an ultimate return of that alienation, *whatever* the new circumstances.

There is also a more dire and direct set of retributions in the California myth. A mountain pass between Reno and Sacramento is named Donner Pass. The referent, indeed the occasion for its bearing that name, is a party of migrants led by George Donner, one of the many parties that joined the Great Migration in 1846, when it was believed that the route to California was passable. The Donner story is simple and tragic: the party became stranded in the Sierras in November 1846 by heavy snows. Despite heroic escape efforts, many of them perished. The reason the story has not joined the dozens of unremembered stories of its kind, however, is that the surviving members of the Donner party cannibalized their dead in order to gain strength to move forward (Stewart, 1960). What better retribution for greed than to die and be devoured? What better reason for the story to become part of the California myth of plenty and passivity?

The famous earthquake is another part of the California myth dramatized by the great San Francisco tragedy of 1906. The precise symbolism of the earthquake in the popular mind is difficult to discern, but two recurrent fantasies are that the earth will open and swallow people, and as a kind of variant, California will break away from the continent and either be swallowed by the Pacific Ocean or again become an isolated island, as it was drawn on the imaginary maps of the Spanish dreamers. Once noted, the symbolism of oral destruction is, perhaps, too obvious to call to attention. It is, nonetheless, consistent with the notion that the California myth has a precise retributional counterpart.

The reason for my impatience with the dictionary definitions of "myth" must now be clear. A myth need not be a purely fictional account; the fate of the Donner party is a documented historical episode. The threat of earthquakes is clearly real to this day, though perhaps not in the precise sense called forth by the fantasies. The point is not fiction versus fact; it is, rather, the psychodynamic blending of fiction and fact to complete the inevitable logic of ambivalence in myth. My impatience with the exclusively positive and visionary definition of myth stems from the same considerations; there is no happy myth without its unhappy side and no dark myth without its light side.

The dismal, negating side of the California myth goes further. Consider the following themes:

- On material plenty: The words of a recent popular song, played to the point of tedium on California country and Western radio stations, run as follows: "All the gold in California/ Is in a bank/ In the middle of Beverly Hills/ In somebody else's name."
- On stardom: As a matter of fact, Hollywood actors and actresses have a variety of lifestyles, some very humdrum. As a matter of collective fantasy, however, the stars of Hollywood, in addition to receiving the earthly gratifications due to the gods, drink themselves to death, pop overdoses of drugs and sleeping pills, and generally live ruined, dissolute, and miserable lives. Such is the power of myth to select and distort.
- On social relations: Californians may be guiltless and freed from social obligations, but by the same token, their lives are believed to be anomic, plagued by divorce and separation, isolation, and loneliness. Such are the themes extracted by James Hughes in his survey of post-industrial California novelists (1980).
- On craziness: Californians may be liberated, but the mythological cost is the danger of going berserk: both Los Angeles and San Francisco are known as places of refuge for the wild, the cultish, and the bizarre.
- On ultimate retribution: The bridge connecting San Francisco and Marin County may be Golden, crossing the gate to the Golden State, but it is one of the most well-known symbols of violent suicide in the world.

All these blended elements of the California myth are rooted in a certain social reality—a reality perhaps engendered in part by the myth itself—but I am stressing another dimension of that myth. Its elements manifest themselves as a series of dialogues with the Puritan past; the common theme of this dialogue is that in our revelries in California's paradise we have, in fact, perpetrated a betrayal and must ultimately pay the terrible cost.

Further Social and Political Significance of Myth

Up to this point I have stressed what might be called the cultural and psychological dimensions of myths, their tensions and ambivalences. Myths have their place in the drama of social interaction as well, and to close my exploration, I will note a few of the social uses and significances of myths, staying with the illustrative example I have been following.

To choose the most obvious social significance first, a myth may have a certain commercial value: people will pay to see fantasies enacted on stage and screen or to read them in literary representations. Our illustrative myth of California lends itself well to commercial use, if not exploitation. Generations of real estate brokers, surfboard manufacturers, and sellers of bathing suits and suntan lotions have made free use of elements of the myth to vend their wares. So myths are, in one capacity, a free resource to advertisers and producers.

There is a more subtle function of myth that appears in the fabric of daily, informal intercourse among people. We use myths to express our normative postures and to secure the same from others, thereby binding ourselves in a kind of momentary solidarity. Permit a biographical example. In the late 1970s, I served as a director of a student exchange program in the United Kingdom, supervising the work of about 130 University of California undergraduates as they spent their junior year abroad. They were scattered around the British Isles: from time to time they came through London on their way to Paris, Rome, Athens, or other places with distinctive myths of their own. When they visited my office in London, I asked them, in the course of conversation, where they were going, and if they said Paris, for example, I immediately conspired with them in their romance and euphoria; told them of experiences to have, food to eat, and atmosphere to absorb; and generally envied them. As often as not, however, when they went to Paris, they froze while standing outside American Express waiting to check their mail, slept in fleabags, were unable to afford the Parisian cuisine, and perhaps were accosted by abusive people. Yet when they returned to London and I asked them how it was, they said "fantastic"; and I envied them again. In this way we conspired to deny reality and shared in that denial, thereby doing our bit to perpetuate the myth of Paris.

These kinds of episodes are daily and repeated occurrences, and taken as an accumulation, they constitute a mechanism for building and reproducing myths. We Californians in England did the same with our myth as well, maintaining our suntans as long as can be done in Britain, romanticizing California to the natives and to one another. The main social significance of these thousands of collective little crimes of distortion, I believe, lies in sustaining solidarity with our fellow humans. Our own inner realities are so idiosyncratic and complex at any given moment that comparison or relation to another inner reality is almost impossible. Sharing in a myth for a moment is a way to unify two selves in a kind of regressive solidarity, to orient to the same object, to evoke the same affect, and to become temporarily one.

In addition to being an economic and social resource, the myth may be a political resource, constituting the framework within which political dialogue occurs and permitting politicians to seize one ingredient of a myth, mobilize support in its name, and use it as a weapon to discredit others. To illustrate this significance, we might turn to the political rhetoric of two of California's governors, Ronald Reagan and Jerry Brown. During the campaign of 1966, when the Great Society was reaching its full expression and when California higher education was in full turmoil, Reagan hammered home two primary themes: high welfare costs and the mess in higher education, both of which he promised to clean up. On welfare, his campaign was a positively Franklinian attack on sloth and ideas: "It's hard to figure," he said, "how welfare costs are going up while need and unemployment are going down" (*Los Angeles Times,* October 1, 1966). When the *Los Angeles Times* (October 16, 1966) endorsed him for governor, it predicted he would "rescue discouraged men from the economic junkheap, and get them into gainful employment." In a variation on that theme, Reagan described welfare as "prepaid vacations for a segment of our society which has made this a way of life" (*Los Angeles Times,* October 6, 1966). Was not this an assault on one central ingredient of the myth of California—getting something for nothing? It was, and in part, it was a play on our guilt for having entertained that desire ourselves and an invitation to displace that guilt on others. On the student front, Reagan's attack was more complex, but the same theme emerged: the students were privileged to receive an education from the state of California, and they should work to justify it instead of assaulting university authorities and engaging in what Reagan referred vaguely to as "sex orgies on the Berkeley campus." These themes show Reagan maneuvering in, and exploiting, that family of myths I have ranged from the Calvinist to the Californian. They reveal him as adopting not only a politically but also a morally reactionary stance.

We do not often put Jerry Brown in the same category as Reagan, but Brown can be regarded as moving within the same family of myths. Whatever else Brown is known for, he is known for his romance with the pessimistic futurists and the environmentalists. He has repeatedly borrowed from their vernacular of "spaceship earth" and "small is beautiful," and he has spoken of the need for collective sacrifice in the face of the exhaustion of world resources. While we may question the ultimate political effectiveness of these messages, it is worth observing that his theme is fundamentally Calvinist: our California myth of plenty is a sinful, corrupting nightmare, and the only answer is renunciation. We must turn the California myth into its negation, and we should celebrate that negation: salvation through denial.

A Concluding Note

At the end of his famous essay on Protestantism and capitalism, Weber remarked that capitalism, while originating in the heartless discipline of Calvinism, had by the twentieth century established itself as an autonomous system, no longer dependent on that particular theological impulse. Industrial capitalism, he argued, now resting on its own institutional foundations, feeds itself and constitutes a sort of iron cage for us all; but "the spirit of religious asceticism . . . has escaped from the cage" (Weber, 1958, p. 181). Weber may have been right about industrial capitalism, but I hope I have demonstrated that we have not escaped from the cage of salvation through asceticism and its family of related myths. In many respects, that complex of myths dictates our internal and interpersonal discourses as well as our internal and interpersonal conflicts. At the same time, it constitutes a set of limits. Whether stressing cold asceticism and recognition of worldly accumulation as an incidental by-product of salvation, whether worshipping individual success, or whether revelling in some version of a myth of plenty, these possibilities—all of which end with economic mastery of the world and materialism—seem to be growing increasingly inappropriate to the changing economic and historical circumstances of the world. There is something stale about all of them, and I think that staleness stems from our own realization of inappropriateness; new solutions do not seem to be forthcoming or even suggested by that family of myths. We keep running around the same sets of mythological tracks. It would be foolish to envision a radical break with the dualism of a mythical past that has been a part of our psychic structure for so many centuries. But given its apparently increasing irrelevance, I would, personally, hope that we might expand our horizons for some more appropriate mythical alternatives in the decades to come.

References

Alger, H., Jr.
1879 *The Young Miner: Or, Tom Nelson in California.* Philadelphia: Coates.
Freud, S.
1959 [1908] "Creative Writers and Day-Dreaming." In *Standard Edition of the Complete Psychological Works of Sigmund Freud,* Vol. 9, edited by James Strachey. London: Hogarth Press. Pp. 141–53.
1959 [1910] "Preface to Sandor Ferenczi's *Psycho-analysis: Essays in the Field of Psycho-analysis.*" In *Standard Edition of the Complete Psychological Works of Sigmund Freud,* Vol. 9, edited by James Strachey. London: Hogarth Press. P. 252.
1960 [1901] "The Psychopathology of Everyday Life." In *Standard Edition of the Complete Psychological Works of Sigmund Freud,* Vol. 6, edited by James Strachey. London: Hogarth Press.
Gudde, E. G.
1969 *California Places Names: The Origin and Etymology of Current Geographical Place Names.* Berkeley and Los Angeles: University of California Press.
Hughes, J.
1980 *California's Frontier Ethos in Post-Industria: A Literary Interpretation.* Paper presented at the meetings of the American Association for the Advancement of Science, San Francisco, January 7.
Jurgensmeyer, M.
1980 *California as Religion.* Paper delivered at the meetings of the American Association for the Advancement of Science, San Francisco, January 7.
Malinowski, B.
1971 *Myth of Primitive Psychology.* Westport, CT: Negro Universities Press.
Seelye, J.
1965 "Horatio Alger Out West: A Marriage of Myths." Introduction to Horatio Alger, *The Young Miner: Or, Tom Nelson in California.* San Francisco: The Book Club of California.
Sorokin, P.
1937 *Social and Cultural Dynamics.* New York: American Books.
Stewart, G. R.
1960 *Donner Pass: And Those Who Crossed It.* San Francisco: The California Historical Society.
Weber, M.
1958 *The Protestant Ethic and the Spirit of Capitalism.* Translated by T. Parsons. New York: Charles Scribner's and Sons.
1968 *Economy and Society.* Edited by Guenther Roth and Claus Wittich. New York: Bedminster Press.

7

The Politics of Ambivalence: Diversity in the Research Universities

Debates over cultural diversity, multiculturalism, and the integrity of the community are perennial in American history. They extend back at least to colonial times, when religious heterogeneity posed major social and political problems for many of the colonies. They became chronic in the nineteenth and early twentieth centuries, as waves of immigrants diversified the population. The movement of the black population northward and westward, beginning in earnest in the early twentieth century, generated a new heterogeneity, racial tensions, and alarms about the integrity of affected communities.

The current debates are thus properly regarded as the latest episode in the long history of the cultural diversification of America. What is new about them is the historically specific confluence of social forces from which they emanate: the civil rights movements of the 1950s and 1960s; the campus and antiwar turbulence of the 1960s; the women's movement; the "sexual preference revolution"; the increasing political self-consciousness of many ethnic groups, including "white ethnics"; and the extraordinary increase of immigration—mainly but not exclusively Latin and Asian—during the past several decades.

Conflicts involving cultural diversity are not new in American academic circles: the historic flood of children from farm families into the teaching profession via colleges and universities; the entry of Irish Catholic Americans into the professions, notably engineering, through colleges; the struggle over Jewish quotas in elite private institutions; and

Originally published in *Daedalus,* Journal of the American Academy of Arts and Sciences, from the special issue titled *The American Research University* 122, no. 4 (Fall 1993): 37–53. Reprinted by permission.

the evolution of Eastern private institutions from regional/social elite to national/intellectual elite institutions all are episodes that involved issues of cultural diversity in academia. At the same time, the contemporary situation has some novel elements and is grounded in a distinctive cultural setting.

Social and Political Dimensions

THE UNIVERSITY CONTEXT

The national debates about diversity affect all research universities across the nation. Within research universities these debates are reproduced as microcosms of the national political arena, with some notable regional differences. The debates occur in the context of the culture of those universities, which imparts a special form and flavor. It is necessary, therefore, to remind ourselves of a few characteristics of that culture.

First, the major research universities in the United States constitute a national *elite* among institutions. This status is evident in all measures—prestige, quality of faculty, quality of students, occupational placement of graduating students, and, not least, cultural voice. They share this elite status with liberal arts colleges on some of these measures. One implication of elevated status for institutions is that the real and symbolic stakes associated with access to them are high. Those who enter as students secure both status and enhanced life opportunities; those who enter as faculty share in their prestige.

Second, the research universities' cultural traditions give the highest premium to the values of *competitive excellence* and *meritocracy.* They compete aggressively with one another for outstanding faculty and students. They assess both their faculty and their students primarily on meritocratic criteria—that is, universalistic standards of judgment. The successful application of these criteria is, indeed, one of the conditions that sustain the elite status of research universities.

Third, the culture of research universities is *liberal* in several senses of the term. They, along with the rest of the academy, are the seat and the defenders of that special class of civil liberties known as academic freedom. They are committed, above all, to standards of freedom of inquiry and expression. And, in the national political spectrum, both faculty and students at research institutions, while internally diverse, lean in a liberal direction.

Fourth, because of their unique intellectual missions, controversies and debates in universities—perhaps especially in elite universities—take on a special *symbolic intensity.* As institutions, universities do not house much power, but they specialize in and are good at cultural symbolism. Debates in universities tend to take on an intellectualized, back-to-square-one quality. Being shrouded in symbolic discourse, these debates are likely to confound and irritate outsiders.

THE PECULIARITIES OF THE CURRENT DEBATES

Viewed simply, the current debates about cultural diversity derive historically from the political pressure that built up in the 1960s and 1970s, as one categorical group after another began expressing a collective claim for increased access to and more equitable recognition in academic institutions. Universities reacted to these demands—and the demands of governmental and other pressures for affirmative action—with varying degrees of responsiveness and effectiveness. Now both the values of and procedures for affirmative action are in place, and the increased presence of most of these groups is visible. Recently, the debates have taken a more distinctively *cultural* turn—hence the salience of the terms "cultural diversity" and "multiculturalism."

The debates, as they have built up over the past decades, have generated a historically unique configuration of components:

1. The challenge has come from an unprecedented number and scope of sources—racial and ethnic minorities, women, and homosexuals—in many cases with the willing and active support of government and other public groups affecting the universities.
2. The challenge is not only to *gain access* to the dominant culture and opportunities of the university, but also to *question the legitimacy* of, and perhaps *unseat,* that culture—though, interestingly, not so much its associated opportunities. The traditional curriculum is challenged as being Eurocentric. Its language and assumptions are assaulted as being racist or sexist, and the world of heterosexual, older, white males is depicted as a bastion of illegitimate privilege and power.
3. The challenge is a *collective* one, involving the political efforts of identified groups. The logic of affirmative action should not conceal the fact that it is simultaneously an organized effort on the part of traditionally disadvantaged minority and gender groups

aimed at the collective upgrading of those groups, as defined on the basis of ascribed *categories*, not simply at individual mobility for selected members of the groups.

4. Because the identifying (and self-identified) characteristics of the challenging groups are categorical, the challenge has overtones of *the entitlement of groups* to student, faculty, and administrative places in the university and to full citizenship and respect in these places. This feature arises simultaneously from three sources: the character of the demands of the claimants, the efforts of opponents of those demands to label them as illegitimate claims to entitlement, and the tendency of authorities (government officials and administrators) to acknowledge the entitlement aspect by responding to demands as *claims by categorical groups*.

PARADOXES AND VULNERABILITIES

These special features of the current debates pose a range of institutional dilemmas and anomalies that have not been encountered as such by universities in the past. Not the least of these is the dilemma posed for the dominant liberal culture of the current administrative/faculty "establishment." Historically the elements of liberalism, egalitarianism, and meritocracy have been comfortably fused, as nineteenth-century middle-class liberals challenged the entitlement claims of monarchy, aristocracy, and church in the names of democracy and meritocracy. In the contemporary scene, those components have become strangely disassociated from one another. Liberal academic administrators and faculty generally applaud and welcome "diversity" if it is carried out within the confines of meritocracy and the preservation of the values of the academy. When those values themselves come under attack, however, and when the attacks on them appear to be made in the context of antimeritocratic demands for entitlement, liberals are cast in an uncomfortable role, in which they experience a dissociation of—indeed a conflict between—meritocracy and egalitarianism. Their role now becomes one of a conservative elite, jealously guarding those values of universalism that were invented and best suited to challenge conservative elites.

A closely related feature of the contemporary struggles over diversity is the creation of new, improbable, and unstable combinations of bedfellows. Traditional struggles in academia have involved issues of academic freedom, in which liberal faculty stand up against bastions of power—usually coalitions of business-legal-political representatives of the Right—who are alarmed at the liberal/radical ideologies and teachings of academics. (The courts have usually acted as friends to academic freedom, and thus are countervailing forces to the external Right.) In these struggles, academic administrators sometimes have sided with the outside "Right," sometimes with the internal faculty "Left." Students have tended to be either indifferent or supportive of the faculty Left.

The contemporary political situation has torpedoed those comfortable political alliances and fashioned a new, unfamiliar political quilt. The challenge now comes from a new Left, made up of vocal representatives of different "minority" claimants—themselves standing in unstable coalition; of outside left political forces, often governmental, who are cognizant of their own dependence on minority constituencies in their political environments; of academic administrators who are directly in the line of fire from the external Left; of representatives of a generation of radical faculty—perhaps socialized in their student days in the 1960s; and of "new" minority members of the faculty and the administration. On the Right are liberal faculty (and sometimes administrators and students), cast in the role of conservatives, evoking universalistic values and meritocracy as a defense rather than a challenge, and eliciting arguments of academic freedom as a conservative defense against "political correctness," laws and rules against "hate speech," and other initiatives emanating from the Left. These liberal faculty are bolstered by their conservative colleagues and by other conservative groups, usually white, in the larger political community, who are alarmed at the challenge from various minority and other Left sources.

If one translates these coalitions into the collective emotions that are typically associated with each, on the one side one finds a fusion of anger, guilt, uncertainty, and anxiety of minorities and liberal/radical white supporters. On the other, one finds the associated anger and guilt of the liberal/conservative forces. Furthermore, *both* of these affective mixes find support in a legitimate ideology—the ideology of egalitarianism, social justice, and past wrongfulness on the one side, and the ideology of universalism, meritocracy, and appeals to traditional liberal values of freedom on the other. In controversies in which such emotions fuse with ideologies based on such legitimate first principles, the resultant conflict produces high levels of righteousness and vindictiveness and low levels of self-insight on both sides.

The new battle lines are tenuous, however, because every subgroup in both major coalitions has its own particular agenda and its own particular ambivalence, which may surface at any time and occasion a subtle or open realignment. Liberal faculty are torn between their egalitarianism and their commitment to their cherished academic values of universalism. They are also often uncomfortable with being found in common cause with political conservatives. Asian Americans, like Jews in the past, are torn between the strategies of representing themselves with entitlement-like claims on the one hand, and "making it" within the context of meritocracy, in which they have been effective competitors, on the other. And Hispanic and black minorities, more drawn toward entitlement-like claims, forever wonder whether admission on an entitlement-like basis does not doom them to second-class citizenship in a world dominated by meritocratic values. All this makes for the greatest political fluidity, and for frustration on the part of observers and analysts who savor the neatness of political division.

To add to the confusion, the polity of the research university is not very well equipped to handle controversies of the sort that have developed. That polity itself is a strange historical mélange, incorporating several different principles of maintaining order and community in the university. It contains historical residues of a *religious calling*, which combines self-imposed discipline and personal freedom, and elements of *collegiality*, a company of equals whose main political cement is civility and mutual influence (within this kind of polity, above all, resides the myth of the university as a unified community); elements of *formal bureaucracy*, superimposed over time by the exigencies of growing size and multifunctionality; and a system of dual governance that is simultaneously *hierarchical* (with administrators retaining final authority) and *democratic* (with administrators delegating widely to academic senates and consulting with faculty, and to a certain extent with staff, students, and alumni). Needless to say, these different principles of polity often stand in tension with one another.

Whatever the mix of these ingredients in any university, it is the case that representatives of that polity are peculiarly ill-equipped to handle *collective* struggles among categorical groups. Universities are institutionalized in large part in the name of values of individual achievement and are best equipped to deal with individuals. They admit individuals, give instruction to and grade individuals, discipline individuals, graduate individuals, and prepare individuals for and place them in occupational positions. That institutional "tilt" also reveals a shortage of mechanisms to deal with group conflict. This deficit became evident during the turbulence experienced in higher education in the 1960s.

Colleges and universities, reasonably able to handle traditional individual academic problems and individual disciplinary offenses, found themselves ill-equipped to deal with group phenomena such as mass demonstrations, protests, and violations of rules. They also discovered that they lacked—and had to invent—machinery to negotiate with such groups.

Two other factors contribute to the vulnerability of universities to group conflict. First, because they are generally liberal and tolerant, if not permissive—as institutions go—some political groups see them as especially inept at playing political hardball when confronted with protest and conflict. As such, universities are magnets for political action. Second, campus conflict is typically dramatized and magnified by the media, which gravitate toward conflict situations in any case, and perhaps take special glee in publicizing group conflict and disruption in institutions that have traditionally presented themselves as seats of collegiality, civility, and community.

Even with several decades of experience with group conflict, universities are still more comfortable in dealing with individuals than with groups. This constitutes a special vulnerability in the current conflict over diversity because so many of the groups involved define themselves in collective, if not primordial, ways—along gender, racial, ethnic, cultural, and lifestyle lines—and present themselves politically as groups, not as individuals. If one adds to these the "group" challenges from environmental, community action, animal rights, and other groups that impinge on the university's political environment, it becomes apparent that the university stands in a kind of political situation for which its history has not equipped it well.

Results of institutionalized ineptness in dealing with collective conflict are seen in the kinds of "impossible" political situations in which many universities find themselves. Two examples follow. First, the admissions policies of most universities have accepted the "numbers game" logic of admitting a percentage of different claimant groups, either by pointing with pride to achieved results or by vowing to do better in the future. The "impossible" aspect of this definition of the situation is that, in the end, the university is trapped in a zero-sum game. An increase in the percentage of *any* group means a decrease for another, which in the current atmosphere is politically unacceptable to the losing group. And even an increase does not silence the demands for greater increases. Second, in faculty hiring policies universities have likewise committed themselves to increase the numbers of women and minorities in an absolute sense. Particularly with respect to certain minorities—Native

Americans, blacks, and Hispanics—this is currently a collectively impossible goal because of the small pool of doctoral candidates who appear in the market in any given year. The resultant situation is a heady competition for scarce minority candidates, including the practice of one institution pirating such candidates from another. Individual minority candidates may benefit from this process, but it does not seem to address the general problem of improving access for all minorities.

PROGNOSIS

The upshot of the foregoing assessment is that the contemporary debates over diversity are particularly intractable and unclear. All sides find themselves successfully able to appeal to ideological and cultural arguments that still enjoy legitimacy, but which, by a turn of history, have become opposed to one another.

The special character of the present debates also defies those who would write simple scenarios for the future. Rather, it is more advisable to envision a separable set of ideal-type outcomes, all of which are plausible, given the special alignment of social forces at the present time. The following three scenarios can be imagined:

1. The program of assimilation of racially, ethnically, and culturally diverse groups to the existing values and roles of higher education. This is the liberal view and envisions continuing traditional patterns of liberal education and occupational and professional training, with students being socialized into these patterns, accommodating to them, and preparing themselves for participation in the institutions of the larger society.
2. The program of altering the traditional mission of higher liberal education—which, it is argued, is biased along racial/ethnic, class, and gender lines in any event—to some mission that gives greater recognition to nonmainstream groups. The recent episodes of pressure for curricular change are signs of this tendency, as are the recent debates on campus about "political correctness" and its possible threat to principles of academic freedom.
3. The program of converting campuses into a microcosm of the pluralistic polity, with racial, ethnic, cultural, gender, and other groups competing for the resources as well as the symbolic and real control of the institutional life of universities. This scenario, too, while not novel in the history of education, would mark a further change in the traditional, liberal mission of educational

institutions. And, given the frail capacities of colleges and universities to manage group conflict, such a "political pluralism" model would prove difficult to stabilize.

Like the future of any complex social institution that is based on multiple values and principles, the future of research universities with respect to diversity will not reveal a clear victory for *any* of these scenarios. Some aspects of all will continue to be visible. Each one will persist, and each one will have its vicissitudes. With respect to the issue of diversity, then, the future will bring "process" rather than "product" as an outcome, with all involved parties struggling for but never finally gaining new and satisfactory definitions of the situation, institutional advantages, or political domination.

Cultural and Psychological Dimensions

Because so much of the contemporary discussion of the diversity debate is "externalized" into the social and political arenas, reference to psychological dimensions that might be involved in the experience of those who are "diversifying" and those who are being "diversified" is neglected. The reason for this neglect is at least in part ideological. If one ventures into the psychological arena, it is often regarded as a means (if not a ploy) to "psychologize the issues away" as expressions of individual problems and, therefore, not matters for political concern. I do not accept this implication. To explore the psychological dimensions of a social problem is not to ignore the problem, but, instead, to probe into ever-present aspects of any process of change in institutional and group life. The remainder of this essay will focus on these aspects.

OLD AND NEW DIVERSIFICATION

At the outset it is essential to note that the cultures of universities are *already* culturally heterogeneous and diversified. With regard to the cultures of undergraduate student bodies of these institutions, for example, the following subtypes manifest themselves in varying degrees of visibility, coherence, and self-consciousness:

- a *collegiate* culture, which is highly social; has close links to fraternities, sororities, athletics, and alumni; and manifests a kind of innocent anti-intellectualism

- a *preprofessional* culture of serious, competitive students, who are academic but not always intellectual in orientation
- a culture of *free, intellectual spirits* who identify with the faculty and treasure intellectualism and the life of the mind
- a *politically active culture,* typically liberal/radical in political tone, and often manifesting a species of anti-intellectualism
- a culture of *expressive protest,* manifested in personal appearance, drug use, sexual liberty, and countercultural values
- various *niche* cultures, including functionally based groups such as drama, band, and undergraduate and graduate academic clubs and associations.

Similarly, graduate student cultures in research universities have never been homogeneous. They vary first of all by disciplinary commitment—field by field in the sciences, social sciences, humanities, and professional schools. Within fields, they vary by level of professional commitment and identification with the field of study. They differ in the degree to which graduate students are politically active *within* the university context, and the degree to which they give priority to intellectual, political, or moral concerns. Faculty cultures are also diversified within the research university, both by academic fields and by rank/age cohorts. They vary according to the priority they accord to the major sub-missions of the university—for example, excellence and national recognition in research, commitment to undergraduate teaching, and public and professional service. Faculties also differ along lines of their level of loyalty to or suspicion of academic administrators, of their level of commitment to traditional academic values and their derived hierarchies of prestige, and, like graduate students, in the salience of intellectual, political, and moral concerns in their outlook.

Formal and informal groups based on particular racial and ethnic backgrounds, gender, and sexual preference have always been a feature of collegiate and university life, but with the increasing heterogeneity of undergraduate student bodies—and to a lesser extent, of graduate students and faculty—these groups have increased in size, visibility, and social and political salience. However, it must be underscored that the new groups are entering into an arena that is already culturally highly diversified, and in which distinct subcultures can be identified.

THE OMNIPRESENCE OF AMBIVALENCE IN THE DIVERSIFYING PROCESS

The preexisting subcultures in a university community *all* constitute opportunities for personal identification for their incoming members. They also extend implicit cultural invitations for any new member so interested or so inclined to join.

To point this out is not to ignore the barriers to participation in all the cultural and lifestyle opportunities that campuses hold. The most obvious barriers are found in the fraternity and sorority world—a special subculture of the "collegiate" alternative for students—which, even if legally and formally barred from discrimination, certainly continues to be formally segregated along gender lines, and informally along class and racial/ethnic lines. In addition, any distinct subculture develops its own mechanisms of closing ranks and of discouraging entry through informal social sanctions of ignoring, snubbing, and making life generally uncomfortable for those regarded as alien to their subculture.

At the same time, the university campus, as a liberal and voluntaristic arena, has a range of freedom of choice. Within some limits, an individual student can choose to be serious or flippant in his or her commitments to academic study; to become "intellectual" or "anti-intellectual"; to take a vocational or a liberal route in the curriculum; to adopt a traditional "Joe College" or "coed" role; to become politically active; to become bohemian; to go out for different kinds of activities such as athletics, band, or drama if able and interested; to join clubs; or to go it alone. Similarly, a faculty member has an element of choice as to whether to be a scholarly loner, a conscientious teacher, a participating or nonparticipating citizen in the academic community, a faculty conformist, or a faculty protester.

These choices, moreover, inevitably become invitations to incoming members to become something culturally *different* from what they were before entering that community. This principle is most vividly seen in the case of entering undergraduates. They are typically leaving their family and community of residence, whereas graduate students and faculty have presumably already been more fully socialized into the university cultures of their choice. Let us now consider this process from the standpoint of the undergraduate student, with special reference to racial and ethnic diversity.

There are three reasons why the collegiate experience is destined to pull students away from the cultural values and attitudes of their family, their social class, and their community. The first is found in the still viable philosophy embodied in the idea of a liberal education. Such an education is meant to be broadening, indeed *liberating* in its essence. It exposes students to new ranges of factual information, new perspectives, different ways of looking at the world, and, above all, challenges to what they have previously been taught and learned. A liberal education is thus intended to "diversify" the student to make him or her more universal, more cosmopolitan. Put more dramatically, a liberal education is based on the premise that "the student is always wrong." The sense in which that declaration is true is that the conscientious teacher takes as his or her mission the idea that students' existing knowledge and perspectives are limited; they are meant to be broadened in the educational process. The other corollary of the idea of liberal education is that, in the process, teachers are not supposed to hold out some kind of final, correct worldview, personal philosophy, or set of cultural values to the student, but rather to equip that student better to choose his or her preferred combination of these. Needless to say, this is an ideal representation of a liberal education, which does not always work out according to the ideal; nonetheless, it is still a discernible ingredient of the collegiate experience. The diverse student subcultures—serious youth culture, political activism, and bohemianism—also provide opportunities to experiment and broaden, even though they do not constitute part of the philosophy of liberal education as such.

Second, these ingredients of the collegiate experience promise not only to make the student different from his or her parents, class, and community; they also provide an opportunity for that student to *reject* those origins—to break from them in a process of rebellion that may range from polite to violent. The history of undergraduate education in America is a history of "liberated" sophomores bringing home the "enlightened" perspectives of Darwinism, Freudianism, Marxism, philosophical relativism—and nowadays deconstructionism—during vacations and torturing their stodgy and unenlightened parents with those perspectives. They may also bring home new lifestyle commitments as well—dissolute carousing, countercultural values, political radicalism, arrest records—and inflict the same torture on parents, even those (or perhaps especially those) who regard themselves as liberal.

Third, the collegiate experience is culturally defined as an avenue for *social mobility.* This cultural ideal is a deeply American one, namely to use higher education as a means to improve one's social standing by advancing occupationally and by gaining status-endowing credentials. Parents themselves usually conspire to assist in this mobility, by saving and paying for college for their children. Sometimes the mobility is not upward but simply "different"—the lawyer's daughter does not become a lawyer, the doctor's son does not become a doctor—and parents may not necessarily approve, but it is a kind of mobility all the same.

Liberation, rejection, and mobility invariably have some features in common. They are integral parts of an individual's personal growth and self-realization. But equally important—and this is where ambivalence makes its entrance—they always involve feelings of guilt. Guilt is always there for the student; it appears *no matter how* he or she resolves the tension between the culture of origin and the cultures that invite one to forsake that culture of origin. If one rejects the invitations of collegiate life, one is guilty for not having seized the opportunities—and perhaps for having disappointed one's parents in the process. If one rejects the cultural values of origin, one is guilty for having rejected them—and thus for having disappointed one's parents in another way. If one tries to strike some kind of middle ground between the two, one is certain to feel guilty on both counts. With guilt, moreover, comes anger, and that anger is likely to be directed at any and all parties who have conspired to set up the conflict that has generated the guilt in the first place.

The developmental ambivalence I have described is more or less universal, no matter what the origin of the student. However, it is particularly salient when the student comes *from* a subculture that regards itself as distinct, homogeneous, and discriminated against as a minority. Ironically, such students are often incorporated into the "middle-class," "Anglo," or "mainstream" American culture. One of the most vivid accounts of this ambivalence was described by William Foote Whyte fifty years ago in *Street Corner Society* (1955 [1943]), an ethnographic study of life in the Italian community of North Boston. The two protagonists of the study constitute the two faces of the ambivalence—"Doc," the successful local politician who never left the family values, congeniality, and loyalty to friends of the Italian community, and "Chick," the successful businessman who went to a private college and forsook all of those. Both suffered the characteristic regret and guilt associated with the distinctive route he took.

Because of the increasing numbers of racial/ethnic minorities that have entered the college and university scene in recent decades—numbers that promise only to increase in the decades to come—this phenomenon of ambivalence toward culture of origin and cultures of invitation is and will be correspondingly more widespread. The core psychological tension is between a real or imagined "home" culture of parents and community who stress continuity, loyalty to group, and perhaps endogamy on the one side, and between a real or imagined "campus" culture—an amalgam of the diverse opportunities which constitute an invitation to leave and reject the home culture and enter some real or imagined larger, cosmopolitan, and alternative world. The "home" pressure emanates not only from home; any campus with a sizable group of minority students will have an association of conscious spokespersons for that group who stress cultural identity, loyalty, and demands for respect and participation. The ambivalence is thus real and present, and constantly stirs that range of effects—including especially guilt and anger—generated by ambivalence.

As a psychological phenomenon, ambivalence is difficult to deal with and tends to be unstable; it is forever being resolved into simpler alternatives that are easier to live with. The following resolutions are identifiable on university campuses: (1) Accepting—either silently or rebelliously—the invitation to leave the "home" culture and take on one of the available cultural alternatives of the campus; in this case the loyalty to the "home" culture is uneasily repressed or openly rejected. (2) Affirming the "home" culture and repressing or rejecting the real or imagined "establishment" of the university, either by withdrawing from it or by actively assuming an alienated and critical stance toward it. (3) Striking some compromise between the two sides of the ambivalence and thus trying to have it both ways; the student may be the loyal, conformist child when at home, while simultaneously exploring and adopting other cultural styles when on campus—hiding the two adaptations from one another; the student may be politically active in varying degrees on behalf of his or her group but remain in good standing with the academic culture of the university at the same time; or the student may major in something like ethnic studies, which is simultaneously a commitment to an academic path and an affirmation of group identification and loyalty. Some kind of compromise of this sort seems the most frequent resolution of cultural ambivalence in contemporary American campus life.

The common tendency of racial and ethnic groups to "ghettoize" on campuses is often ignored or regretted. When recognized, it is typically explained by a simple formula like "people being comfortable with their own kind." I believe the phenomenon is more than that and can be interpreted consistently within the framework of the ambivalence that I have noted. Associating informally with one's "kind" is one—probably the most typical—mode of resolving that ambivalence. The campus ghetto is a kind of way station: a means of declaring one's loyalty to a real or imagined home community while participating in and presumably reaping the real or imagined benefits of the alternative cultures that university life has to offer.

The logic of ambivalence also applies to those who are part of the supposed "majority" on diversifying campuses—whether these are referred to as majority, white, Anglo, mainstream, or whatever. This group may, incidentally, include—psychologically—members of minority groups who have opted for the first-noted resolution of *their* ambivalence. On the one hand, they may experience the feeling that the dominant academic and collegiate cultures are historically "theirs" in some vague sense and that they are therefore being "invaded"; they are likely to interpret their own presence in the community as resulting from their having "made it" on traditional meritocratic grounds while others have not. On the other hand—many being liberal themselves and all being exposed to the traditionally liberal culture of the university—they welcome, or feel the pressure to welcome, historically less privileged minority and other groups to that culture. This ambivalence of the majority group tends to be resolved in a number of different ways:

1. Asserting the traditional dominance of "their" historic university, whether this is expressed in the affirmation of meritocratic ideals which others have presumably not met, the conviction that the "diversifying" groups are aliens or less than first-class citizens, or, in some cases, outright racism.
2. Espousing egalitarian causes—liberal admissions policies, affirmative action, and multicultural curricular reform—and identifying with the incoming minority groups, their aspirations, their political positions, their social movements, and perhaps their social life.
3. Striking some compromise between the two sides, and thus having it both ways; perhaps to espouse liberal values but to associate informally with other "majority" students, or periodically to espouse "causes," which, however, do not disturb the basic contours of traditional collegiate life. This kind of compromise is probably the most frequent among "majority" groups as well.

These are some of the manifestations of the complex process of personal and social adaptation to ambivalence. Let me end with two final observations. First, the analysis of ambivalence and its complications has been carried out mainly with reference to undergraduate students. The same dynamics and their resolutions, with different weights and in different contexts, apply equally well to graduate student bodies and faculties that are in the process of diversifying. Second, the politics emanating from the adaptations to multiple ambivalences generate an enormously complex mosaic. Not only does one find "minorities" and "majorities" opposed to one another—which is the relationship enunciated most frequently in public rhetoric—but one also finds these groups in common cause with one another, depending on the resolutions of the ambivalences on each side. Moreover, the politics of ambivalence means that many political subdivisions *within* both minorities and majorities emanate from the multiple resolutions of ambivalence. Finally, because these resolutions are superimposed on *other* divisions in the university—divisions among undergraduates, graduate students, faculty, administration, and staff—the possible permutations and combinations of political alliance and political division are even greater. These considerations carry us some distance toward understanding the special fluidity and volatility of politics on the campuses of research universities.

The conclusion to this psychological line of reasoning is similar to the conclusion emanating from the sociopolitical reasoning laid out in the first part of this essay. The political divisions that arise from the ambivalences of diversification are profound, multiple, and omnipresent, and the bases for these divisions are endemic. These politics show no signs either of abating or of yielding any simple social-psychological or political resolution. The political forces of the nation are such that the march of diversification in universities is becoming and will become an established historical fact. However, from the standpoint of the social psychology of diversification and its political manifestations, we must expect continuous process and flux, not a finished product.

Reference

Whyte, William Foote
1955 [1943] *Street Corner Society: The Social Structure of an Italian Slum.* Chicago: University of Chicago Press.

8

Problematics of Affirmative Action: A View from California

Affirmative Action in Historical Context

From colonial times—and consolidated in the moment of constitutional founding—American society has found its legitimacy in four central cultural values: individual liberty and freedom, democracy, progress manifested in mastery of nature and economic expansion, and equality of opportunity. It is a matter of historical fascination that human slavery—an institution that ran contrary to most of these values—persisted for almost a century after the birth of a republic founded on them. It is also, however, a confirmation of the power of those values that slavery was brought down in their name, and that discriminatory practices established after the Civil War were also curtailed in their name. Yet during World War II Gunnar Myrdal could still write of an American dilemma—a society that simultaneously institutionalized those values (Myrdal focused above all on freedom, democracy, and equality of opportunity) and a system of racial inequality that denied those values.

Affirmative action, born officially about two decades after Myrdal wrote, must be regarded as a continuation of the conversation about that dilemma, but it was not simply an extension of past assaults on inequality. It arose in a new historical context and differed qualitatively from past struggles. What was that context, and what was new about it?

The 1960s witnessed a confluence of three historical circumstances that created the facilitating if not necessary conditions for affirmative action:

- A civil rights movement, focused mainly on the South but drawing participation from both black leaders and citizens and liberal whites around the country. This movement was named properly, since it concerned above all civil—or public—society and worked to end traditional denials of rights in that arena. The major battlegrounds were the polity, with voting the focus; public education, with integration the focus; and access to public places, with transportation and businesses such as restaurants the foci. While economic discrimination became the target of some protest, the main emphasis was civil. Furthermore, the battle for civil rights was about *racial* injustices affecting black Americans and did not extend to disadvantaged groups in general.

- Eight years of political domination by the Democratic Party, which, through the leadership of John Kennedy, Robert Kennedy, and Lyndon Johnson, proved to be sympathetic and responsive to the goals of the civil rights movement. Moreover, especially under Johnson, the Democrats went beyond civil rights and introduced economic and educational reforms. The war on poverty was couched in general terms—linked to the generic problem of poverty—but in practice it encompassed educational programs (such as Head Start) and welfare reforms directed disproportionately toward the poor black population.
- A *generalization* of political protest and alienation, some of it inspired by the goals, methods, and successes of the civil rights movement. The new directions included the student movement, targeting the universities and social—including racial—injustices generally; the antiwar movement, which consumed the country from 1965 until the beginning of the 1970s; the mobilization of other disadvantaged racial and ethnic groups—notably Native American and Hispanic/Latino—in protest against injustices specific to them; a mobilization of protest against racial injustice in South Africa; and a revitalization of the feminist movement, with a more explicit emphasis on economic, educational, and other institutional disadvantages than ever before.

These circumstances set the stage for affirmative action. As an institutional innovation it combined ingredients from all of them and added a few new ones. In its essence, affirmative action was a set of policies and procedures intended to give disadvantaged groups differential access to economic and educational opportunities and to their associated rewards. Like the civil rights movement, affirmative action aimed to improve the situation of the disadvantaged. Like Johnson's Good Society, it focused on educational and occupational arenas. It was thus a *synthesis* or *convergence* of themes found in the civil rights movement and the programs of the Democratic administrations. It remained conscious of civil and political rights, but it focused more on social and economic rights.

In addition, affirmative action involved a number of extensions beyond the themes of the 1960s:

- It included but moved beyond the removal of obstacles to participation in society's institutions. It actively *promoted* such participation, in the form of preferential treatment in hiring, contracting, and educational admissions.
- It included the rationale that it would redress *past* as well as present institutional disadvantages, wrongs, and sufferings. This rationale was explicit in the case of African Americans and Native Americans but came to pervade the entire logic of affirmative action.
- It involved a generalization of concern beyond the civil rights movement focus on race. Affirmative action's initial focus was on American blacks but it soon came to include other racial and ethnic groups—Native Americans, Hispanic/Latinos, Asians, South Sea Island peoples. It early included gender as well, and subsequently physically disabled persons. What makes affirmative action sociologically interesting is that it generalized in *ascriptive* directions. Ascription refers to categories that are, by birth or social designation, defined as largely *unalterable* by personal choice or behavior. Another ascriptive category, age, also entered the picture, not principally as demands for preferred treatment but as demands to end job discrimination against the elderly and the disadvantages imposed by retirement. Finally, sexual preference, a category that lies ambiguously between ascribed and voluntary, also came on the scene, but this, too, involved protest against discrimination rather than active, preferential treatment.

  (Ascription is only an approximate sociological category. In the case of age it is pure, since chronological age, sociologically defined, is unalterable by choice or behavior, even though one might "feel" or "act" older or younger than one "is." Other areas are less clear. "Passing for white," renouncing ethnic identification, and sex changes give the lie to the adjective "unalterable."

At the same time, such changes are regarded as unusual or exceptional, thus confirming the sociological reality of the notion of ascription.)

Some Additional Features of Affirmative Action

THE CULTURAL CONTEXT

No institutional practice exists without explicit or implicit reference to some legitimizing, presumably consensual cultural value that gives meaning and defensibility to that practice. For example, voting procedures, electoral districting, political primaries, and political conventions make sense and gain their institutional desirability by reference to the cultural ideal of representative democracy.

Advocates of affirmative action seek legitimacy in the values of social justice and equality of opportunity. From these values derive the argument that those who have experienced past or do experience present disadvantage through some form of oppression have been unjustly treated and deprived of equality of opportunity and merit compensation by preferential treatment. At the same time, preferential treatment can be regarded as running *counter* to another connotation of equality of opportunity—namely, meritocracy, or the reward of talent and ability without regard to other considerations. University of California Regent Ward Connerly, for example, who spearheaded the movement to repeal existing affirmative action provisions, said the initiative was a way to achieve "an inclusive society in which people of all races, religions, and sexual preference have a right to have our talents considered" (*San Francisco Chronicle,* December 1, 1995). In the immediate wake of the passage of the California Civil Rights Initiative in the November 1996 election, the *New York Times* (November 10, p. 26) quoted an advocate of the measure as saying "Equal opportunity is what America is all about—*not* preferences." In the very next paragraph, an opponent of the legislation spoke as follows:

> We believe the vote in California in no way reflects the general public's sentiment on the value and viability of affirmative action programs. Most Americans support preservation of equal opportunity, especially in the workplace.

Because of this circumstance, the nation has been faced with a situation in which *both* advocates and opponents of affirmative action policies and practices have legitimized their arguments by referring to the *same* cultural value, equality of opportunity.

This situation—while not unheard of—is not typical. Debates over welfare policies, for example, often invoke conflicting value perspectives: competitive individualism versus humanitarianism or collective responsibility. Furthermore, the simultaneous reference to the same legitimizing context often gives rise to some interesting formulas. For example, one instruction that appears in affirmative action manuals is the following: if two applicants for a position are equally qualified, but one falls in a preferential treatment category and the other does not, the position should go to the former. This formula attempts to accommodate, through compromise, the tension involved in the simultaneous appeal to equality of opportunity and preferential treatment: to recognize talent and qualification, but to tilt judgments in marginal cases. (It is also true that such a formula creates a difficult if not impossible assignment in practice—how to judge objectively and exactly if two people are equally qualified when such a judgment inevitably involves multiple criteria, some subjective? But when conflicts over meaning and legitimacy are at hand, the closest attention is not always paid to practical issues of workability.)

In addition, when advocates and opponents of affirmative action appeal simultaneously to the same values, this may create a specter of ambiguity and tension for participants. Those who benefit from preferential attention may experience a sense of vindication for past or present wrongs, but they may also experience a sense that they have not "made it" on the basis of their own abilities and achievements. Those who oppose affirmative action may harbor the same suspicion that those who benefited have not "really" made it on their own, and, on that basis, may resent or "tolerate" the "less deserving" in their midst—a particularly subtle and evasive form of racism or sexism. Indeed, the argument that affirmative action "demeans" the beneficiaries by elevating them artificially in a merit-based world was one of the principal claims made by those who wished to dismantle affirmative action policies during the debates before the University of California Regents in 1995.

THE POLITICAL CONTEXT

As noted, affirmative action was born in the context of and sustained by a number of social movements—movements by racial and ethnic groups, different wings of the feminist movement, gay and lesbian movements, and more diffuse sentiments against social injustices of all kinds. The project also gave rise to counter or "backlash" political movements with varying degrees of articulation, energy, and mobilization. This circumstance, if no other, confirms that affirmative action has been a *political* phenomenon: an institutional crucible in which social movements and countermovements clash.

The politics of affirmative action are complicated by another political peculiarity. For many social movements, the response of government authorities is to regard them as something "out there," whether they are something to crush, oppose, resist, handle, become divided over, accommodate, or give in to—in a word, to maintain a certain distance from them. Revolutionary political movements, the labor union movement, and the antiwar movement are cases that illustrate this point. In the case of affirmative action, the federal government and some state governments *joined* the movement. For whatever motives, government agencies were often the leaders in promoting affirmative action. Through administrative and judicial pressure, the government encouraged if not coerced others to pursue its policies. In higher education, for example, agencies such as the Department of Health, Education and Welfare and the Department of Labor threatened to withhold research funds from universities unless they instituted and followed affirmative action policies. This government stance not only endowed the relevant social movements for affirmative action with legitimacy, influence, and boldness; it also gave additional momentum to the affirmative action project as a whole.

Another political dynamic invited the extension and generalization of the affirmative action project. Two necessary conditions for a group to derive advantage from affirmative action are (1) to identify itself as a tangible group, presumably with a consciousness and identity; and (2) to make a claim—and make that claim "stick"—that it is suffering or has suffered disadvantage. The government played a role in establishing these conditions by indicating that it was prepared to respond to claims of ascription and disadvantage. The result was to encourage a special kind of politics, called, variously, the politics of ascription, ethnic politics, or the politics of identity. (It is interesting to note that political scientists and sociologists have recently turned their attention to identity-based social movements and "identity politics," thereby acknowledging a social reality that had been created for them.)

As a corollary, there is only limited evidence for the salience of *social class* as a feature of affirmative action. By and large, advocates of affirmative action do not claim to represent class from an economic point of view, even though they often frame their protests and demands in the language of class oppression. Some might regard this as an oddity, given the significance of class in other eras of American politics—for example, the politics of class in the early history of labor unionism and during the Great Depression. In education, too, class has played a major part in the history of preferential treatment. The preferential admission of children of alumni—long a practice of private and some public institutions—can be seen in some cases as affirmative action in favor of the wealthy. Another example is the preferential treatment of able students from backgrounds too modest to afford a college education, which is class-based preference as well. Preferential admission of athletes, while based in the first instance on athletic talent, is in some cases, such as the recruitment of male football players, class preference in practice. (There is, however, great variation among sports and between the sexes with respect to class origins.)

Identity politics, if we may term it that, may turn against the political authorities who acknowledge them. As we will see, identity-based demands tend to develop into claims to entitlement, because advocates of the identity groups often base their arguments on primordial or quasi-sacred considerations—such as common blood or ancestry—which demand dignity and respect. This imparts an uncompromising character to their claims and demands. This circumstance creates difficulties for politicians, because politicians in democracies engage in compromise if nothing else, and, as a rule, are less comfortable with absolute demands than they are with contingent, negotiable ones.

Finally, if demands for entitlement by identity groups come to be translated into quotas for positions, this creates additional difficulties for political resolution. Consider an example from my former university, the University of California, Berkeley. That campus has a deserved reputation of being one of the most aggressive in pressing the project of affirmative action. As noted in the foregoing chapter, it has pursued this project in such a way as to create a permanent presence of complaining groups for campus authorities. Its policies have resulted, furthermore, in the slow but steady reduction of students from the white population, who (and whose parents) have not, until recently, been as mobilized or as articulate as minority groups have.

POINTS OF AMBIGUITY IN IMPLEMENTING AFFIRMATIVE ACTION PROGRAMS

While definite phrases (e.g., Equal Opportunity Employer) characterize affirmative action, and while manuals and procedures guide implementation, affirmative action has experienced a certain vagueness and ambiguity about both goals and processes. With respect to goals, the following points of uncertainty can be noted:

- Should affirmative action be defined in terms of specific substantive goals or as a general process aimed at ameliorating present and past disadvantages?
- If the former, how should goals be characterized? Should they be regarded as definite quotas or targets? Should they be regarded as aimed at achieving some proportion of a population, or should they be regarded as efforts to move toward "more" or "better" representation of groups, without further specification?
- Which groups qualify for affirmative action? Certain groups, such as African Americans, Latinos, and Native Americans come to mind as unambiguous cases, but their recognition has come about at different points in time. Furthermore, different groups *within* the Latino population have had different salience, with Cuban Americans being the most ambiguous case. Pacific Island peoples are typically listed officially as qualifying minorities but figure only little in practice. Asian Americans constitute another ambiguous case. To take a vivid example at the University of California, Asian American groups are, de facto, not considered an affirmative action minority in undergraduate admissions. (Indeed, Asian American groups have argued that they have been discriminated *against*, and would fare better under completely meritocratic standards.) At the same time, some academic departments, de facto, consider Asian Americans as minorities meriting special attention in graduate admissions and faculty hiring. The salience of gender as an object of affirmative action has also varied over time. It has been an insignificant issue in undergraduate admissions and has diminished in significance in some other arenas. In the end, the effective qualification of different groups has been largely a function of their capacity to make their case and mobilize politically. In practice, finally, there are great regional and institutional differences in the recognition of different groups as qualifying for affirmative action.
- How are members of groups to be identified as belonging to those groups? Recognition by name is a reasonably but not completely accurate way of identifying Latino groups and women. Recogni-

> tion of African Americans and Native Americans by name and sometimes by appearance is difficult, sometimes impossible. Asking applicants to identify their group is another measure, but requests of this sort are almost always voluntary, and, as a result, incomplete. In 1975—when affirmative action was entering into a high gear—I was chairman of my department at U.C. Berkeley. I was requested, in the interests of affirmative action, to specify the racial, ethnic, and gender distributions of a pool of candidates for academic appointment, but discovered, at the same time, that I was forbidden by administrative rule to request identification from the candidates! The example is extreme but illustrates the ambiguity.

With respect to procedures for implementing affirmative action, a comparable list of uncertainties emerges:

- Is active discrimination in favor of a group permissible? And does this imply active discrimination against another group? One judicial decision—the Bakke case at the medical school of the University of California, Davis—suggested that the answer to the former is negative and the answer to the latter is positive, since the ruling was in favor of a white applicant to medical school, who claimed he was denied admission because places were reserved for minority students. However, such a ruling has not necessarily controlled informal practices in all situations.
- What constitutes a proper search in affirmative action hiring? Is advertising in a few outlets likely to reach women and minorities sufficient, or should the search be more aggressive? Most institutions have developed definite procedures for searching, but, again, the variation is great.
- What constitutes a proper accounting for affirmative action efforts? While formulas have emerged (for example, reporting the character of the search, describing the pool of applicants by race/ethnicity and gender, defending why minority candidates were not hired), these have sometimes produced stock, uninformative answers. Some maintain that to require reporting produces positive results; others complain that reporting has little effect and serves mainly to increase paperwork and costs.
- How and in what detail should affirmative action be policed? Should monitors be satisfied when proper procedures have been

carried out, or should they be interested in accounting for and influencing results in hiring and admissions?

To summarize up to this point, affirmative action policies, while conceptually clear in intent and yielding significant results, have been matters of cultural ambivalence, political conflict, and institutional ambiguity. The origins of this, moreover, lie in the uncertain legitimacy that affirmative action enjoys in the context of American values, the political competition that results, and the practical difficulties in implementation—the last derived in part from the first two. These persistent features of ambivalence, conflict, and ambiguity have contributed in part—but only in part—to the potential for reaction and backlash, which appeared in earnest in the 1990s.

Three Interrelated Trends

I have been able to discern three irregular trends in affirmative action practices during the past quarter century. When viewed together, they may cast some additional light on why a significant opposition to the program has developed. I confess that I have less than full documentation for these trends and have more confidence in some of the following statements than others.

1. We may detect a movement from an emphasis on *substantive* goals (initiating affirmative action programs, achieving results in the form of targets) toward an emphasis on *procedures.* To note this trend is to state the sociologically obvious. It is what Max Weber called routinization. Weber's main illustration was the routinization of charismatic leadership into more stable forms, but his point may be generalized. Any innovation or reform produces an initial period of enthusiasm and vision, but as the innovative becomes the normal, practice comes to be regulated by more explicit and stable norms.

   This has been the case with affirmative action. Most employers, both public and private, have sooner or later established modes of searching, evaluating, and monitoring affirmative action policies. Two additional observations can be made about routinization. The first concerns the general ambiguity—noted earlier—in the project of affirmative action. As a general principle, the more ambiguous the project, the greater the urgency to establish understood ways of administering it. The objective—seldom explicit—of this adaptation, moreover, is to turn the novel and uncertain into the established and certain.

The second observation has to do with the management of conflict. The substantive goal of affirmative action is to alter practices associated with inequalities in race, ethnic, and gender relations. Such efforts often challenge people's personal beliefs and identities. Resistance to change is invariably strong, and conflicts often become bitter and explosive. To focus on the rules of the game—on due process, as it were—often has the effect of diverting conflict away from its hot substantive core and toward more neutral grounds of procedure. In the 1970s, when the University of California and other research universities were under pressure from federal agencies to move forward on affirmative action, U.C. President Charles Hitch negotiated a kind of truce whereby the agencies would forgo insistence on establishing short-term targets if the university would establish procedures designed to further affirmative action. Such a compromise tended to defuse direct conflict and focus attention on the process.

Under such circumstances, discourse and debate tends to move away from substantive conflict and focus on methodological issues. In the early 1980s, as chair of the Berkeley Division of the U.C. Academic Senate, I was sometimes asked to sit in on visits to the Berkeley campus of representatives of federal agencies who were to monitor its progress on affirmative action. A fascinating feature of the exchanges in these visits was the focus on methodological points—estimating the size and quality of pools of minority group members and women in the academic market, disputing the accuracy of measurements, challenging and defending the university's estimates of progress it was making, and even arguing about statistical techniques. Some of these discussions became heated. At the same time, they amounted to a way of avoiding confrontations over the substantive rights and wrongs of affirmative action and the conflicts between government bureaucrats who were under political pressure to achieve results and the university officials who were pleading for patience and flexibility because of the political exigencies they faced in their own institutions. The substantive conflicts were hidden in the methodological agenda, but, with that agenda, discussion could proceed under the tacit—but possibly mistaken—assumption that the parties agreed on goals and differed only about means. As a result, discussions could proceed with a lower probability of open, bitter, and explosive conflict.

2. Another trend is the movement from preferential treatment to entitlement. The aim of affirmative action was to improve the institutional fortunes of disadvantaged groups. The means were to intervene in the labor and contracting markets and in the admissions policies of educational institutions. Over time, tangible results began to appear—in different degrees—in government offices, in colleges and universities, and in business and professional firms. With such progress there often develops a subtle but definite shift in expectations among groups that have benefited: that those gains should be consolidated and protected, and that further advances should be made. It is only a short step from such expectations to the mentality of entitlement.

   Such developments create a difficult political situation. The expectations of all groups simply cannot be met unless positions available in the institutions and organizations involved continue to expand. If those positions expand slowly, remain stable, or decline, then a zero-sum game is at hand. The logic of that game is that if one party gains, the others necessarily lose. This logic conflicts directly with the logic of entitlement to past and future gains. The consequences of that conflict are three: latent or open conflicts among the groups struggling for scarce positions, resistance to further change on the part of those who regard themselves as potential losers, and heightened political pressure on those regarded as responsible for policies—in this case employers, administrators, and government officials. All three consequences have been visible in the history of affirmative action.

3. A final trend is from a focus on economic and institutional justice to a focus on cultural conflict. There is nothing necessary about this trend, but it also expresses a certain logic. Affirmative action promises, above all, an improvement for the groups affected—from second-class citizenship to something better. But the process does not stop there. As Alexis de Tocqueville demonstrated in the cases of the middle classes and the peasantry in eighteenth-century France, advances in one social sphere generated higher levels of dissatisfaction. This is the dynamic of relative deprivation: the wounds of exclusion from spheres not yet improved become all the sorer when advance is attained in one.

   That dynamic is evident in the history of affirmative action.

One demand that followed the increased admissions of minorities to colleges and universities in the late 1960s and early 1970s was for programs, departments, and schools of ethnic studies. This demand was for equity in educational institutions in which minorities now had greater numbers. Many such academic units were put in place after a period of faculty resistance and political conflict. Despite some successes, most of these units continue to hold a second-class status in the eyes of older and more established academic enterprises in the colleges and universities.

In the 1980s, the demand for academic inclusion and respect took a new turn: a call for the reform of long-established curricula. This involved not only a demand for inclusion but also a *cultural* attack on traditional college and university curricula and on those believed responsible for them. Those who had demanded Third World and ethnic programs were bidding for inclusion as equals. Those who called for ending the traditional "Western Civ" requirement at Stanford and for an "American cultures" requirement at Berkeley were also demanding inclusion, but they combined that with an assault on "Eurocentrism" and a "white male establishment" that exercised its "hegemony" by imposing its Eurocentric views on peoples with different but equally if not more dignified cultures.

The movement for curricular reform in the 1980s—along with related debates on cultural diversity, multiculturalism, and the "culture wars"—was a confluence of two major historical forces: first, an escalation of demands to the cultural level by advocates for minority groups and women who still felt disadvantaged on college and university campuses; and second, the postmodernist movement, the appearance of which coincided with the collapse of radical Marxism in the 1980s and which developed, as a barely-beneath-the-surface agenda, a critique and political protest against those who impose power-as-knowledge on disadvantaged groups.

This escalation to the cultural level has not affected the majority of working people in the country, whose main interest is still in the improvement of their economic and institutional positions and rewards. The cultural debates have been confined largely to spokespersons for social movements, academics, intellectuals, and the sophisticated press. In those circles, however, that escalation poses a deeper and in some respects more difficult political situation than demands for institutional access. The cultural critique is

> more aggressive than the institutional one. In addition, it excites conflicts over cultural values as well as group interests, thus making the conflicts more fundamental and encompassing.

To summarize this section, I would propose a connection among the three trends mentioned: A combination of increased political consciousness of and political pressure by disadvantaged groups and reformers produced a series of economic and educational reforms. The resulting programs and procedures produced a significant incorporation of previously excluded groups. That success generated increased expectations of two kinds—those based on a sense of entitlement and those stemming from a bid for cultural dignity as well as institutional inclusion. These demands, in turn, created a more aggressive and threatening face on the part of the movement, and thus increased the likelihood of backlash and countermovement. This line of analysis may fill in another piece of the puzzle of explaining the backlash of the 1990s. But the story is not yet finished. To complete it, I turn to some specifics of the California situation which reveal some factors not yet considered and help explain the strength of the backlash in that state.

The California and the University of California Situations

In one respect, the situation in California has already been addressed. Most of the general aspects and trends already discussed apply to California, and many illustrations refer to the California scene. That state's situation, however, has been extreme in two senses: its scene is one of extreme racial and ethnic diversity, and the "rollback" of affirmative action by both the University of California Regents and the voters of California mark two of the most dramatic events in the history of affirmative action.

AFFIRMATIVE ACTION IN THE UNIVERSITY OF CALIFORNIA

As indicated, the main external pressure for affirmative action in the university came from federal research agencies, the government of California, and demands of minority and women's groups. One should not conclude from this, however, that the university itself was completely passive or resistant. Its campuses—most notably Berkeley and Santa Cruz—have political cultures that welcome reforms to improve disadvantaged populations.

Affirmative action affected every sector of the university, but the effects varied by sector. To mention the major variations:

- Administrative staff. Affirmative action policies—expressed mainly in the hiring and advancement of women and minority employees—proceeded earlier and further with respect to staff. There are several reasons for this. First, the administration, as direct target of political demands, was most sensitive to pressures to institute affirmative action policies. Second, the administration can effect changes in personnel policies in its own ranks more easily than it can in areas such as graduate student admissions and faculty recruitment, which are usually delegated to largely autonomous academic departments. Third, administrative staff, in contrast to faculty, requires a diversity of skill levels among its personnel. While applying criteria of competence and quality in hiring decisions, the administration does not have such an elaborate machinery as faculty recruitment to ensure quality and competitive excellence. Finally, employee turnover is higher for administrative staff than for faculty, thus providing greater opportunity for rapid changes in hiring policy.
- Undergraduate admissions. Affirmative action proceeded faster and further in undergraduate admissions than in other academic sectors. Admissions at that level is centralized on the campuses and thus more easily affected by central administrative decisions. Furthermore, the characteristics of its recruitment pool—the top one-eighth of graduates from the state's high schools (as required by the California Master Plan for Higher Education)—are well known. Third, a mechanism for preferential treatment of undergraduates was already in place. For years the university had used a "2 percent rule," instituted mainly in the interest of recruiting athletes, that permitted campuses to extend admissions beyond the eligible academic pool for 2 percent of its entering class. Subsequently, and in the interest of extending affirmative action, this rule was extended to 4 percent, then to 6 percent. This afforded campuses greater flexibility in recruiting and greater capacity to bring in minority students.

In practice, the experiences of the different campuses of the university were diverse. They varied according to the aggressiveness of individual administrators and according to the size of minority populations in their respective "catchment areas." The large urban campuses of Berkeley and Los Angeles were most diversified, and by the late 1980s they had student bodies with a minority of "Anglo" students. The process went less far on less urban campuses such as Davis and Santa Cruz. In the lore of undergraduate applicants in Southern California—a lore which does not mince words—the Irvine campus was known as the "yellow campus," the Los Angeles campus as the "black and brown campus," and the Santa Barbara campus as the "white campus." Regarded as a whole, however, the University of California carried affirmative action policies in undergraduate admissions very far in comparison with other educational institutions in the country.

- Graduate admissions. Graduate admissions also vary by academic unit and campus, but the general pattern is to evaluate applicants first at the unit level (professional school, academic department), with recommendations going to a central Graduate Division for approval. The latter very seldom challenges the units' judgments, and when it does, it is typically on procedural, not substantive, grounds. This decentralization has meant that affirmative action has been pursued variably at the unit level. Some fields, such as engineering and economics, have small pools, and recruitment of qualified women and minorities has been low; others, such as education and sociology, have larger pools. Furthermore, pools cannot be easily expanded, since strong performance in college is a condition for finding a place in them. In addition, disciplinary "cultures" differ along conservative-liberal-radical lines, and these differences affect the degree to which academic units push or resist affirmative action goals and procedures. Despite these barriers, many schools and departments in the University of California have significantly altered the racial, ethnic, and gender composition of their graduate student bodies.

- Faculty recruitment. The factors affecting graduate recruitment apply even more to faculty recruitment. Recruitment pools are even more restricted, since a condition for becoming part of them is to have attained a Ph.D. or advanced professional degree. Furthermore, the campuses of the University of California, like those of all major research institutions, are engaged in a constant and vigorous competitive struggle to hire only "the best." This means that many doctoral and professional graduates are not even considered. Finally, the institution of academic tenure restricts the rate at which the goals of affirmative action can be realized. With an annual turnover rate of 3–5 percent through retirement and resignation through the 1970s and 1980s (and before the mass exodus of senior faculty via early retirement in the 1990s), the opportunities to hire women and minorities were modest. This combination of factors yielded the smallest quantitative results of affirmative action among faculties, compared to other sectors in the university. Once again, however, the University of California was a national leader in implementing affirmative action at the faculty level.

The faculty, however, expressed the strongest political resistance to affirmative action programs. The basis for this opposition rose mainly from its deep commitment to standards of "quality" and "excellence" in recruitment and advancement, and in its highly developed machinery (multiple reviews of faculty members by department faculty, committees on academic personnel, and administrators). Many faculty, themselves politically liberal, shared the belief that hiring and advancement on any standards other than merit was a violation of those standards. Many academic units experienced their bitterest internal conflicts over the hiring of minorities and women. The 1970s and 1980s also witnessed incidents of faculty outrage over administrative reversal of faculty recommendations on minority and women candidates. On the Berkeley campus, the only really systematic faculty alienation and opposition to I. Michael Heyman—whose tenure as chancellor spanned the 1980s—came from groups of faculty members who believed that he was going "too far, too fast" in pressing affirmative action and compromising standards of academic excellence long embraced on that campus.

Despite the ambivalence, ambiguity, resistance, and conflict associated with affirmative action, by the early 1990s the principles, policies, and procedures of that project were firmly established in the University of California and were legitimate in the minds—if not entirely in the hearts—of most of its constituencies. The most direct evidence of this is that every constituency—the president and his office, the chancellors, the faculty through the Academic Senate, and students through their representative institutions—spoke out officially *against* the initiative of the Board of Regents' resolution of July 1995. This polarization between the regents and all other constituencies is a remarkable political fact and will—as remarks later will indicate—reverberate throughout the university system for a long time.

The Politics of the Regental Action

By the end of 1994, the American nation confronted a unique historical situation that set the stage for a popular and governmental backlash against affirmative action, especially its racial and ethnic components. Among the factors contributing to this situation were the following:

- Since 1973, the real wages of Americans had remained virtually stagnant, after a period of steady but variable increase in real wages dating back to World War II. In addition, traditionally secure middle-class positions became less secure as firms and other agencies resorted to downsizing as a competitive strategy. For a country historically committed to material progress and the expectation that the next generation will be better off than the last, this economic fact contributed, perhaps more than all others, to the mood of national sourness about its institutions, including its government.
- This stagnation was aggravated—especially from the early 1980s on—by a regressive movement in the distribution of income, accompanied by social problems such as increases in poverty and homelessness. The causes of the stagnation and regression are complex; they include technological change, international wage competition, a weakening of labor unionism, and tax and housing policies of the Reagan administration. Whatever the causes, they were a recipe for dissatisfaction among many groups. The significant economic recession of the early 1990s only exaggerated these economic conditions.
- The combination of stagnation and regression often gives rise to protest from the left. Contrary to this expectation, the electoral politics of the country in the last two decades have been dominated by the right and the Republican Party. From the presidency of Richard Nixon to the presidency of Bill Clinton, the country expe-

rienced only one episode of Democratic dominance—the unpopular presidency of Jimmy Carter—and the politics of the Reagan and to some extent the Bush administration emanated from ideologies of the right. Clinton's administration promised a reversal, but most of Clinton's liberal initiatives either failed or stalled, and the election of a Republican Congress in 1994 was interpreted by the winners as a mandate against government in general and governmental involvement in domestic policies in particular.

- One reason why difficult economic conditions were expressed in a right-wing mode is that the country experienced, during the same decades, the greatest wave of foreign immigration since the late nineteenth and early twentieth centuries. That fact provided many with an explanation for their economic difficulties—immigrants compete for jobs, are willing to work for less, and increase expenditures on welfare.
- An early initiative of the Republication Congress of 1994 was an aggressive move on the part of influential Republicans to reverse—by radical revision or even abolition—affirmative action as a governmental policy. That initiative put the Clinton administration on the defensive, and while that administration opposed the movement against affirmative action, it promised a thoroughgoing review of affirmative action programs with an eye to correcting excesses.

All these long-term and short-term developments constituted a relevant national environment for California; in particular, the national move to weaken or abolish affirmative action was a green light for the state. In addition, some social conditions specific to California intensified those national developments:

- Immigration rates in California were higher than those of the nation. The inflow was mainly Mexicans and Central Americans, but Asians also contributed. It was repeatedly reported in the media and elsewhere that California was becoming a state of minorities, and that by sometime after the year 2000 minority populations would outnumber the Anglo population. Equally common were reports that businesses and wealthier Anglo residents of California were leaving the state and that the overall increase of its population was because of the inflow of immigrants.
- The recession of the early 1990s was more severe in California than it was in the rest of the nation. California's unemployment rates

were consistently 2 or 3 percent higher than the national rate. California's unhappy economic fortunes were generated in part by reductions in government defense spending, concentrated in Southern California, in the wake of events in Eastern Europe and Russia in 1989–90.

- California politics have been dominated since 1982 by Republican governors—George Deukmejian and Pete Wilson. The latter built much of his campaign and political program on antiwelfare and anti-immigration issues, and he threw his weight behind Proposition 187, the 1994 action that would deny the state's educational, medical, and other institutions to illegal immigrants. The constitutional status and impact of that proposition are still unclear, but the political message was clear. On June 1, 1995, Wilson issued an executive order to "End Preferential Treatment and to Promote Individual Opportunity Based on Merit." In the summer of 1995, he exploited the themes of antiwelfare, anti-immigration, and anti-affirmative action in his brief, ill-fated bid for the Republican presidential nomination.
- One consequence of the Republican gubernatorial domination was a radical change in the composition of the University of California's Board of Regents. Regents are appointed by the governor; those appointments almost always go to political supporters of the incumbent governor. Since regental terms are for twelve years, it transpired that every appointment by Democratic Governor Jerry Brown (who preceded Deukmejian as governor) left the regents and no Democrats were appointed to replace them. So, as of the mid-1990s, the entire Board of Regents was composed of Republican appointments by Deukmejian and Wilson. Many of those regents, moreover, were indebted to Wilson, since appointment to the Board is widely considered to be an important political reward and a source of recognition and prestige for those appointed.
- One regental appointment was of crucial significance, that of Ward Connerly, an African American businessman from Sacramento, in 1993. Himself a recipient of contracts under affirmative action provisions for contracting with minority businessmen, Connerly nevertheless had developed a special antagonism toward affirmative action. This attitude was manifested from the beginning of his term, at which time, he recalled he was "instantly struck by the extent to which group classifications, particularly that of race,

> were being used in the activities of the University" (Connerly news release, July 5, 1995). He began a campaign of criticism of the university's admission policies, but in the early stages this attracted the open support of only a few regents, though Connerly maintained that many of them "privately shared similar concerns" (ibid.). He complained that the university did not take his concern seriously (he spoke of his "Lone Ranger" image), so in January of 1995 he decided "to increase [the issue's] public visibility" (ibid.).

Three additional, interrelated contextual features of California politics should be mentioned as background. Those features concern the popular—if not populist—character of its democracy and the public character of its politics. First, dating from its state constitution, California has institutionalized many features of direct democracy, including provisions for initiatives, referenda, and the recall of public officials. These features—especially the referendum—have lent a certain cumbersomeness to California politics, and, from time to time, a certain timidity on the part of politicians, who pass difficult and explosive political issues on to the voting public. Second, California's political parties, in comparison with states to the east, are weak in structure and in capacity to control and discipline their members. The history of California politics has witnessed many unpredictable elections and many political mavericks, traceable in part to this weakness of parties. Third, and derivative in large part from the first two, many political battles are fought in the public media rather than negotiated in party caucuses and meetings. The advent of the television age has augmented this tendency, and as a result, California politics are conspicuous for public free-for-alls. The public airing of political conflict during the debate over affirmative action in the U.C. Regents in the summer of 1995 fit this political style.

THE AFFIRMATIVE ACTION DEBATE OF 1995

As of early 1995, and as a result of the contextual factors just reviewed, the political climate in California was ripe for an assault on affirmative action. It began in July in the context of the brief campaign on the part of Governor Wilson for the Republican nomination for the United States presidency. This campaign included conservative statements on immigration, welfare, and affirmative action.

Regent Connerly's introduction of the "rollback" motion on July 5—for consideration at the July 20 Board of Regents' meeting—was clearly an instance of "outside" national and state politics coming into the university. Though Connerly had been pressing the issue for some time within the regents, and though denials of intervention by the governor were issued, the governor's presence was clear. Up to this point, there was no significant evidence of initiatives within the university to change the policies and procedures of affirmative action.

Connerly's principal justification for his initiative was that the university, by pursuing its policies, was breaking the law (as manifested in the Bakke decision) in its admissions policies. He claimed it was actively discriminating in favor of African Americans, Latinos, and Native Americans by using race as a criterion for admission (automatically admitting students in those categories on the Davis and Irvine campuses, and giving them special consideration on the Berkeley and Los Angeles campuses). Asian and white students, correspondingly, were being "harmed" because higher standards were being demanded of them. He maintained that the university's standards had been lowered; that the public opinion of California citizens, students, and alumni supported the renunciation of race as an admissions category; that the practices did not promote "racial harmony and integration" but aggravated conflict through practices of racial segregation on the campuses; and that "some of our administrators" were raising the false specter of student protests in opposing his initiative. In the end, Connerly applauded the principle of diversity and argued that his initiative did not mean that the "University is . . . turning its back on affirmative action." He appealed, furthermore, to the principle of equality of opportunity by reminding his audiences that "We need to make clear that there is a difference . . . between providing people with equal opportunity and providing preferences."

Other parties joined the debate in early July. On the date of Connerly's July 5 news release, the university released a statement by the General Counsel, stating that the Bakke decision permitted colleges and universities to take race and ethnicity into account so long as it is only one factor and so long as "no places are set aside on this basis" (news release, July 5, 1995). The release also promised that "[changes] will be made at UC Berkeley, UCLA, UC Davis, and UC Irvine to assure that the potential qualifications and experiences of all applicants are reviewed competitively" (ibid.).

Extended releases by the Office of the President on July 10 also struck a defensive tone. An individual statement by U.C. President Jack Peltason, a joint statement by vice presidents and chancellors, and a resolution by the Executive Committee of the systemwide Academic Senate all praised affirmative action for furthering diversity and the American egalitarian tradition. Peltason argued that the July initiative was premature, that the decision should wait until the state election initiative of November 1996, and that, in the meantime, extended review by administrators and faculty should begin. At the same time, he promised investigation and action on the four campuses in question, and he promised to modify faculty and employee recruiting away from reliance on minority status. The resolution passed by the faculty leadership argued that affirmative action had made the university "a better institution" and called for it to "continue to act affirmatively to increase the participation of individuals from underrepresented groups, evaluating and modifying these programs in order to strengthen them." The resolution did not, however, take an explicit stand on the use of racial and other group membership as criteria for admission, recruitment, and contracting.

The wording of the resolution adopted by the Board of Regents on July 20 was strong and decisive in several respects, but equivocal in others. On the one hand, it prohibited the university from using "race, religion, sex, color, ethnicity, or national origin as criteria for admission to the University or its programs," either in regular or "exceptional" admission. It also called for admission of between 50 and 75 percent of any entering class "on the basis of academic achievement" (the previous policies specified 40 and 60 percent, respectively). On the other hand, it gave until 1997 to put these policies in place and called upon the administration to consult with faculty with respect to "supplemental criteria," such as giving special consideration to eligible individuals who have shown "character and determination" despite "having suffered disadvantage economically and in terms of their social environment." Furthermore, it ruled out any policies that might conflict with eligibility for receiving funds from any federal or state agency, and it did not mention faculty or employee recruitment at all. A final provision contained a statement of principle in favor of diversity but against preferential treatment:

> Because individual members of all of California's diverse races have the intelligence and capacity to succeed at the University of California, this policy will achieve a UC population that reflects this state's diversity through the preparation and empowerment of all in this state to succeed rather than through a system of arbitrary preferences.

(May I digress and point out the general sociological significance of this action? It signaled a shift in the definition of social justice and equality of opportunity—and conflict about these issues—*away* from race and ethnicity and *toward* social and economic class, as the reference to "economic disadvantage" suggests. If the regents' actions were to be carried out, this would mark a dramatic shift in the political, legal, and public definition of social inequality and social divisions. We cannot know the precise consequences of such a shift. On the one hand, it could be argued that it would be healthy, because racial and ethnic divisions have such a primordial, enduring, and bitter quality about them and because class and class conflict are more manageable as permanent divisions in American society. On the other hand, at this moment in history class divisions may have an unappreciated volatility in this country, because of the trends toward income stagnation of a more regressive income distribution. In all events, however, it is difficult to overestimate the profundity of such a shift.)

Several days after the resolution passed, Peltason issued a statement on it. He, too, reaffirmed the principle of diversity, saying that "it is important to make clear . . . that [the resolutions] have to do with means not with goals." He predicted few changes in contracting and employment programs, because these are constrained by federal and state laws. Noting the January 1997 deadline for action on admissions, he promised to consult with chancellors and faculty on how best to implement admissions policies, "the area in which we expect most change." In the meantime, he promised to set up a multiconstituency task force on improving the preparation of underrepresented minorities and other students for college. He also promised to press forward on the changes in admissions and appointments promised in his July 10 press release. By late October, four intra-university task forces—on contracting, academic and staff employment, undergraduate admissions criteria, and graduate and professional school admissions—had been formed, all with instructions to come back with recommendations for implementing the regents' resolution.

The peace and calm achieved by these actions, however, was only apparent. Virtually every constituency in the university remained in a state of ambivalence and conflict about the summer actions, and, as a result, very little appears to have been resolved by them. To illustrate:

- Regents. Some members of the minority of the regents who opposed the resolutions made an effort, at the January meeting of the Board of Regents, to reverse the July resolutions. Their efforts failed as the regents voted to table the motion. The effort to reverse appears to have had little short-run hope, particularly in light of the fact that the voters of the state passed an anti-affirmative action initiative, the California Civil Rights Initiative, similar in wording to the regents' resolutions, in the election of November 1996. Should that initiative be declared unconstitutional, should California state politics take a turn to the left in the future, and should that reflect itself in an altered composition of the Board of Regents—a process many years in the making—then a reversal or some other modification of the resolutions of July 1995 might appear on the horizon.

In February 1996, a dramatic confrontation between regents and the university president revealed the political salience and volatility of the affirmative action issue. In an administrative act, the new president, Richard Atkinson, delayed the implementation of the regents' resolution on undergraduate admissions from 1997 until 1998. This action prompted a summons to the president to appear in Sacramento for a dressing down by Governor Wilson, and it led Connerly and some other regents to call a special meeting of the Board of Regents to "review the performance" of Atkinson. (The last time such a meeting was held was 1967, when Clark Kerr was fired as president of the university.) The meeting was canceled only after a public, written apology by Atkinson. In the wake of that episode, several dozen Democratic assemblymen and senators signed a document accusing Regent Connerly of abusing his office and using the incident to stir up support for the California Civil Rights Initiative.

- Students. The editorial board of the Berkeley campus student newspaper, *The Daily Californian,* cast a divided vote in favor of the regents' actions. To those who have followed the editorial preferences of that publication over the years, this was something like hell freezing over. An equally dramatic thunderbolt occurred in November 1996, when the student newspaper came out in favor of the California Civil Rights Initiative. On the other hand, a modest amount of student activity against the resolutions continued to bubble up on the various campuses. In late February 1996, the student newspaper filed a suit against the Board of Regents which charged that the July vote was decided in secret and in advance and should be voided because it violated Board of Regents' policies calling for public meetings.
- Faculty. Most of the faculty "establishment" appeared to wish to accept the passage of the summer resolution and work out sen-

sible, informed means of implementing it while working by other means to seek diversity. Another wing of the faculty continued to protest, submitting petitions and seeking faculty expressions of opposition on grounds that the regents violated the principles of university governance by passing the resolutions. The faculty as a whole, however, appeared to be of mixed mind. A poll of faculty conducted by the Roper organization in December 1995 yielded the finding that about half the faculty favored the renunciation of race and other group criteria (that is, pro-resolution), and half favored their explicit incorporation.

- Administration. While campus administrations have no official choice other than to implement the resolutions, matters are not as simple as that. A difficult atmosphere persists because of the possibility of unofficial subversion of the official nonrecognition of group criteria in the actual work of admitting and recruiting. Regent Connerly issued statements about undermining the regents' resolutions, and so long as even a small group of regents continue to be in a policing frame of mind, a tension and potential conflict between regents and administration remains alive.
- The state political context. California politics remained embroiled in affirmative action and other controversies related to the California Civil Rights Initiative, introduced in 1995 as an amendment to the California state constitution. That initiative proposed to end all preferences related to gender, race, national origin, and other related categories. The movement to gain signatures for this met with early difficulties, and late in 1995 Republican supporters of the measure persuaded Regent Connerly to head the campaign to put the measure on the ballot. The movement gained momentum after that time, and by the end of February enough signatures had been secured to place the measure on the November 1996 ballot. After a long campaign, which heated as election day appeared, the measure passed by 10 percentage points, thereby generalizing the regents' action to employment, educational, and contracting activities to the state of California as a whole.

The success of the civil rights initiative is hardly surprising, given the confluence of social and political forces I have outlined. The measure was bottled up in the courts—with one judge having ordered the state to stay its effects, a panel of three appeals judges declaring it constitutional, and an appellate court ordering its im-

> plementation—and the United States Supreme Court finally declared it constitutional. The measure's passage had one interesting consequence for the University of California. Every constituency in the university, save the Board of Regents, had gone on record as favoring affirmative action for the university, that is, opposing the initiative. At the same time, its passage at the state level took the university out of the limelight; affirmative action went to the state and even national political level (with President Clinton and the Department of Justice weighing in against the referendum). If the measure had been defeated, the regents would have been under enormous pressure to rescind their vote, and the university would have been rocked with internal conflict once again. One can only surmise, therefore, that the university regarded the passage of the civil rights referendum with a distinct ambivalence.

To conclude, the prospect for affirmative action's future may be put as follows. In California, as in the nation as a whole, the advances achieved for both minorities and women have been enormous, and in that respect the affirmative action project may be considered to have been an *institutional* success. However, it can be claimed only with greater difficulty that it has been a *political* success. Neither its adoption nor its implementation nor the efforts to reverse it seem to have had—or will have—a calming effect on the racial, ethnic, and gender politics of the country. This suggests that the country's main agenda is not really affirmative action; rather, the most important underlying agenda concerns the racial, ethnic, and gender struggles *themselves.* As a result, any institutional contrivance affecting the terms of this struggle—whether affirmative action or something else—will be bound to generate the ambiguity, ambivalence, conflict, and instability that we have witnessed over the past three decades of affirmative action.

9

The Rational and the Ambivalent in the Social Sciences

The idea of the rational holds a noble place in the history of philosophy. In that tradition it is closely linked to reason, a mental faculty through which humans are able to think logically, reflect on right reasons for conduct, and discover the rational life, which in its turn is connected with a virtuous life. The idea of reason reached both a turning point and an apex in the Age of Reason in eighteenth-century France, when it came to dwell on the capacity of humankind to devise an orderly, rational *society*, free from the encumbrances of religion, aristocracy, and tradition (Taine, 1881; Tocqueville, 1856).

"Rational" has always been a positive word. Alan Sica (1988) observes that "'rationality' has attained totemic status, having served more often during the past two centuries as slogan or symbol than as convincing analytic concept. It connotes secularization and the eclipse of mythological explanation" (p. 4). An exception to this glorious history is the

Delivered as the Presidential Address at the meetings of the American Sociological Association, Toronto, August 1997, and published in the *American Sociological Review* 63, no. 1 (February 1998): 1–16. My thanks to those who have helped me develop and hone my ideas on rationality and ambivalence over the years are so many that I cannot begin to report them. I would like to thank Christine Williams of the University of Texas, Austin, for giving me encouragement to pursue the idea on ambivalence as the core of the ASA Presidential Address. Mary Waters of Harvard echoed Chris's advice. I also received encouragement, advice, and a certain amount of helpful flack from Maureen Hallinan, my predecessor as president of ASA. During the academic year 1996–97, I gave three presentations of my ideas to groups of Fellows at the Center for Advanced Study in the Behavioral Sciences. I will not single out particular individuals to thank, out of dread of omitting someone, but I will say that they know who they are, and they should know that the suggestions they gave me make the quality of the Presidential Address much higher than it would have been had I worked alone.

idea of psychological "rationalization," or creating phony good reasons for ignoble motives.

The rational survives in the contemporary social sciences but, except in psychology, the link with reflective capacity has largely dissolved, and the idea of a virtuous life derived from reason seems to have disappeared altogether. The major contemporary meanings are as follows:

- Rational choice. This derives from the British utilitarian tradition, via neoclassical economics. It is the theoretical core of economics, though it has been greatly qualified and elaborated through parametric modifications and other developments such as game theory. It has also spread, with varying success and opposition, into political science, sociology, anthropology, law, organization theory, management science, and other fields. The central tenet of rational choice is that individual and corporate actors take into account their preferences and relevant external conditions and behave so as to maximize utility or advantage.
- Rationality as an organizational or institutional strategy. This is conveyed in Weber's concept of "rational bourgeois capitalism," which connotes the *systematic* organization of ideas, people, and resources in the interests of instrumental efficiency and effectiveness (Weber, 1968). This idea is also found—though with less positive connotations—in Habermas's notion of instrumental rationality (Habermas, 1975) embodied in the administrative-legal bureaucracy of the contemporary state. Weber's idea sometimes implies *differentiation* and *elaboration*, so that administrative structures, legal systems, musical styles, and religious traditions—as well as the economy—may become rationalized. In this connotation "rationality" and "rationalization" are almost synonyms; both refer to systematic social-structural and cultural development. Some postmodern and globalist writers regard this meaning of the rational as a distinctive feature of modern society, which is giving way to postmodern forces (Albrow, 1996, pp. 34–37).
- Scientific rationality. This refers to the assumptions, values, norms, and procedures of scientific inquiry. It is the conduct of research and the production of theory and empirical findings in line with scientific logic and methods. Those committed to sociology and other social sciences *as sciences* accept some version of scientific rationality, though its tenets have come under attack within our own fields.

The first two types of rationality have become increasingly dominant in the second half of the twentieth century. I mentioned the march of rational-choice analysis. Consider several other examples:

- In psychology, the overwhelming success of the cognitive revolution, with offshoots of cognitive science and information science
- In organizational theory, the emergence of theories of rational management of organizations, including management science in schools of business administration
- In psychoanalysis, the shift from drive and instinct psychology toward ego psychology and object-relations theory, and the downplaying of the unconscious and the irrational
- In the study of social movements, less emphasis on affect and ideology and more emphasis on the instrumental/rational perspectives of resource mobilization and social-movement organizations
- In the revolution made possible by the computer, a rationalizing device par excellence
- In the spectacular expansion of global capitalism, accompanied by extended rationalization of world resources, organizations, and markets

Correspondingly, nonrationalist and irrationalist perspectives in the social sciences have diminished. Nietzsche finds few adherents; Freud must be considered marginal (even in anthropology, where the Freudian-inspired "culture and personality" approach has waned); Le Bon has been passé for decades; Mosca and Michels are remembered not for their "irrationalism" but for their theories on the distribution of power; Pareto is famous not for his residues and derivations (the ideological and emotional dimensions of life) but for his optimum, a rational principle of welfare economics and social policy; and Simmel's sociology of emotion and eroticism remains unappreciated. We see current stirrings in the psychology and sociology of emotion, but these are flickers in relation to the larger trends.

The main countertrend in the contemporary world is a certain *anti*-rationality directed at all three forms of rationality identified. I have in mind the cumulative impact of strands of thought such as neo-Marxism, critical theory, varieties of phenomenology, some parts of feminist and gender studies, cultural studies, and postmodernism. Some neo-Marxist and critical thought has rejected much social science as an apology for capitalism and the state; the phenomenological impulse has sought to undermine the positivistic and generalizing aspects of social science investigation; some feminist writers have attacked rational-choice theory and other lines of social science analysis as male-dominated and male-biased; and postmodernism combines an alienation from "rational" aspects of modern society with an antiscience impulse, an identification with the oppressed, and a fascination with "difference" and the uniqueness of "the other," which rejects general principles and grand narratives. At the same time, representatives of these approaches themselves appeal to reason and logic and occasionally marshal empirical data in pressing their perspectives.

Thus we witness a polarization between various kinds of rationality and a reactive antirationality that includes a curious right-left opposition, with serious analysis of the nonrational and irrational abandoned somehow by the wayside. I will suggest a way of resuscitating the role of nonrational forces in individual, group, and institutional behavior, employing the idea of ambivalence. I hope that, along the way, we will liberate ourselves to a degree from the worldview implied in the enduring distinctions among the rational, the nonrational, and the irrational.

Some Notes on Rational Choice

I now turn to rational choice as theoretical assumption and as psychological construct. Some of my observations will be critical, but I intend neither to applaud nor to bash the rational-choice approach yet again. Rather, I will be looking toward developing a supplement to it.

The ingredients of rational choice, as refined in neoclassical economics, are the following:

- Individual actors, uninfluenced by others and "unconstrained by norms" (Coleman, 1990, p. 503), are motivated to maximize their well-being (utility).
- Actors possess complete information about their tastes, their resources, and the availability, quality, and price of products, as well as job opportunities and other market conditions.
- Actors calculate and behave rationally. They do not make errors, they do not forget what they know, and they do not act on impulse or otherwise irrationally.

- Tastes are "given," that is, stable and not to be explained; they are the starting point, not the object of analysis.
- The interaction between two actors—buyer and seller—produces an equilibrium point at which exchange occurs. This point marks a convergence of supply and demand, utility and cost.

In the recent history of rational-choice analysis, economists and others have relaxed every one of these assumptions and now analyze situations of incomplete information, risk and uncertainty, unstable preferences, power differentials among actors, "satisficing" rather than maximizing, and so on. Furthermore, rational-choice analysts have moved beyond market interchanges and analyzed contest situations (game theory), voting and other political behavior (Downs, 1957), participation in social movements (Olson, 1965; Oberschall, 1973), racial discrimination, decisions to marry and have children (Becker, 1976), and addiction (Becker and Murphy, 1988). Schelling (1996) has even devised a model of coping rationally with lapses in rationality. These developments have meant—according to one's point of view—(1) a relaxation of first assumptions to extend and refine the rational-choice model, or (2) an imperialism on the part of economists and other rational-choice theorists. Above all, these developments involve a conceptual stretching of the idea of rationality and threaten to yield a theoretical degeneration: *everything* becomes rational if you push hard enough, and "rational" becomes more or less synonymous with "adaptive."

Despite these extensions, rational-choice analysis retains a theoretical continuity. Even if conditions of risk, uncertainty, lack of knowledge, third parties, and so forth are incorporated, the rational-choice analyst's strategy is to convert them into parameters and ask, *given them,* how individuals will behave rationally. This query is answered by building a model of rational behavior under new hypothesized conditions, frequently expressed mathematically, and sometimes related to hypothetical or real empirical data. This is the kernel of continuity, the enduring "culture" of rational-choice analysis (Smelser, 1995).

I note five additional points about rational-choice analysis:

1. "Rational" is a relative, not an absolute, notion. It varies according to framing perspective and level of analysis. The same item of behavior (smoking) may be rational in the short run (it gratifies) but not in the long run (it increases the probability of death). To sell in a panicking financial market may be rational from the individual's standpoint, but its aggregated effects on markets may lead

to irrational outcomes. To dump toxic waste in the river may be rational for the firm (as cost minimization) but not rational from the standpoint of preserving the environment.

2. Rational choice is relative in a second sense. For rational-choice behavior to be possible, a number of conditions must be present. Mutual trust and predictability between exchanging partners is a necessary social-psychological condition. At the social level, we might mention a stable institutional setting and rules for exchange (a market), a stable medium (money or its equivalent), and a legal order that prevents theft, fraud, and coercion and enforces rules of property and contract. These conditions are neither rational nor nonrational in themselves. They are best regarded as contextual conditions under which behavior guided by rational choice can occur.

3. Ironically, as rational-choice analysts execute their work, both formulaic words lose their meaning. Explained behavior is not rational in the classical sense of the term (that is, it need not involve reflection and reasoning). It need not even be consciously calculated. This is so because behavior conceived as the product of rational choice is, in the end, determined by a given set of preferences and by a number of objective factors such as price and quantity. Furthermore, even though alternatives are available to the actor, the explanatory power of preferences and conditions is (or should be) complete, and there is no choice. Thus, although the idea of rational choice resonates rhetorically with valued philosophical traditions of rationality and valued cultural traditions of individualism, neither reason nor choice is necessary for what passes as rational-choice analysis. Regarded correctly, rational choice is an intervening psychological constant typically invoked when assigning meaning to and explaining links between market and other conditions and rates of behavior.

4. Rational-choice analysis leaves little place for affect and emotional attachments (Lawler, 1997; England, 1989; England and Kilbourne, 1990). In one sense this omission is odd, because the chief principle of utilitarianism is seeking pleasure and avoiding pain, both affective states. In fact, however, anxiety, rage, love (especially blind love), neurotic conflict, and psychosis do not figure in rational-choice analysis, despite some recent general efforts to relate rational action and affect (Hirschleifer, 1993; Collins, 1993; Jasso, 1993) and some research on feelings of regret that

occur after decisions are made in uncertain situations (Loomes and Sudgen, 1982; Lindenberg, 1994).

5. With respect to actors' motivation, rational-choice theory relies almost exclusively on *univalent* orientations. The motivation is maximizing utility or acting on the basis of a hierarchy of preferences. True, negative factors are involved, as in the conception of disutility and costs, but these are conceptualized separately from preferences and weighed alongside them. Equilibrium states are reached when the positive and negative balance out in relation to one another. Rational-choice theory does not deal with the possibility that we actively love and hate the same object simultaneously, or the possibility that these affective orientations cannot come into an equilibrium with one another so as to permit optimizing choice and action based on that choice.

These issues of affect and valence open the door to another psychological foundation of behavior—human ambivalence.

The Nature of Ambivalence

I have treated rational choice as a psychological postulate, not as a general psychological principle. As a postulate it has two advantages: (1) as a simplification, it permits the creation of formal models capable of mathematical expression and capable of generating predictions about behavior; and (2) as an ingredient of explanations, it has value when applied to those socially structured situations (markets, competitive games, political contests, arranged marriage systems) in which interests are given a place and in which gain and advantage are rewarded.

Now I turn to another psychological postulate that also has wide applicability. This is the postulate of ambivalence, the combination of attraction and repulsion, of love and hate. Ambivalence is inclusive in that it can focus on people, objects, and symbols. Experience alone demonstrates the importance of this phenomenon. We may, for example, divide the world into people we love and people we hate, but on examination that distinction fades. If we think only of those we love or like most, we almost always discover this feeling accompanied by something we do not like, and even the most hateful people turn out to hold out some morbid attraction or redeeming feature.

In picking the topic of ambivalence, I am in good company. I point out Robert Merton's superb essay on sociological ambivalence (1976 [1963]), in which he masterfully crafted an account of how socially structured roles call on incumbents simultaneously to embrace and reject the same object or norm. My approach to ambivalence takes intrapsychic processes, not roles, as the starting point, but Merton's and my analyses greet one another in a friendly fashion even though they come from different directions. In another sense I am in unfriendly territory. In reviewing Merton's "Sociological Ambivalence," Donald Levine pointed to American culture's tendency "to eschew dualistic or ambivalent constructs in favor of univalent statements." American sociologists, he added, are part of this culture; they like to search for "dominant patterns, univalent metrics, monochromatic path diagrams, and unilineal logical derivations" (Levine, 1977, p. 1278; see also Levine, 1985, chap. 2).

Two other initial remarks are in order. I hope they will deflect misunderstanding and misinterpretation:

- The postulate of ambivalence is meant to differ from that of rational choice in at least two senses: (1) Preferences are generally formulated in positive terms—as what people want. Preferences can be expressed negatively—as what people do *not* prefer—but they tend to be univalent, either positive or negative. The nature of ambivalence is to hold *opposing affective orientations* toward the same person, object, or symbol. (2) With some exceptions, preferences are regarded as relatively stable; ambivalence tends to be unstable, expressing itself in different and sometimes contradictory ways as actors cope with it.
- Although the postulate of ambivalence differs from that of rational choice, it is not a theoretical competitor, certainly not opposed to the postulate of rational choice. Both are generated for purposes of understanding, analysis, and explanation. My argument is that the notion of ambivalence leads us to understand and explain a range of behaviors and situations beyond the scope of rational-choice explanations, however far the latter may be stretched.

The term "ambivalence" was first used by the psychologist Bleuler in 1910, though the idea was not novel. He gave the term a number of meanings, one of which was simultaneously opposing affects—love and hate—toward the same object. This meaning caught the attention of Sigmund Freud, the great theorist of ambivalence. It pervaded all his works. Many elements of his psychoanalytic theories have been discredited (see chap. 10, p. 201), but the principle of ambivalence remains a cornerstone of psychoanalytic thought.

Freud applied the idea of ambivalence widely. In his *The Interpretation of Dreams,* he noted that often one dreams of a dead person, who subsequently comes alive, and then is again dead in the same dream. Freud argued that this sequence "help[s] the dreamer to repudiate his very intense and often contradictory emotional attitudes" (Freud 1953 [1900], p. 41). Ambivalence may become eroticized, as in sado-masochism (Freud, 1953 [1905], p. 159). It is at the core of the oedipal relations between child and parent. Of Little Hans, for example, Freud remarked: "We know that . . . Hans's anxiety had two constituents: there was fear *of* his father and fear *for* his father. The former was derived from his hostility towards his father [a competitor for his mother], and the latter from the conflict between his affection . . . and his hostility" (Freud, 1955b [1909], p. 45). Ambivalence is at the core of obsessional and compulsive disorders, in which the person continuously does and undoes the two sides of "a conflict between two opposing impulses of approximately equal strength" (Freud, 1955a [1909], p. 192). Indeed, the development of *conscience* itself is rooted in ambivalence—"one of the opposing feelings involved shall be unconscious and kept under repression by the compulsive domination of the other one" (Freud, 1955 [1912–13], p. 68).

Combing through Freud's writings, one discovers the following characteristics of ambivalence:

- Its origins lie in the intimate relations between a child and his or her parents and siblings. These relations, I might add, are those *from which the child cannot escape.* This will turn out to be a critical point.
- The stronger the positive side of ambivalence, the stronger the negative. Freud said, "[the] king or chief arouses envy on account of his privileges: everyone, perhaps, would like to be a king. Dead men, new-born babies and women menstruating or in labour stimulate desires by their special helplessness; a man who has just reached maturity stimulates them by the promise of new enjoyment. For that reason all of these persons and all of these states are taboo, since temptation must be resisted" (ibid., p. 33). Elsewhere he wrote of the "law of ambivalence of feeling, which to this day governs our emotional relations with *those whom we love most*" (Freud, 1957 [1915], p. 293). (Incidentally, this premise con-

trasts with Homans's proposition that "the more frequently persons interact with one another, the stronger their sentiments of friendship for one another are apt to be" [Homans, 1950, p. 133]. Homans's proposition is only half true; the "law of ambivalence" brings negative sentiments back in.)

- Ambivalence becomes established in the psyche. It cannot be resolved once and for all. Speaking of the child's desire to masturbate and its prohibition (both by parents and by the child's conscience), Freud noted that "the prohibition does not succeed in *abolishing* the instinct. Its only result is to *repress* the instinct (the desire to touch) and banish it into the unconscious. Both the prohibition and the instinct persist . . . the psychological constellation becomes fixed . . . as the subject's *ambivalent* attitude toward a single object" (Freud, 1955b [1909], p. 29).
- Although fixed mainly in childhood, ambivalences generalize readily to other real and symbolic situations. The most dramatic evidence is the patient's positive and negative transferences toward the psychoanalyst, evoked in the absence of any stimulus that might excite strong reactions. Ambivalence finds expression in religious systems. Says Freud, "The contradictions in the original nature of God are . . . a reflection of the ambivalence which governs the relation of the individual to his personal father. If the benevolent and righteous God is a substitute for his father, it is not to be wondered at that his hostile attitude to his father, too, which is one of hating and fearing him and of making complaints against him, should have come to expression in the creation of Satan" (Freud, 1961 [1922], p. 85). Erikson applied the idea of splitting repeatedly in explaining the psychology and theology of Martin Luther's Protestantism (Erikson, 1962 [1958]).

The psychology of ambivalence has one final ingredient. Because ambivalence is such a *powerful, persistent, unresolvable, volatile, generalizable,* and *anxiety-provoking* feature of the human condition, people defend against experiencing it in many ways. To select only those mechanisms of defense mentioned by Freud:

- Reversing one side of the ambivalent feeling, usually by turning the negative side into a positive ("love thine enemy")
- Repressing one side and rigidifying the other side into a reaction-formation, for example, in the idealization of a parent

- Displacing, or substituting a remote object or symbol for the real object
- Projecting; for example, resolving one's own ambivalent feelings toward a loved one who has died by blaming evil spirits
- Splitting, or transferring the positive side of the ambivalence into an unqualified love of one person or object, and the negative side into an unqualified hatred of another (see also Klein, 1986 [1935], pp. 141–43).

The sequence beginning with ambivalence, proceeding to defense, and then moving to behavior does not fit comfortably with the logic of rational choice. Many of the dynamics of ambivalence occur beyond the range of consciousness and calculation. The psychological and behavioral reactions involved are likely to be immediate responses to emotions—principally anxiety—that escape reflection altogether. We might say that this kind of behavior is *adaptive*—though with varying success—and *reasonable* in that it is understandable within the logic of ambivalence. (We might even suggest that ambivalence forces us to reason more than preferences do, because conflict may be a stronger motive for thinking than desire is.) It is also possible to develop models of behavior based on the dynamics of ambivalence. But to subsume it under the logic of "rational" or "choice" or "rational choice" is not helpful analytically. To do so involves serious conceptual stretching and adds little except a false sense of precision and the positive hortatory effect that invoking the idea of "rational" typically produces.

Applications of the Logic of Ambivalence

DEATH AND SEPARATION

We begin with an obvious example, the loss—especially unanticipated loss—of loved ones, which evokes the strongest ambivalent reactions. The classic study of bereavement is that of Lindemann (1944), a psychiatrist who interviewed the survivors of the Cocoanut Grove nightclub fire and panic in Boston during World War II. He found among survivors several affective and behavioral reactions, sometimes occurring in rough sequence—numbing and denial, blaming the lost victim, blaming oneself and idealizing the victim, blaming others, and then a gradual "working through" the grief by resuming routines and building old and new social relationships. All these reactions were accompanied by strong affects. Even those not suffering personal loss were shocked, and the tragedy was followed by episodes of scapegoating—the bellboy who presumably started the fire, the nightclub management, city inspectors, and others (Veltford and Lee, 1943).

This mourning syndrome has been documented in other settings, including the battlefield death of comrades in World War II and the Vietnam War (Grinker and Spiegel, 1945; Lifton, 1973), and the loss of loved ones, friends, and neighbors in natural disasters (Erikson, 1976). It is also seen in the natural death of parents, spouses, children, and other loved ones, though in the case of long-expected deaths, anticipatory grief and its associated reactions mitigate the bereavement process.

Shock, anger, grieving, and recovery from grief are also witnessed in the wake of deaths of political leaders and cultural idols. These figures are often endowed with charisma, especially in times of crisis, but beneath this idealization lies a deep ambivalence, which probably accounts for "the fragility of charisma" (Aberbach, 1996). Research has documented the ambivalent reactions to the death of Franklin Roosevelt (de Grazia, 1948) and the assassinations of Abraham Lincoln, John Kennedy, Robert Kennedy, and Martin Luther King Jr. (Turner, 1982; Sheatsley and Feldman, 1965; Bonjean, Hill, and Martin, 1965). The attempted assassination of Ronald Reagan in 1981 excited a similar range of reactions, including expressions by some that they wished the assassination had succeeded (Mortensen, 1987). The idealization of Richard Nixon—perhaps the target of more ambivalence than any other president in the twentieth century—in the days after his death is also notable. Leadership succession—the loss of one leader and the arrival of a new one—often produces instability and turbulence (Weber, 1968; Gouldner, 1954). If more evidence is needed, we need only point to the charged and often idealized memories of figures such as Marilyn Monroe and Elvis Presley—sometimes including the belief that they are still alive (see Fowles, 1992). We are bound affectively to our leaders and secular gods and goddesses, both because of what they are and because we bring powerful childhood transferences—both positive and negative—to them. So when they are lost, we react with feelings of loss and bereavement.

These observations do not stop with death. Divorce and separation, often voluntary and even wished, produce reactions of ambivalence and working-through as complex and deep as death reactions. Typically, one never completely forgets or recovers from a past marriage or similar love attachment (Goode, 1965). The departure of children from home, though sometimes welcomed by parents and children alike, is also shrouded with continuing ambivalence.

Milder though similar reactions occur with other separations, such as retirement and moving from a community. In this connection, it might be observed that at the end of the twentieth century the world is experiencing an acceleration of these kinds of separations—through continuing high rates of divorce, estrangement, and breaking up; through sustained rates of geographical mobility and increased rates of international migration; through the tenuousness of neighborhood and community resulting from that mobility; through the "temp revolution," which brings workers to and from the workplace with greater frequency; and through the increased mobility *within* the workplace associated with the phenomenon of flexible specialization (Piore and Sabel, 1984). Ours might be called the age of temporariness, or the age of intermittency, or perhaps the age of sequential bonding. The human being has enormous capacity to adapt to these circumstances, but we must also acknowledge that those involved are not immune from recurrent ambivalent reactions that accompany the comings and goings.

A single principle underlies all these examples: when we bond with people deeply or even superficially, we become to some degree less free emotionally as a result. Those relations invariably become fused with some ambivalence, and when we lose or separate from others, dealing with that ambivalence becomes a necessity, even though the coping process is often mild and passing.

This principle invites generalization, and I now turn to some less self-evident applications of it.

DEPENDENCE, LIMITATIONS ON CHOICE, AND AMBIVALENCE

Let us recall the kinds of situations to which models of rational choice appear to apply best: situations in which both calculation and choice are institutionalized and rewarded, and in which standards for calculation are known. Another ingredient of these situations is that the actor may enter into and withdraw from exchange relations. We call this ingredient choice, which is a type of *freedom*. Markets for consumer goods and free labor are its prototypes. In Hirschman's words, "some customers stop buying the firm's products or some members leave the organization" (Hirschman, 1970, p. 4). This is Hirschman's *exit option*, of which we will hear more later. Of course, this freedom is relative. Deciding *not* to buy a product may involve a psychological cost. Furthermore, one usually has to work *somewhere*, and it is often both costly and risky for an employee to quit and search for another job. I should note, however, that rational choice theorists (especially game theorists) have also analyzed situations in which choice is limited—for example, relations to authority, blackmail situations, and international relations.

With this reference to freedom in mind, I now call attention to a contrasting range of situations in which actors are *dependent* on one another. The form of dependence may vary. A subordinated person in a power relationship is politically dependent, a person who is committed to a religious or social movement cause is ideologically dependent, and a person in love is emotionally dependent. The common element, however, is that freedom to leave—choice—is restricted because it is costly politically, ideologically, or emotionally. Dependence entails a certain entrapment. Although the relation between dependence and solidarity—the positive side of ambivalence—is well articulated (Hechter, 1987), the negative side of dependence has not been given anything like equal time. My general proposition is that these situations breed ambivalence, and, correspondingly, models of behavior based on the postulate of ambivalence are best applicable to them. I illustrate this proposition in several situations:

1. Let us return to Freud. His prototypical setting for the development of ambivalence is the young child, dependent on his or her parents in many ways—dependent on them for survival as an organism, dependent on them as authorities, and emotionally dependent on them because he or she loves them. Childhood entails a type of enslavement, from which one cannot escape. The child's objects of ambivalence are those by whom he or she is entrapped—parents and siblings (and perhaps increasingly these days, day care personnel). Adolescence is the protracted experience of partial escape, a period in which ambivalence toward parents and siblings is repeatedly "acted out," sometimes in extreme ways. Once the escape into independence has been more or less accomplished, we often observe a return to the positive side of the ambivalence, because the entrapment is diminished. This process is captured in Mark Twain's remark that when he was sixteen years old he thought his father the stupidest man in the world,

but by the time he reached twenty-one he was surprised at how much the old man had learned in five years. The escape is never complete, however. The enslaved child in us never sheds the ambivalence toward parents and siblings, and this ambivalence finds expression in recurrent "transference" to authorities, colleagues, subordinates, loved ones, friends, gods, demons, heroes, and scapegoats.

2. The common adult relationships in which ambivalence is most evident are those between lovers, partners, intimates, and friends—in a word, those on whom we are dependent. One might appropriately term these relations "voluntary emotional dependence," or perhaps the dependence arising from the half-voluntary, half-involuntary actions of falling in love and becoming friends. These relationships often involve other kinds of dependence as well—for example, in marriage, the dependence deriving from the differential power of husband and wife, and in friendships among political and status unequals. Emotional dependence, however, is always a part of the picture.

3. Lawler's experimental and theoretical work on group membership and affect suggests that "positive emotion generated by choice processes strengthens affective ties to groups credited with making choice opportunities available; negative emotion weakens ties to those blamed for constraining choice" (Lawler, 1997; also Lawler, 1992). The general principle is that constraint generates ambivalence, and that, as a special case, the difficulty involved in withdrawing from a group into which one is "locked" increases the ambivalence toward that group and its members.

4. Certain types of organization are seedbeds of ambivalence and its consequences—spite, petty wrangling, struggles for recognition, and vicious politics—even though the political stakes are often not very high. These are Goffman's "total institutions"—mental institutions, military camps, prisons, and private schools (Goffman, 1962), as well as monasteries, convents, psychoanalytic institutes, and academic departments. What these organizations have in common is that their members are "locked in" by personal or institutional commitment or other situational circumstances and can escape only at great cost. In academic departments people are "locked in" by tenure or by the yearning and struggle for tenure, and can escape only at great cost unless a more attractive oppor-

tunity arises. People have to live with one another, but this does not mean that they have to love one another; it implies, rather, that they both love and hate one another.

These organizational settings contrast with situations in which people live temporarily but from which they know they are going to withdraw or escape. I refer to these as "odyssey" situations, which have a known beginning, duration, and end. They include ocean voyages, summer camps, junior years abroad, and the college years generally. I would also include the residential years at my own Center for Advanced Study in the Behavioral Sciences. People, sometimes strangers, are thrown together in physical proximity, but they know this close contact is going to end in one year. They can thus afford to love one another and more or less bury the negative side of the ambivalence that is associated with intimacy. This circumstance, I am certain, goes a long way toward explaining why these odyssey experiences are typically experienced and remembered with such unalloyed sentimentality and nostalgia.

5. Another setting for ambivalence is those groups, organizations, and social movements that demand commitment, adherence, and faithfulness from their believer members. These include churches, ethnic and racial identity groups and movements, labor unions and other social-class movements, and social movements generally. Some of these have salience in contemporary times—namely in the apparent worldwide challenge to the nation-state by identity groups and identity movements. The dependence created in these settings comes through commitment to a belief, cause, or common goal and through membership in a demanding organization. Three observations are in order:

   - These groups and organizations manifest the principle of in-group solidarity and out-group hostility. This principle was enunciated forcefully in the sociology of Georg Simmel (Simmel, 1950, pp. 368–70; Coser, 1956). Almost all groupings regard the world dichotomously—as friends or enemies, believers or nonbelievers, good or evil. We do not understand the full significance of this categorization, but one of its apparent functions is to diminish the internal ambivalence bred by commitment by splitting it between inside and outside. I know of no mechanism that better protects the fragile solidarity of these intense groupings.

- Many social movements—those we classify as protest movements—act *against* political authorities or against social arrangements put in place and legitimized by them. They express the negative side of ambivalence that colors most orientations toward authority. At the same time, many such movements exhibit opposite tendencies within—adoration of leaders and strong demands for conformity and commitment. But, finally, leaders of movements are themselves subject to the vicissitudes of their followers' ambivalence, and they stand in constant danger of experiencing a negative turn.
- Just as the defiant child excites ambivalence in his or her parents—generated by struggles with their *own* inherited ambivalences—so political authorities almost invariably assume an ambivalent attitude toward those who protest against them. Accordingly, authorities are forever tempted to punish, ironically contributing to their own vulnerability. The delicate relationship between protesters and authorities is often a double-dance of ambivalence, a game of last-tag in which each forever tries to avoid illegitimate expression of the negative side of their ambivalence and to push antagonists into it.

6. In consumer markets we see ambivalence toward some kinds of products such as jewelry, fine clothing, furs, and luxury automobiles. This ambivalence finds expression especially among those who cannot afford extravagance or luxuries and sometimes among those who can. Attitudes toward these products contrast with those toward primarily instrumental items, such as hammers, nails, garden hoses, and toothpaste. The reason for the ambivalence and controversy does not reside in any material characteristics of the products. It arises because they are symbols of the *status systems* in the community and society. People's places in these systems are largely involuntary; these are systems from which it is difficult to escape, and symbols of them are bound to draw mixed reactions.
7. Finally, in our search for applications of the idea of ambivalence, we would do well to look in our own sociological backyard. There is almost no facet of our existence as sociologists about which we do not show ambivalence and its derivative, dividing into groups or quasi-groups of advocacy and counteradvocacy. We are ambivalent toward one another; toward the competing notions of our

discipline as a science, as a humanistic study, as a political enterprise, and as an art; toward the different methodologies we employ; toward the academic departments that house us; toward the administrators and funding agencies that sustain and feed us; toward other disciplines; and last but not least, toward our subject matter itself—the community as simultaneously embracing and suffocating, the deviant as simultaneously troublemaker and critical innovator. You name it, we have mixed feelings about it. We do not think much about these ambivalences; we mainly voice and act on them unreflectively. The sobering paradox is that although we as sociologists are perhaps best equipped to understand them, we scarcely think about or study them at all. Yet to understand them would lead us toward explaining our own sectarian and schismatic tendencies, as well as those in academic life in general.

SOCIAL STRUCTURE, SOCIAL PROCESS, AND POLITICAL AMBIVALENCE

To carry the analysis further, I call attention to some social structures and social processes that serve, among other things, as vehicles for the expression, play, and never-to-be-realized resolution of individual and group ambivalence. Let me address one possible misunderstanding at the outset. I have no interest in the origin of these illustrative structures and processes, and, more important, I disown any claim that they are conscious or unconscious *inventions* to deal with ambivalence. That special function, however, may have something to do with the passion they excite and their tendency to endure.

Many if not all societies institutionalize rituals that reverse, temporarily, ambivalently regarded situations—for example, giving high school students the opportunity to run the city government for a day and the widespread practice of ritual rebellion (Gluckman, 1963). In our own and other societies, athletic contests, organized around institutional memberships (high schools, colleges, and universities) and communities or territories (professional sports), offer endless opportunities for the splitting of ambivalence—solidarity with the one side, hostility toward the other. Because athletic contests are usually carefully controlled and defined as "only games" that do not matter in the serious business of life, the splitting is relatively benign, except when it spills over into barroom brawls, mob violence and looting, and marauding soccer crowds. One could also mention in the same light local and regional pride (which invariably includes some hostility toward *other* localities and regions) as well as uneasily institutionalized urban gangs, known both for their fierce solidarity and their violent potential.

Familiar political institutions and processes also offer opportunities for converting ambivalent feelings into univalent preferences and, in the meantime, delegitimizing in a certain way one side or the other of ambivalence. Consider the following illustrations:

- The public opinion survey—a special invention of the social sciences—has, in time, evolved into a full-scale political institution. Its essence is this: a representative sample of citizens is asked a question about a political official (approve or disapprove), a political candidate (how one intends to vote), or some issue of public concern (crime, drugs, abortion, affirmative action, race relations). Most research on public opinion focuses on background social factors (age, race, sex, religion, education) or on cognitive processes involved (complexity theory, balance theory, dissonance theory) (Milburn, 1991). From an affective point of view, however, the interesting fact is that most survey questions are phrased *univalently*—approve or disapprove, favor or not favor, and how strongly. Introspection alone, however, informs us that our feelings about public figures and issues are *ambivalent* if not *multivalent.* Consider only the names of Roosevelt, Truman, Eisenhower, Kennedy, Nixon, Ford, Carter, Reagan, Bush, and Clinton. There is not one of them about whom each of us does not have mixed feelings, even though we have preferred or prefer some over others. Likewise, we are ambivalent on many social issues tapped by surveys, even though we may sometimes confidently represent our opinions to ourselves and others as absolute. This ambivalence is seldom tapped by most surveys. Indeed, it is typically shunted aside by offering forced-choice alternatives. Surveys often depict the world as though it is divided into people who are for and against someone or something—a clear distortion of the social-psychological reality of public feelings. This representation is then reified into an imagined "public opinion," reported as reality in the press, read by market analysts and politicians, and acted upon. Following this reasoning, we must regard attitude surveys not as revealed preferences but as a distorted structure of reality that minimizes and—in the process—delegitimizes both ambiguity and ambivalence. This general diagnosis must be qualified in one important way. Some sociological colleagues (Schuman and Presser, 1981; Turner and Martin, 1984; Smith, 1984) have attacked, with great imagination, the issues of measuring nonattitudes, passion, intensity, subjectivity, and ambiguity, thus moving closer to the kind of methodological sophistication required to tap human ambivalence.

- Other, more binding parts of the political process also redefine, defuse, and pacify—at least temporarily—situations of more or less permanent and never-resolved public ambivalence. In the electoral process, to vote converts individual ambivalence into absolute preference. (Votes, too, are not revealed preferences but conversions of ambivalence into univalence.) The results are aggregated and the winner takes all, at least for a period (see Slater, 1963). At the same time, public ambivalence is temporarily delegitimized, which is why protests against election outcomes seldom occur, or, if they do, they are ineffectual unless they take the form of constitutional challenges. This either-or logic applies to a wide range of political acts—laws enacted, acceptable compromises reached, court decisions made. All these binding political decisions partake of this either-or, winner-take-all character, and can thus be regarded as "truce points" in the eternal process of temporarily resolving ambivalent and conflictual situations and rendering one side of public ambivalence temporarily unacceptable and nonlegitimate.

Following this logic, I have found it profitable to re-read Hirschman's remarkable book, *Exit, Voice, and Loyalty* (1970), as a treatise on ambivalence. Hirschman's treatment concerns the market mainly, but it also applies to organizations and nation-states. In what follows I will consider the political aspects. Viewed from the perspectives of citizen and state,

- Exit is the capacity of citizens to react to the negative side of their ambivalence toward the nation. The nation, is, of course, a social entity on which we are dependent, because we are locked into it by membership from birth and under its laws and power. The exit option is to withdraw from it.
- Loyalty represses the negative side of the ambivalence and accentuates the positive.

Exit, however, is costly for individuals, and Hirschman perceives ambivalence—as well as splitting—involved in exiting:

> In leaving his country the emigrant makes a difficult decision and usually pays a high price in severing many strong affective ties. Additional payment is extracted as he is being initiated into a new environment and adjusting to it. The result is a strong psychological compulsion to like that for which so large a payment has been made. In retrospect, the "old country" will appear more abominable than ever while the new country will be declared to be the greatest, "the last hope of mankind," and all manner of other superlatives. (Hirschman, 1970, pp. 112–13)

Hirschman's "splitting" resolution may be typical, but a truer account would take into account the continuing ambivalence toward both old and new, just as colonies that have "exited" the empire experience a continuing ambivalence toward the former colonial power.

Voice, finally, is intermediate; some degree of loyalty is presupposed, and some degree of alienation and opposition—a wish to exit, as it were—is acknowledged. Some arena is established for "working out" public ambivalence and conflict—with varying effectiveness—and "working it into" institutional arrangements. Voice is, in Hirschman's words, "any attempt at all to change, rather than to escape from, an objectionable state of affairs" (ibid., p. 30). Voice is manifested in democratic institutions. It is especially important when exit is unavailable or costly. As Hirschman noted, "[t]his is very nearly the situation in such basic social organization as the family, the state, or the church" (ibid., p. 33).

Many combinations of exit, voice, and loyalty are possible as resolutions of ambivalence in binding organizations. In classical Judaism, self-defined as tribal, exit was impossible and extreme loyalty demanded. In classical Catholicism, exit was virtually impossible (except through excommunication) and voice (heterodoxy) prohibited, except in the case of "orders," which did not exit and retained some voice while proclaiming loyalty. In much of Protestantism, loyalty has been a matter of individual commitment; more voice is permitted, and exit (schism) is relatively easy. In its uneasy history, East Germany suppressed both exit and voice, and demanded extreme loyalty. When at a critical moment exit became possible, that option *became* voice, and the regime, which commanded ambivalence at best and little true loyalty, collapsed (Joppke, 1995).

Finally, this line of reasoning adds to our understanding of democracy and democratic institutions. If we may simplify, the French Revolution provided the West (and the world, as it turns out) two great political legacies that crystallized in the unfolding of that revolution. The first is the values of a free democratic community, which were expressed in the first word of the Revolution's slogan—*liberté*—which implies that the state will not intrude on citizens except in instances when they threaten to do harm to others. The second is the idea of the modern nation-state—*la patrie*—which was to become the modern basis of political integration above all others. The nation-state is envisioned as the single seat of sovereignty and governance, a bounded territory, the locus of economic self-sufficiency, the monopolistic wielder of legitimate force and violence, the focus of a common culture (including language), and the object of loyalty and group identity. (Our own pledge of allegiance to the flag, which refers to "one nation . . . indivisible, with liberty . . . for all" compresses both legacies into a single phrase.)

Both sets of ideals are evidently utopias, unrealizable in pure form. Moreover, they often pull in opposite directions, and, as a result, create a range of political ambivalences that have never been resolved and that continue to dominate our political life (Wagner, 1994). In this context, most democratic institutions appear as "voices"—available mechanisms to work these ambivalences through, continuously if never entirely satisfactorily.

Here is my reasoning: Liberty can be regarded as a principle of limited exit within a context of loyalty—a way of minimizing governmental involvement in the lives of citizens. This principle, however, stands in permanent tension with the political imperatives of the sovereign nation, which are to discourage exit and to demand loyalty, both of which impinge on liberty, absolutely defined. By institutionalizing a democratic principle—or fiction, if one prefers—that the rulers are ruled by the people they rule, limited intrusions on liberty are defended as legitimate, particularly if rulers are policed by a quasi-independent agency, the courts.

Concluding Remark

If we move toward the broader implications of my line of argument, it becomes clear that we are dealing with a fundamental existential dilemma in the human condition. It goes by various names—freedom vs. constraint, independence vs. dependence, autonomy vs. dependence, maturity vs. infancy, and perhaps more—but whatever the name, the dilemma appears to be insoluble. Neither pole is a separable state or condition. Neither freedom nor dependence can be realized in full or exclusive form. Human beings strive for both, but when they achieve a measure of either, the other reasserts itself. As in the nature of ambivalence itself, we want both sides at once but cannot fully satisfy either side.

We social scientists, in our brief history, have fashioned a certain division of labor that is understandable in the dilemma I have described. Economics and part of political science (democratic theory and the study of democracy) have stressed the freedom side; parts of sociology, anthropology, and social psychology—which stress the interpersonal as well as normative and other constraining forces—have fallen toward the other. I have argued that the traditions of rational choice apply best to situations in which relative freedom of choice reigns. Coleman appears to confirm my point in his advocacy of the rational-action model. He argues that its principles are "grounded in a humanistically congenial image of man" (Coleman, 1990, p. 4). By this he refers to a classical liberal image—"the freedom of individuals to act as they will" and a concern over "constraints that social interdependence places on that freedom" (ibid.). To me that says that rational-choice principles are *applicable* to situations in which choice is institutionalized. I have also argued that psychological models based on ambivalence have special power in social situations in which political, group, and emotional dependence is salient. We find both sides of the dilemma between freedom and dependence stressed—in relative degrees—in our social arrangements. I argue, finally, that we must be driven to understand both sides by employing different assumptions and different explanatory strategies. In dealing with dependence as well as freedom, we reach toward a fuller understanding of human action, social institutions, and the human condition.

References

Aberbach, David

1996 *Charisma in Politics, Religion and the Media: Private Trauma, Public Ideals.* London: Macmillan.

Albrow, Martin

1996 *The Global Age: State and Society Beyond Modernity.* Cambridge, MA: Polity Press.

Becker, Gary S.
1976 *The Economic Approach to Human Behavior.* Chicago: University of Chicago Press.

Becker, Gary S., and Kevin M. Murphy
1988 "A Theory of Rational Addiction." *Journal of Political Economy,* Vol. 96, pp. 675–700.

Bonjean, Charles M., Richard J. Hill, and Harry W. Martin
1965 "Reactions to the Assassination in Dallas." In *The Kennedy Assassination and the American Public: Social Communication in Crisis,* edited by Bradley S. Greenberg and Edwin B. Parker. Stanford, CA: Stanford University Press. Pp. 178–98.

Coleman, James S.
1990 *Foundations of Social Theory.* Cambridge, MA: The Belknap Press of Harvard University Press.

Collins, Randall
1993 "Emotional Energy as the Common Denominator of Rational Action." *Rationality and Society,* Vol. 5, pp. 203–30.

Coser, Lewis
1956 *The Functions of Social Conflict.* Glencoe, IL: The Free Press.

de Grazia, Sebastian
1948 *The Political Community.* Chicago: University of Chicago Press.

Downs, Anthony
1957 *An Economic Theory of Democracy.* New York: Harper & Row.

England, Paula
1989 "A Feminist Critique of Rational-Choice Theories: Implications for Sociology." *American Sociologist,* Vol. 20, pp. 14–28.

England, Paula, and Barbara Stanek Kilbourne
1990 "Feminist Critiques of a Separate Model of Self: Implications for Rational Choice Theory." *Rationality and Society,* Vol. 2, pp. 156–71.

Erikson, Erik H.
1962 [1958] *Young Man Luther: A Study in Psychoanalysis and History.* New York: Norton.

Erikson, Kai
1976 *Everything in Its Path: Destruction of Community in the Buffalo Creek Flood.* New York: Simon & Schuster.

Fowles, Jib
1992 *Starstruck: Celebrity Performers and the American Public.* Washington, DC: Smithsonian Institution Press.

Freud, Sigmund
1953 [1900] "The Interpretation of Dreams." In *The Standard Edition of the Complete Psychological Works of Sigmund Freud,* Vols. 4 and 5, edited by James Strachey. London: Hogarth Press.

1953 [1905] "Three Essays on Sexuality." In *The Standard Edition of the Complete Psychological Works of Sigmund Freud,* Vol. 7, edited by James Strachey. London: Hogarth Press. Pp. 125–243.

1955a [1909] "Notes Upon a Case of Obsessional Neurosis." In *The Standard Edition of the Complete Psychological Works of Sigmund*

Freud, Vol. 10, edited by James Strachey. London: Hogarth Press. Pp. 153–249.

1955b [1909] "A Phobia in a Five-Year-Old Boy." In *The Standard Edition of the Complete Psychological Works of Sigmund Freud*, Vol. 10, edited by James Strachey. London: Hogarth Press. Pp. 3–149.

1955 [1912–13] "Totem and Taboo." In *The Standard Edition of the Complete Psychological Works of Sigmund Freud*, Vol. 4, edited by James Strachey. London: Hogarth Press. Pp. 1–161.

1957 [1915] "Thoughts for the Times on War and Death." In *The Standard Edition of the Complete Psychological Works of Sigmund Freud*, Vol. 14, edited by James Strachey. London: Hogarth Press. Pp. 275–300.

1961 [1922] "A Seventeenth-Century Demonological Neurosis." In *The Standard Edition of the Complete Psychological Works of Sigmund Freud*, Vol. 19, edited by James Strachey. London: Hogarth Press. Pp. 72–105.

Gluckman, Max

1963 *Rituals of Rebellion in Tribal Africa*. London: Cohen & West.

Goffman, Erving

1962 *Asylums: Essays on the Social Situation of Mental Patients and Other Inmates*. Garden City, NY: Doubleday.

Goode, William J.

1965 *Women in Divorce*. New York: The Free Press.

Gouldner, Alvin W.

1954 *Wildcat Strike*. Yellow Springs, OH: Antioch Press.

Grinker, Roy, and John Spiegel

1945 *Men Under Stress*. Philadelphia: Blakiston.

Habermas, Jürgen

1975 *Legitimation Crisis*. Boston: Beacon Press.

Hechter, Michael

1987 *Principles of Group Solidarity*. Berkeley and Los Angeles: University of California Press.

Hirschleifer, Jack

1993 "The Affections and the Passions: Their Economic Logic." *Rationality and Society*, Vol. 5, pp. 185–202.

Hirschman, Albert O.

1970 *Exit, Voice, and Loyalty: Responses to Decline in Firms, Organizations, and States*. Cambridge, MA: Harvard University Press.

Homans, George

1950 *The Human Group*. New York: Harcourt, Brace & World.

Jasso, Guillermina

1993 "Choice and Emotion in Comparison Theory." *Rationality and Society*, Vol. 5, pp. 231–74.

Joppke, Christian

1995 *East German Dissidents and the Revolution of 1989*. New York: New York University Press.

Klein, Melanie

1986 [1935] "A Contribution to the Psychogenesis of Manic-Depressive States." In *The Selected Melanie Klein*, edited by Juliet Mitchell. Harmondsworth, UK: Penguin Books. Pp. 115–45.

Lawler, Edward J.
1992 "Choice Processes and Affective Attachments to Nested Groups: A Theoretical Analysis." *American Sociological Review,* Vol. 57, pp. 327–39.
1997 "Affective Attachments to Nested Groups: The Role of Rational Choice Processes." In *Status, Networks, and Structures: Theory Development in Group Processes,* edited by John Skvoretz, Jacek Szmatka, and Joseph Berger. Stanford, CA: Stanford University Press.
Levine, Donald N.
1977 "Review of *Sociological Ambivalence and Other Essays,* by Robert K. Merton." *American Journal of Sociology,* Vol. 83, No. 5, pp. 1277–79.
1985 *The Flight from Ambiguity: Essays in Social and Cultural Theory.* Chicago: University of Chicago Press.
Lifton, Robert
1973 *Home from the War: Vietnam Veterans, Neither Victims Nor Executioners.* New York: Simon & Schuster.
Lindemann, Erich
1944 "Symptomatology and Management of Acute Grief." *American Journal of Psychiatry,* Vol. 101, pp. 141–48.
Lindenberg, Siegwart
1994 "Norms and the Power of Loss: Ellickson's Theory and Beyond." In *The New Institutional Economics: Bounded Rationality and the Analysis of State and Society,* special issue of *Journal of Institutional and Theoretical Economics,* edited by E. G. Furubotn and R. Richter. Pp. 101–13.
Loomes, G., and R. Sudgen
1982 "Regret Theory: An Alternative Theory of Rational Choice under Uncertainty." *Economic Journal,* Vol. 12, pp. 805–25.
Merton, Robert K. (with Elinor Barber)
1976 [1963] *Sociological Ambivalence and Other Essays.* New York: The Free Press.
Milburn, Michael A.
1991 *Persuasion and Politics: The Social Psychology of Public Opinion.* Pacific Grove, CA: Brooks/Cole.
Mortensen, C. David
1987 *Violence and Communication: Public Reactions to an Attempted Presidential Assassination.* Lanham, MD: University Press of America.
Oberschall, Anthony
1973 *Social Conflict and Social Movements.* Englewood Cliffs, NJ: Prentice-Hall.
Olson, Mancur
1965 *The Logic of Collective Action.* Cambridge, MA: Harvard University Press.
Piore, Michael, and Charles Sabel
1984 *The Second Industrial Divide.* New York: Basic Books.
Schelling, Thomas C.
1996 "Coping Rationally with Lapses from Rationality." *Eastern Economic Journal,* Vol. 22, No. 3, pp. 251–69.

Schuman, Howard, and Stanley Presser
1981 *Questions and Answers in Attitude Surveys: Experiments on Question Form, Wording, and Context.* New York: Academic Press.

Sheatsley, Paul B., and Jacob J. Feldman
1965 "A National Survey on Public Reactions and Behavior." In *The Kennedy Assassination and the American Public: Social Communication in Crisis,* edited by Bradley S. Greenberg and Edwin B. Parker. Stanford, CA: Stanford University Press. Pp. 149–77.

Sica, Alan
1988 *Weber, Irrationality, and Social Order.* Berkeley and Los Angeles: University of California Press.

Simmel, Georg
1950 *The Sociology of Georg Simmel.* Translated, edited, and with an introduction by Kurt H. Wolff. Glencoe, IL: The Free Press.

Slater, Philip E.
1963 "On Social Regression." *American Sociological Review,* Vol. 28, pp. 339–63.

Smelser, Neil J.
1995 "Economic Rationality as a Religious System." In *Rethinking Materialism: Perspectives on the Spiritual Dimension of Economic Behavior,* edited by Robert Wuthnow. Grand Rapids, MI: William B. Eerdmans. Pp. 73–92.

Smith, Tom W.
1984 "The Subjectivity of Ethnicity." In *Surveying Subjective Phenomena,* Vol. 2, edited by Charles F. Turner and Elizabeth Martin. New York: Russell Sage Foundation. Pp. 117–28.

Taine, Hippolyte
1881 *The Ancient Regime.* London: Sampson Low, Marston, Searle & Rivington.

Tocqueville, Alexis de
1856 *The Old Regime and the French Revolution.* New York: Harper.

Turner, Charles F., and Elizabeth Martin (eds.)
1984 *Surveying Subjective Phenomena.* New York: Russell Sage Foundation.

Turner, Thomas Reed
1982 *Beware the People Weeping: Public Opinion and the Assassination of Abraham Lincoln.* Baton Rouge: Louisiana State University Press.

Veltford, H. R., and S. E. Lee
1943 "The Cocoanut Grove Fire: A Study in Scapegoating." *Journal of Abnormal and Social Psychology,* Vol. 38 (Clinical Supplement), pp. 138–43.

Wagner, Peter
1994 *A Sociology of Modernity: Liberty and Discipline.* New York and London: Routledge.

Weber, Max
1968 *Economy and Society.* Edited by Guenther Roth and Claus Wittich. New York: Bedminster Press.

PART IV

Micro-Macro Connections

10

Depth Psychology and the Social Order

It has been remarked that any kind of interdisciplinary marriage between the psychoanalytic and the sociological perspectives is difficult, if not impossible, to attain (Wallerstein and Smelser, 1969; Parsons, 1953; Rabow, 1983). As one who has explored each extensively, I share this view. In this essay I will first adduce a number of fundamental obstacles to synthesis between the two sets of perspectives; second, note a number of possible and actual points of contact found in the literature; and third, modestly try my own hand at striking a synthetic chord, taking the theory of the mechanisms of defense as a starting point.

The Psychoanalytic Tradition and the Sociological Tradition

Actually, it is an error to speak of these two traditions in general terms because both have become differentiated into a number of traditions, characterized by varying assumptions, theoretical emphases, research styles, and methodologies. It is possible, however, to point out several reasons for "noncontact" between one or another facet of the two sets of traditions.

Originally published in Jeffrey C. Alexander, Bernard Giesen, Richard Münch, and Neil J. Smelser (eds.), *The Micro-Macro Link* (Berkeley and Los Angeles: University of California Press, 1987), pp. 267–86. Reprinted by permission of the University of California Press.

1. In Freud's writings on society, particularly in *Civilization and Its Discontents* (1961 [1930]), he tended to place stress almost exclusively on the antagonistic relations between civilization and the instinctual side of individuals' lives; he spoke of "hostility to civilization which is produced by the pressure that civilization exercises, the renunciation of instinct which it demands" (Freud, 1961 [1927], p. 15). Such a dualistic formulation would be unwelcome to many sociologists, including myself. In particular, it leaves out the fundamental fact that "civilization" is not a monolithic entity; it should be divided, at the very least, into culture and social structure, with the latter (including institutions such as the family, courts and other legal agencies, and the church) regarded as *mediating* between the strictures of culture and the desires and tendencies of individuals. To put the matter differently, Freud projected the antagonism between the id and superego onto society but neglected to note that there is also a functional sociological equivalent to ego.

2. Despite his early efforts to develop a scientific physiological model in the *Project for a Scientific Psychology,* Freud's model of science, mainly a psychological adaptation of a medical model, rests on epistemological and methodological bases different from those of the positivistic strands of sociology, associated with the positions of Durkheim (1958 [1893]) and Ogburn (1930). The latter stressed causal association among *aggregated* social facts as the basis for scientific knowledge, whereas Freud stressed clinical inference about uniquely convergent *patterns* of forces in the individual's psyche. In addition, a sociologist such as Durkheim was hostile to what he called "internal facts" (i.e., dispositional psychological forces)—a hostility shared by behaviorists in psychology—and insisted on objectively measurable "external facts." For Freud, the sole field of study was *intrapsychic* representations of instinctual forces and external realities.

3. More generally, the fundamental units and levels of analysis of sociology and psychoanalysis differ from one another in apparently unsynthesizable ways. Sociologists are concerned mainly with the objectively determinable opportunities and constraints of the social structure for individuals and groups; psychoanalysts are concerned with various forces, including the external reality of social structure. What is real for sociologists is external reality; what is

real for psychoanalysts is the internal representation (including distortion) of that reality. This discontinuity of levels of analysis plagues efforts to synthesize the microscopic and macroscopic generally.

4. The psychoanalytic model of unconscious motivation and conflict, often irrational in character, is difficult to square with two alternative models of the mind often employed in sociology and the other social sciences: the rational-choice model, in which the actor is in full possession of knowledge about alternative lines of action, calculates costs and gains from each, and acts accordingly; and various phenomenological models, which take the actors' conscious intentions and meanings as the proper representation of psychological reality.

5. For scholars and practitioners in both traditions interested in the potential for change, the psychoanalyst regards the decisive locus of change to be in the pattern of conflicts and defenses in the individual person. Sociologists view the decisive locus of change as existing in the social, political, and economic environments of the individual.

Thus, when different parts of the psychoanalytic tradition touch different parts of the sociological tradition, it is difficult to envision any kind of fit or mutual exchange because of discrepancies in fundamental assumptions and formulations. Nevertheless, a number of points of contact can be seen in the literature, among which the following are illustrative:

1. Ogburn, a positivist sociologist, himself underwent psychoanalysis and regarded it as a *means* by which irrational misunderstandings, myths, and fantasies—all antipathetic to the rational, scientific organization of knowledge—could be dispelled (Duncan, 1964).

2. Certain formal *analogies* between psychoanalytic and sociological thought can be noted. (See chap. 11, p. 222, for an extended analogy between the structure of Freudian and Marxian theory.

3. One particular tradition in anthropology, known as "culture and personality," interpreted various kinds of social institutions and belief systems as *projections* of intrapsychic conflicts generated by particular kinds of child-training practices (Kardiner, 1945; Whit-

ing and Child, 1953). The main theme of *The Authoritarian Personality* (Adorno, et al., 1950) and related studies—that one main determinant of prejudice, discrimination, and its attendant inequalities is the projection of ambivalences acquired in dealing with parental authorities—is consistent with this tradition. Also closely related is the work of a number of small-group theorists, such as Slater (1966) and Cottle (1976), who treat the dynamics of authority and affiliation in small groups in part as reenactments of earlier family dramas and the ambivalences and conflicts created in those dramas.

4. Another tradition, a kind of mirror image of that just noted, treats the structure of personality (conceived in psychoanalytic terms) as purely a product of internalization of objects, role relations, collectivities, and values that constitute the sociocultural environment of the individual. Parsons's (1953; Parsons, Bales, et al., 1955) treatment of personality development and personality structure is perhaps the most notable example of this line of work. The more recent theoretical work of Chodorow (1978) on the perpetuation of the mothering motive through early mother-daughter relations, though differing in emphasis from that of Parsons, is in the same genre of interpretation.

5. A number of sociologists and others have employed different facets of the psychoanalytic tradition in attempting to *diagnose* and *evaluate* the contemporary human condition. This characterization applies to many of the works of the early critical theorists, especially Horkheimer, Adorno, Fromm, Marcuse, and Lowenthal (Jay, 1973), as well as, in a certain degree, to writers such as Norman O. Brown and Christopher Lasch.

6. Finally, some theorists have found the psychoanalytic method useful in their foundations. Habermas (1973), for example, likened the psychoanalytic technique to Marxist study, in that both constitute a critical means of cutting through obfuscation and ideological distortion and reaching to the deeper structural dynamics of a situation.

The foregoing are some of the linkages that have appeared, in varying degrees of seriousness and strength, over the decades. It is not within the frame of this essay to evaluate these illustrative efforts, except to say that some of these lines of work, such as the culture and personality approach, appear to have run their course (Spindler, 1978), and that, taken together, these linkages do not appear to add up to anything resembling a synthesis of theory or empirical research.

A Reformulation and Reclassification of the Defense Mechanisms

Over the generations, many aspects of psychoanalytic theory as originally formulated by Freud have experienced both discrediting and reformulation: the dualism of Eros and Thanatos as the primary instincts; the psychosexual theory of development (modified, for example, by Erikson [1950]); female development, female sexuality, and anatomical determination; and the primacy of the Oedipus conflict in psychic disorders (in the work of Kohut [1971], for example); to say nothing of the psychoanalytic classification of neurotic and other disorders. The status of all these aspects must be regarded as clouded at best.

Other aspects of psychoanalytic theory, though having experienced many vicissitudes, have remained vital elements in that theory. I have in mind the centrality of the notion of ambivalence toward internal representations and external objects (including persons) in the development of character traits, symptoms, and interpersonal relations; the importance of the transference phenomenon, both within and outside psychoanalytic treatment; and the concept of the mechanisms of defense as characteristic modes of dealing with intrapsychic conflict and anxiety (see Abend, 1981). The idea of the mechanisms of defense proves a particularly valuable guideline in psychoanalytic technique, serving as a basis for recognizing resistances, in the psychoanalytic theory of personality and character, and in various metapsychological frameworks—economic, genetic, and developmental.

Despite this persistence and vitality, however, the theory of defense mechanisms remains problematical on a number of counts. First, the classification of defenses has always had a kind of incomplete, ad hoc quality. The defenses most commonly referred to are those recited by Freud in *Inhibitions, Symptoms, and Anxiety* (1959 [1926]) and by Anna Freud in *The Ego and the Mechanisms of Defense* (1937)—repression, regression, reaction formation, displacement, undoing, isolation, projection, introjection, reversal, sublimation, and intellectualization. Since that time, other kinds of complex combinations, such as "depersonalization" (Feigenbaum, 1937) have been added, as well as such specific items as "infertility" (Benedek, 1958) and "humor" (Mishkinsky, 1977) as instances of defense mechanisms. To bring this to its logical extension, Greenson (see Pumpian-Mindlin, 1967) remarked that every kind of psychic phenomenon can be used for defensive purposes. Clearly this kind of classification is not systematic, and clearly the various defenses lie at different levels of conceptual generality.

More important for the purposes of this essay, the concept of defense mechanism has had a primarily intrapsychic reference. Although Freud acknowledged a reference to the external world when he said that "an instinctual demand only becomes an (internal) danger because its satisfaction would bring on an external danger—that is, because the internal danger represents the external one" (1959 [1926], p. 164), the reference is still to the instinct and to the *reactive* character of the external agent. Anna Freud more or less repeated the point, indicating that the main source of external (objective) threat is in relation to punishments that may be or imagined to be inflicted if a prohibited instinctual impulse is gratified. In this formulation, external reality become virtually an extension of the superego. Although Hartmann (1958) and others stressed the continuity between defense and adaptation—thereby taking a more positive view of defense and looking in the external direction—as late as 1981 Brenner could define defense in terms of its internal consequence, namely, "the reduction of unpleasure associated with a drive derivative, i.e., with an instinctual wish, or with superego functioning" (1981, p. 559). My view is directly contrary to this and includes the notion that objective threats must receive a definition independent of instinctual drive representation and the superego, though in fact they are always reacted to and perceived in relation to the latter two establishments in the personality.

In working to overcome these two deficiencies in the theory of defense mechanisms, I shall proceed by two stages: first, to systematize the classification of defense mechanisms themselves, in reference only to intrapsychic impulses and conflicts (which is the psychoanalyst's point of emphasis); and second, to attempt to generalize this categorization to encompass external (objective) dangers and deprivations as well. In dealing with the latter we come directly into contact with social structure and the social order.

The first basis for classifying defenses is to recognize that defensive operations can be activated at different stages in a model of the process beginning with instinctual arousal and terminating with instinctual gratification. This model, based on Freud's (1953 [1900]) early presentation and formalized later by Rappoport (1951), constructs a highly generalized sequence, beginning with mounting drive tension, which, when its gratification is delayed, gives rise to the establishment of psychic drive representation, characteristic discharges of affect that are associated with these representations, and characteristic hallucinatory representations of potentially gratifying objects. The tension is reduced when the drive is gratified by some kind of motor activity leading to a change in the state of the organism.

With respect to defense mechanisms, it appears that they can be activated at different stages in this process beginning with instinctual arousal and ending with gratification. Repression, for example, appears to involve a frontal attack on the mental representation of the instinctual drive and to prevent its appearance in the conscious life. Other defenses operate against conscious, though possibly distorted, representations of instincts (Freud, 1959 [1926], p. 117). Freud (ibid., pp. 90, 117) also spoke of the "suppression of affect" and suggested that repression can eliminate the "accompanying affective character" of aggressive impulses. At least two of the mechanisms of defense—undoing and isolation—were said by Freud to "take place in the motor sphere" (ibid., pp. 119–20). Evidently, then, the defenses can be considered in terms of the different stages between the excitation of some behavioral tendency and its expression in motor activity.

The second dimension by which defense mechanisms can be classified has to do with the basic mode of defense employed by the ego against threatening intrusions (see Suppes and Warren, 1975). In reviewing the central psychoanalytic writings on the mechanisms of defense, I have found it possible to classify the major defense mechanisms into four basic modes or directional tendencies:

1. to block the threatening intrusion;
2. to reverse the threatening intrusion into its opposite;
3. to shift the reference of the threatening intrusion; and
4. to insulate the threatening intrusion from its associative connections.

(This categorization omits "sublimation," which is considered here not to be primarily defensive in its significance but rather a form of indirect gratification of instincts. I also omit "regression" as a special form of defense, as it typically involves substituting one of the major forms of defense, employed at an earlier developmental stage, for another.)

These modes are very general in their formulation. They are formulated without regard to what psychic content is used for defensive purposes; that is, whether the ego uses an interpersonal situation, an affect, a fantasy, or another defense, among others. The modes are formulated without regard to the degree of their effectiveness as maneuvers. Now I shall discuss each basic mode in somewhat more detail, indicating some of the subtypes of each.

1. *Blocking the threatening intrusion.* The most obvious defense is repression, or the turning of the instinctual representation away from the conscious ego (Freud, 1957b [1915]). The suppression of affect is another. Denial of the meaning of the instinctual representation is still another. The appropriate form of defense in the behavioral sphere would be the inhibition of motor activity that is threatening to the ego, either directly or because it involves the gratification of a reprehensible impulse.
2. *Reversing the intrusion into its opposite.* In the essay "Instincts and Their Vicissitudes" (Freud, 1957a [1915]), Freud identified two forms of this reversal: first, reversal of the direction of the instinctual aim from passive to active (for example, from scopophilia to exhibitionism); and second, reversal of the content, when an instinct is turned around from an object to oneself. Affects also may be reversed (for example, when contempt is transformed into awe or worship). Finally, two of the mechanisms of defense involve new patterns of motor activity which attempt to reverse or nullify the reprehensible quality of other behavioral tendencies; these are reaction formation and undoing.
3. *Shifting the reference of the threatening intrusion.* This category involves the "relocation" of the intrusive element to another place in the ego's environment. Thus, it includes various kinds of externalization—for example, the projection of id impulses onto external objects, and the projection of the sources of superego anxiety (guilt) onto a remote authority figure. In addition, this mode includes two familiar forms of distortion by the ego: displacement, which shifts the reprehensible impulse from the original object to a substitute object, and rationalization, which, by means of giving new "reasons," proliferating new categories, and so on, shifts the original conflict to a more remote symbolic level. All these shifts are designed by the ego to disguise the threatening intrusion by means of cognitive distortion.

   One final manifestation of shifting must be mentioned. With respect to the therapeutic situation, the term "acting out" refers specifically to the externalization of tendencies excited by the transference relation into the behavior sphere, with the same unconscious intent to conceal the relevant internal psychic conflict. I feel it is appropriate to treat acting out in a somewhat more general sense—that is, as a means of defending against any internal psychic conflict by shifting its reference to motor activity. Defined in this more general sense, acting out takes its place among the other types of defense as shifting the reference of the threatening intrusion.

4. *Insulation from associative connections.* This involves the psychic phenomena that have been referred to variously as isolation of instinctual representations, isolation of affects, depersonalization, "splitting" (Akhtar and Byrne, 1983), and isolation of a behavioral event that "is not forgotten, but, instead . . . deprived of its affect, and its associative connections are suppressed or interrupted so that it remains as though isolated and is not reproduced in the ordinary thought. . . . The motor isolation is meant to ensure an interruption of the connection in thought" (Freud, 1959 [1926], pp. 120–21).

The classification resulting from the two sets of dimensions reviewed is presented in Table 1. This type of classification involves a logical ordering of the defense mechanisms in relation to one another, rather than presenting them as a simple list of alternative strategies for the ego. It also suggests a principle by which defenses can be regarded as "layered" or organized into hierarchies that constitute more or less fixed establishments of the personality. Let me illustrate this by a simple example. Suppose the ego's main struggle is with a primitive aggressive impulse against a parental figure which has been repressed at an early stage of childhood development. At some subsequent time, this repression fails and the impulse breaks through. By way of further defending against the impulse, the ego externalizes it by projecting it onto the father himself, thus altering the source of danger from impulse to the external world. In turn, the ego defends against the derived fear of the father by displacing it onto a less immediately threatening object, such as an animal. In turn, this phobic result may be further defended against, for example, by a counterphobic reaction formation, by acting out in the form of avoidance rituals, or by denying the anxiety accompanying the phobic reaction. Any one of these reactions may be even further defended against by rationalization, or an effort of the ego to make reasonable and consistent what might otherwise appear unreasonable and

Table 1 *The Mechanisms of Defense Classified in Terms of Basic Modes and Development Phases of Behavior*

Stages	1	2	3 *Psychic Representation (Hallucination) of Gratification Situation*			4 *Behavioral Outcome*
Modes			3a. Cognitive representation drive	3b. Relevant affect	3c. Relevant object	
Blocking	Libidinal tension	Delay of gratification	Repression	Suppression of affect	Withdrawal, denial	Inhibition
Reversal into opposite			Change of instinctual aim	Reversal of affect	Reversal from other to self as object	Reaction formation; undoing
Shift in reference of			Projection of impulse	Projection of affect	Displacement; identification; rationalization	"Acting out"
Insulation from associative connective			"Splitting" or isolation of impulse	Isolation of affect	Depersonalization of experience	Isolation of behavioral event

inconsistent types of beliefs or behavior. Represented graphically, this model reads as follows:

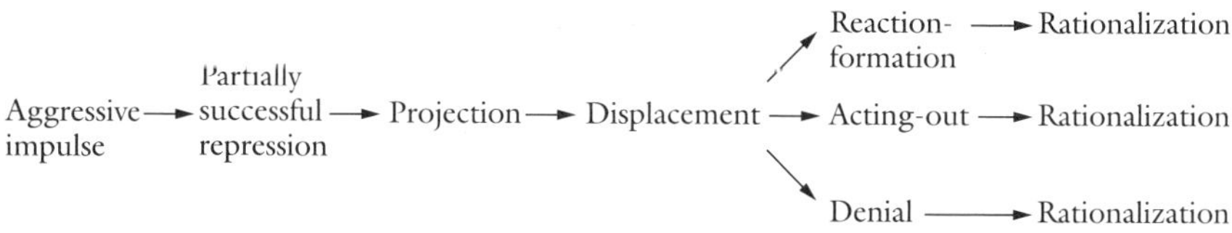

By this process of continuously shifting the source toward which the defenses are directed, the ego builds up layer upon layer of defensive positions, some defending against impulses, some against external threats, some against other defenses, and so on. This process of shifting yields a structural result that has been described by Gill (1961, pp. 122–3) as follows: "What is defense in one layer is impulse in relation to another layer. . . . In general, a behavior is defense in relation to a drive more primitive than itself, and a drive in relation to a defense more advanced than itself." That part of ego structure having to do with defense, then, is best conceived as a hierarchy of defenses, directed toward a multiplicity of different sources and organized in a progression from the deeper, unconscious layers to the more superficial, conscious layers (Sperling, 1958).

One of the accomplishments of Anna Freud's extension of the theory of defense mechanisms is her formulation of a number of different sources of threat or danger to the ego. She mentioned dread of the strength of the instincts themselves, the anxiety that arises from the objective (external) dangers that may arise if instincts are gratified, and, finally, the anxiety that springs from the "ego's need for synthesis" (1937, pp. 59–64). I will now focus on the topic of objective dangers, but first I would like to expand that to include objective reality *beyond* those aspects that are threatening in relation to the gratification of impulses. These additional aspects include uncertainties, threats, and deprivations imposed on the ego from outside.

As a starting point, a model of external excitation can be developed, a model that is precisely parallel to the Freud-Rappoport model relating to instincts and their gratification. The model begins with the appearance (or continuation) of a threat or loss of certain dimensions. The initial response is anxiety on the part of the ego, and in adapting to this anxiety it develops some kind of cognitive representation of the threatening situation (i.e., gives it meaning), mobilizes appropriate affects (primarily fear and anger), and envisions various kinds of behaviors that are, of course, related to and shaped by the meaning assigned to the situation and the relevant affects that are mobilized. The outcome of this process is some line of behavioral action (or inaction) that in turn is related to the ways in which the ego has "shaped" the threatening situation. This is the kind of general model that has emerged in the psychological literature on stress and coping and the more recent literature on risk.

Furthermore, I posit that the ego, in dealing with external threats and deprivations, uses *precisely the same repertoire of defensive modes* as it does in dealing with instinctual representations and conflicts, and that these can be correspondingly classified with respect to external threats. Denial of objective danger, for example, would be the external counterpart of psychological repression—that is, an effort to block the threatening intrusion (Jacobson, 1957). Withdrawal or flight from the scene would be the external counterpart of inhibition. With respect to affective reactions generated by external threats or loss, the same repertoire of suppression, reversal, projection (or, in this case, introjection), and isolation is available.

Empirical studies of coping patterns under stressful or uncertain circumstances seem to give support to such a classification of defensive activities. Defining coping as "the things that people do to avoid being harmed by life-strains," Pearlin and Schooler analyzed reported methods of dealing with strains people encountered as parents, jobholders and breadwinners, and husbands and wives. (The strains themselves were also self-reported.) The interviews included a sample of some 2,300 persons in the Chicago area. In categorizing the responses, Pearlin and Schooler (1978) identified three main clusters: (1) responses that function to control the meaning of the problem, including selective ignoring (denial) and various kinds of rationalizations, such as comparing one's lot favorably with others who are worse off, and devaluation of the importance of that of which one is deprived (e.g., money); (2) responses that function to control the affects generated by hardships (e.g., having faith, keeping calm, trying not to worry, accepting adversity, etc.); and (3) behavioral responses that attempt to modify the situation (e.g., negotiation of problems or seeking advice in marriage, searching for new jobs, etc.). These three categories, generated inductively, correspond to "cognitive representation drive," "relevant affect," and "relevant object" in Table 1, as relevant phases in the excitation of activity.

A recent study of workers in the "dangerous" trades, such as fire fighting, working with toxic chemicals, and the like, showed a similar pattern of reactions. The fact that danger is continuously present and must be confronted on a daily basis makes simple denial of the danger a difficult defense to sustain; evidence of this is the high level of continuous anxiety among workers (Nelkin and Brown, 1984). At the same time, many of the workers apparently try to reduce anxiety by self-assuring phrases such as these: "It's just a normal part of the job," "What you can't change, you accept," "It won't happen to me," and "It's worth the risk" (ibid., pp. 83–99). Another belief that is frequently mobilized is that managers are to blame for dangerous workplace design, failing to provide adequate information about dangers, and cutting corners in order to maximize profits, all with the accompanying affect of anger. Managers, for their part, make an effort to define personal safety as a matter of individual workers' responsibility (ibid., pp. 50–63). These beliefs and affects, of course, set the stage for conflict between the two groups. In the "motor sphere," a number of adaptations are also observable, each depending on the belief and affect that has been picked up by the workers: to quit, to resign oneself to living with danger, to complain to government authorities about dangerous situations, or to agitate politically for preventive and precautionary measures.

The anxiety generated by—and defenses employed against—situations of threat or loss will vary according to whether the threat or loss is severe, whether it is expected or unexpected, whether it is chronic or acute, and whether it is defined as under or out of one's control. Summarizing some of the research evidence from the literature on risk, Douglas notes,

> Apparently, people underestimate risks which are supposed to be under their control. They reckon they can cope with familiar situations. They also underestimate the low probability risk, those which are rarely expected to happen. They get worried by media reported events that seem dramatic (air crashes with film stars on board) and less worried by undramatic losses (such as death from asthma). The media give "salience" to large-scale disasters from recent tornadoes and earthquakes, but presumably salience and recency eventually fade into the familiar background. (Douglas, 1983, p. 6)

Pieczenik (1977) has argued speculatively that the degree of vulnerability that a population feels in relation to a foreign power will determine the "choice" of types of defense mechanisms. To choose the most extreme case, the tension-fraught cold war relations between the United States and the Soviet Union, in which both parties are vulnerable in the extreme, will involve more projection, distortion, and denial, whereas situations of lesser vulnerability, such as relations between the United States and Canada, will involve less extreme defenses, such as the suppression of ambivalence.

The threat of nuclear war stands as the most extreme example of a threat that is severe, unpredictable, both acute and chronic in its dimensions, and seemingly beyond the control of average citizens. One would expect, therefore, denial and suppression of affect. In the early 1970s, psychoanalyst Martin Wangh circulated an inquiry to several thousand psychiatric practitioners in the United States, asking about how patients in treatment dealt with their anxieties about nuclear war. The respondents replied almost unanimously that the subject never came up in treatment (Wangh, 1983). This would suggest a high level of denial, and that even in the psychoanalytic situation, people tend to deal with those areas of suffering over which they can exercise some control. Denial and suppression of affect are, however, often buttressed by self-assuring rationalizations ("The balance of nuclear terror secures the peace," "Limited nuclear wars are possible"). Those who "personalize" the possibility of nuclear war by defining it as mainly in the control of world political and military leaders, moreover, would be those most likely to activate themselves politically on the issue. (I should remind the reader that in referring to various kinds of belief about nuclear war—or any other topic mentioned—as "defenses" I am characterizing them only as psychic reactions to overcome uncertainty and master anxiety. I am not commenting on the empirical validity or invalidity of various claims to knowledge that these beliefs might entail.)

There is also evidence that the employment of defenses in situations of danger or loss may have a sequential character. Lindemann's (1944) classic study of survivors of those who died in a tragic nightclub fire in Boston in 1943 revealed an initial phase of denial of the death itself, followed by episodes of self-accusation and blame as well as episodes of scapegoating others (introjection and projection), then by a longer period of grief work in which the bereaved's social attachments were realigned. A similar kind of sequence apparently occurs among survivors of community disasters, with a period of numbness and disbelief followed by a period of assimilation and giving new definition to the event and to one's relations with others (Erikson, 1976; Rangell, 1976).

These are some of the dimensions of the use of defensive strategies in contending with situations of uncertainty, threat, and loss in the ego's environment. This discussion must be complicated, however, by noting the fundamental fact that the ego does not deal with the external world in isolation. The anxiety and other affects, the meaning patterns assigned, and adaptive reactions envisioned with respect to some kind of external threat inevitably set in motion simultaneous *inner* struggles with those kinds of affects, meanings, symbols, and ambivalences that are aroused by association. Adaptive action, then, always involves a kind of ongoing double dialogue, external and internal, and each side of the dialogue affects (and in some cases distorts) the other.

Societal Linkages with the Defensive Process

In one of its significances, the organization of life into a society is a way of making life more predictable and for that reason less dangerous. Entry into any kind of role (parent-child, employer-employee) simplifies the myriad possibilities of types of interaction by selecting out some as appropriate and others as not appropriate. A commonly shared language with a commonly shared grammar, commonly shared norms and understandings, and commonly shared values and worldview are likewise stabilizing, shaping individuals' lifelong attachments to persons, objects, and symbols.

At the same time, the organization of life into a society brings into being and establishes an almost endless number of possibilities for vulnerability, threat, and loss.

- The organization of social and economic life affects the balance of benefits and threats in the natural environment. The building of reservoirs for purposes of irrigation may reduce the chronic danger of flooding, but it also generates the new danger of massive flooding if reservoirs are destroyed by earthquake. Dozens of additional contemporary examples of environmental poisoning could also be cited.
- The organization of social life also affects the balance of benefits and threats to the health of the organism, as students of sanitation and epidemiology of disease will testify.
- The specialization of social life into roles invariably generates inequalities, which in turn involve real and symbolic deprivations.
- The entry into a social role guided by some kind of expectation inevitably creates the possibility that another will not live up to the rules of the game, which is a source of threat or loss.

- Setting up rules of the social game also establishes the possibility that circumstances may cause changes (including disintegration) of those rules, which is also threatening to those who believe in them.
- The same can be said for the value systems and worldviews that are appealed to in order to legitimize the normative; insofar as these are defined in any way as sacred, attacks on them or their erosion constitute a threat.

Above and beyond these possibilities, it should also be pointed out that society—or, more accurately, culture—selects out and defines specific types of action and symbols as threatening, despite the fact that there may be nothing intrinsically threatening about them. For a male to stand less than a foot from another male while conversing is threatening behavior in many Anglo-Saxon cultures; for a male to stand at a distance while conversing is regarded as unfriendly and therefore threatening in many Mediterranean cultures. It is by virtue of cultural selectivity that menstruating or old people are found disgusting, a style of art found offensive, and communist ideas found menacing. Culture and society, then, contain a reservoir of norms, values, and definitions that determine in large part what is to be defended *against*.

Some of society's social resources are directed toward institutions (medical, law enforcement) that are designed to contend with threatening situations. In addition, society and culture are providers of preferred psychological defenses against many threats. Language and culture are replete with cautionary and sometimes contradictory adages and proverbs ("Look before you leap," "He who hesitates is lost," "A stitch in time saves nine"), which, if believed and made part of one's code of conduct, will presumably fend off some unidentified range of misfortunes implied in the proverb. Superstitions, rituals, and clichés may serve the same function (see Geertz, 1983). As the culture-and-personality scholars were able to show, the world of myths, fairy tales, and religious belief systems constitutes in part enormously complex systems available for projecting, splitting ambivalent feelings, and sublimation. The same functions can be served by the existing reservoir of stereotypes regarding ethnic groups, foreign countries and their peoples, public leaders, movie stars, and famous athletes.

Until this point, it should be acknowledged, the discussion of the role of society and culture in the defensive process has had a certain unrealistic ring; society and culture have been discussed as though they were unified entities. The truth is that modern, complex societies—despite the existence of some forces that make for uniformity, consensus, and integration on the societal level—are differentiated and diversified into literally thousands of divisions and groups along class, ethic, and racial, cultural, political, age, sex, and lifestyle lines. These divisions and groups and subunits within them differ from one another, moreover, along the lines we have been discussing, that is, with respect to what in society they define as threatening and as sources of anxiety, how they define these threats and what kinds of affects they mobilize in relation to these threats, and what kinds of purposive action (if any) they envision as means to contend with them. Indeed, many groups—mainly voluntary associations and social movements—are *built* around the anxiety based on the perception of a grave threat (e.g., alcohol, drugs, crime, environmental abuse) and devote their energies to attempting to persuade others to accept their perception, the anxiety they feel about it, and the need to act. Such groups, when formed, also tend to validate and reinforce the selected combination of threat-definition-affect-action for their members, and, indeed, make it a normative imperative that their members and prospective recruits believe in that combination of elements and act by that belief.

As indicated earlier, these divisions make for a great deal of group conflict; I mentioned the different reactions of workers and managers to environmental hazards in chemical and other industries. In relation to these kinds of conflict, many societal agencies (courts and regulatory agencies of the state are good examples) frequently mediate the conflicts and, in ruling on them, validate one kind of definition of the situation and its associated defensive complex and invalidate others. Following the example given, if upon receiving a complaint from a group of workers about hazardous waste disposal practices a regulatory agency requires managers to take corrective action, the agency is, among other things, giving validity to the workers' particular complex of beliefs and affects. In this way, too, society intervenes in and affects the patterning of defensive belief complexes in it.

Considering this matter more generally, it can be argued that the essential feature of much of contemporary politics—perhaps generally, but certainly in societies with democratic political systems—is a struggle over definitions. Political leaders, parties, groups, and social movements all contend in identifying what is wrong (threatening) in society, giving reasons why it is wrong, blaming others for the wrong, saying how we should feel (anxious, indignant) about the wrong, and saying what ought to be done about the wrong. The media, of course, are crucial in these symbolic dialogues and controversies and play an independent role in their outcomes. The importance of these kinds of political struggles over the legitimate definition of the situation is evident, given that those who can effectively resonate with the electorate's own definition, anxieties, and other affects become the legitimated holders of office and wielders of power.

References

Abend, Sander M.
1981 "Psychic Conflict and the Concept of Defense." *Psychoanalytic Quarterly*, Vol 50, pp. 67–76.

Adorno. T. W., et al.
1950 *The Authoritarian Personality.* New York: Harper.

Akhtar, Salman, and Jessica Price Byrne
1983 "The Concept of Splitting and Its Clinical Relevance." *American Journal of Psychiatry*, Vol. 140, pp. 1013–16.

Benedek, Therese
1958 "Infertility as a Defense Mechanism." Lecture cited in Samuel J. Sperling, "On Denial and the Essential Nature of Defense." *International Journal of Psychoanalysis*, Vol. 39, pp. 25–38.

Brenner, Charles
1981 "Defense and Defense Mechanisms." *Psychoanalytic Quarterly*, Vol. 50, pp. 557–69.

Chodorow, Nancy
1978 *The Reproduction of Mothering.* Berkeley and Los Angeles: University of California Press.

Cottle, Thomas J.
1976 "An Analysis of the Phases of Development of Self-Analytic Groups." In *Explorations in General Theory in General Social Sciences Theory*, Vol. 1, edited by Jan J. Loubser, Rainer C. Baum, Andrew Effrat, and Victor Meyer Lidz. New York: The Free Press. Pp. 328–53.

Douglas, Mary
1983 "Social Factors in the Perception of Risk." Report to the Russell Sage Foundation.

Duncan, Otis Dudley
1964 "Introduction." In *On Culture and Social Change: Selected Papers.* Chicago: University of Chicago Press. Pp. ix–xxii.

Durkheim, Émile
1958 [1893] *The Rules of the Sociological Method.* Translated by Sarah Solway and John H. Mueller. New York: The Free Press.

Erikson, Erik H.
1950 *Childhood and Society.* New York: Norton.

Erikson, Kai
1976 *Everything in Its Path: Destruction of Community in the Buffalo Creek Flood.* New York: Simon & Schuster.
Feigenbaum, D.
1937 "Depersonalization as a Defense Mechanism." *The Psychoanalytic Quarterly,* Vol. 6, pp. 4–11.
Freud, Anna
1937 *The Ego and the Mechanisms of Defense.* London: Hogarth Press.
Freud, Sigmund
1953 [1900] "The Interpretation of Dreams." In *Standard Edition of the Complete Psychological Works of Sigmund Freud,* Vols. 4 and 5, edited by James Strachey. London: Hogarth Press.
1957a [1915] "Instincts and Their Vicissitudes." In *Standard Edition of the Complete Psychological Works of Sigmund Freud,* Vol. 14, edited by James Strachey. London: Hogarth Press. Pp. 117–40.
1957b [1915] "Repression." In *Standard Edition of the Complete Psychological Works of Sigmund Freud,* edited by James Strachey. London: Hogarth Press. Pp. 146–58.
1959 [1926] "Inhibitions, Symptoms, and Anxiety." In *Standard Edition of the Complete Psychological Works of Sigmund Freud,* Vol. 20, edited by James Strachey. London: Hogarth Press. Pp. 73–174.
1961 [1927] "The Future of An Illusion." In *Standard Edition of the Complete Psychological Works of Sigmund Freud,* Vol. 21, edited by James Strachey. London: Hogarth Press. Pp. 5–56.
1961 [1930] "Civilization and Its Discontents." In *Standard Edition of the Complete Psychological Works of Sigmund Freud,* Vol. 21, edited by James Strachey. London: Hogarth Press. Pp. 59–148.
Geertz, Clifford
1983 "Common Sense as a Cultural System." In *Local Knowledge: Further Essays in Interpretive Anthropology.* New York: Basic Books. Pp. 73–92.
Gill, Merton
1961 "Topography and Systems in Psychoanalytic Theory." *Psychological Issues,* Vol. 3, No. 2 (Monograph No. 10).
Habermas, Jürgen
1973 *Theory and Practice.* Translated by M. Viertel. Boston: Beacon Press.
Hartmann, Heinz
1958 *Ego Psychology and the Problem of Adaptation.* New York: International Universities Press.
Jacobson, Edith
1957 "Denial and Repression." *Journal of the American Psychoanalytic Association,* Vol. 5, pp. 74–77.
Jay, Martin
1973 *The Dialectical Imagination: A History of the Frankfurt School and the Institute of Social Research, 1923–1950.* Boston: Little, Brown.
Kardiner, Abram
1945 *The Psychological Frontiers of Society.* New York: Columbia University Press.

Kohut, Heinz
1971 *The Analysis of the Self.* New York: International Universities Press.
Lindemann, Erich
1944 "Symptomology and the Management of Acute Grief." *American Journal of Psychiatry,* Vol. 101, pp. 141–48.
Mishkinsky, Marsha
1977 "Humour as a 'Courage Mechanism.'" *Israeli Annals of Psychology and Related Disciplines,* Vol 15, pp. 352–63.
Nelkin, Dorothy, and Michael S. Brown
1984 *Workers at Risk: Voices at the Workplace.* Chicago: University of Chicago Press.
Ogburn, William F.
1930 "Presidential Address: The Folkways of a Scientific Sociology." In *Studies in Quantitative and Cultural Sociology* (Papers presented at the Twenty-fourth Annual Meeting of the American Sociological Society). Chicago: University of Chicago Press. Pp. 1–11.
Parsons, Talcott
1953 "The Superego and the Theory of Social Systems."In *Working Papers in the Theory of Action,* edited by Talcott Parsons, Robert F. Bales, and Edward A. Shils. New York: The Free Press. Pp. 13–29.
Parsons, Talcott, Robert F. Bales, et al.
1955 *Family, Socialization, and Interaction Process.* Glencoe, IL: The Free Press.
Pearlin, Leonard I., and Carmi Schooler
1978 "The Structure of Coping." *Journal of Health and Human Behavior,* Vol. 12, pp. 2–21.
Pieczenik, Steve R.
1977 "Foreign Policy, Ego-Defense Mechanisms, and Balance-of-Power Vulnerability." *American Journal of Psychotherapy,* Vol. 3, pp. 4–13.
Pumpian-Mindlin, E.
1967 "Report on panel on 'Defensive Organization of the Ego and Psychoanalytic Technique.'" *Journal of the American Psychoanalytic Association,* Vol. 15, pp. 160–75.
Rabow, Jerome
1983 "Psychoanalysis and Sociology." *Annual Review of Sociology,* Vol. 9, pp. 555–78.
Rangell, Leo
1976 "Discussion of the Buffalo Creek Disaster: The Course of Psychic Trauma." *American Journal of Psychiatry,* Vol. 133, pp. 313–16.
Rappoport, David
1951 *Organization and Pathology of Thought: Selected Sources.* New York: Columbia University Press.
Slater, Philip
1966 *Microcosm: Structural, Psychological, and Religious Evolution in Groups.* New York: John Wiley.
Sperling, Samuel J.
1958 "On Denial and the Essential Nature of Defense." *International Journal of Psychoanalysis,* Vol. 39, pp. 25–38.

Spindler, George (ed.)
1978 *The Making of Psychological Anthropology.* Berkeley and Los Angeles: University of California Press.

Suppes, Patrick, and Hermine Warren
1975 "On the Generation and Classification of Defense Mechanisms." *International Journal of Psychoanalysis,* Vol. 56, pp. 405–14.

Wallerstein, Robert S., and Neil J. Smelser
1969 "Psychoanalysis and Sociology: Articulations and Applications." *International Journal of Psychoanalysis,* Vol. 50, pp. 693–710.

Wangh, Martin
1983 *"On Narcissism" in a Changing World.* Paper presented at meeting of the International Psychoanalytic Association, Madrid.

Whiting, John W. M., and Irvin Child
1953 *Child-Training and Personality.* New Haven, CT: Yale University Press.

11

The Psychoanalytic Mode of Inquiry in the Context of the Behavioral and Social Sciences

My objective in this essay is to continue explorations already begun (Smelser, 1968; Wallerstein and Smelser, 1969; Smelser and Erikson, 1980; Smelser, 1983–84; Smelser, 1987) into that still-not-well-charted borderland between psychoanalysis and the other behavioral and social sciences. I will proceed by three stages: (1) to review a number of central characteristics of psychoanalysis, (2) to point out some of the continuities and discontinuities of psychoanalysis—considered primarily as a mode of inquiry—with the other behavioral and social sciences, and (3) to explore the methodological issues and problems that arise when psychoanalysis is turned to the understanding and analysis of data generated *outside* of its clinical setting—in community crisis, in formal organizations, in literature and art, and in history. Psychoanalysis has a long tradition of this kind of inquiry, dating to Freud's interest in religion, art, jokes, and the social psychology of crowds (Freud, 1955 [1912–13], 1955 [1922], 1960 [1905], 1964 [1939]).

Originally published in Jeffrey Prager and Michael Rustin (eds.), *Psychoanalytic Sociology* (Aldershot: Edward Elgar Publishing, 1993), Vol. I, pp. 20–41. Many of the ideas developed in this essay were developed in co-teaching a course with Robert Wallerstein, offered on the San Francisco campus of the University of California to interdisciplinary groups of students. He and I have collaborated before, and in reality I regard him as a silent contributor to this essay.

Central Features of Psychoanalysis

PSYCHOANALYSIS AS THEORY, METHODOLOGY, AND METHOD

Psychoanalysis shares with other perspectives in the behavioral and social sciences the fact that it has both theoretical and methodological aspirations and formulations of a scientific character. While there have been variations and conflicting positions within psychoanalysis as it has unfolded over time, any one of these can be assessed in terms of its first axioms about the basic functioning of the human organism and its psychic life. Examples of first axioms would include the instinct principle, the principles of psychosexual development, structure of the personality, the dynamics of conflict and defense, object relations, identification, the formation of character structure, and so on. At this level of theory, critical assessments are made in terms of whether the first assumptions are valid or invalid, sensible or nonsensical; whether they do or do not form a coherent and consistent conceptual or theoretical structure (i.e., what the relations among the first assumptions are); whether the resultant theory is explicit or vague; whether it is logically complete; and whether it is possible or not possible to derive hypotheses from the theory. At this level of theory the psychoanalytic approach can be compared directly with other theories of personality; in addition, it can be compared formally—i.e., in terms of the structure of theory—with other academic disciplines and subdisciplines, for example, formal economic theory and game theory.

With respect to methodology, psychoanalysis can be described as having a system of rules and procedures by which inferences are made about empirical data and how research is to be designed and executed. The main setting for psychoanalytic inference is the clinical, and the methodological principles are, correspondingly, clinical in character. Psychoanalysts continuously monitor the flow of free association and make inferences as to the avenues by which different associations are connected to one another (common content, common affect, analogy) and how they constitute evidence relating to the major theoretical reference points (impulse, conflict, defense, adaptation) of the psychoanalytic approach. I will have more to say about this methodology throughout the essay, but suffice it to say that this clinical methodology can be compared with different methodologies employed in the behavioral and social sciences, such as the experimental, the archival, the field-observational, and the survey.

So much for several continuities or points of comparability. The principal discontinuity appears when we note that psychoanalysis not only possesses theoretical and methodological ingredients but is simultaneously an *applied* method. The practice of psychoanalysis involves systematic clinical diagnoses of particular disorders and a deliberate effort to intervene in its distinctive therapeutic manner and effect change for the better in the person. Psychoanalysis shares these characteristics with other kinds of psychotherapy and with medical practice generally, but it does not share them with most academic research in the behavioral and social sciences. While it is well known that the latter type of research often unintentionally affects the objects of its study (e.g., interviewer effect, experimenter effect, observer bias), and while variables are sometimes manipulated in field experiments, the main stress in most behavioral and social science research is to maximize the neutrality of the investigator and to minimize directed change. Finally, while the results of this kind of academic research may be useful and used by policymakers, educators, business managers, and others who apply information and knowledge in decision making, such direct application is seldom attempted by those who conduct the research.

A THEORETICAL PRELIMINARY

So much for several very general observations. I will not focus more on psychoanalytic theory, except to make a point regarding the structure of classical psychoanalytic theory in relation to two other classical theoretical positions—those of Thomas Hobbes and Karl Marx. My purpose in making this point is also a preliminary one, that is, to lead to a further discussion of psychoanalysis's methodology and methods.

Hobbes's theory of human nature and the state is simultaneously individualistic and pessimistic. It is individualistic because it does not conceive of any natural or prior basis for organized society, but rather regards human life as a collection of individuals. It is pessimistic in that Hobbes regards these individuals as vain, self-seeking, inhumane, and anarchistic, to the effect that if only individuals are taken into account, human society is impossible. Hobbes solves this problem by postulating further that by virtue of the destructive character of humans, all live in dread fear of their own destruction and will subordinate themselves to an absolute, repressive state. Thus the theoretical closure that was reached by Hobbes is found in his consistent argument that only something as radical and strong as political repression can control individual passions; it is the only way that society is possible.

In one respect it is odd to compare Freud with Hobbes, since Freud was first of all a psychologist, not a theorist of the state and society. That observation is weakened, however, when we realize that Freud himself fashioned a view of the individual and society, particularly in later writings, and realize that while Hobbes was first and foremost a theorist of the state, he felt (correctly) called upon to introduce his treatise on the state with a theory of human nature and psychology.

In Freud's characterization of the id and the superego, and the relations between them (which predated his official recognition of the ego), his formulations bear a striking resemblance to those of Hobbes, though at an intrapsychic rather than a sociopolitical level. The id was represented as a cauldron of instinctual representations, seeking only gratification and knowing no morality, and, if left to themselves, uncontrollable. (The parallels with Hobbes's theory of human nature are obvious; Hobbes's psychology can be regarded, retrospectively, as a psychology of the id, which only external repression by political authorities can check.) Standing in sharp opposition to the id impulses is the superego, whose ultimate function is to engage in a kind of surveillance operation, in which the conscience is maintained, high moral ideals held out, and impulses repressed. The superego, especially in its early formulations, was held to be as moral, strident, and punitive as the impulses were incessant and amoral. Such is the Hobbesian kind of dualism between anarchy and control that is to be found in Freud.

Subsequently, when Freud "discovered" and elaborated the ego as the third great establishment of personality (1923), he introduced a principle of interposition and intermediation between the id, the superego, and external reality. That is to say, the ego was now endowed with a variety of mechanisms of defense (other than repression), which permitted the diversion and disguised expression and gratification of instinctual demands, especially through sublimation. The introduction of the ego, in short, marked a more benign and optimistic turn in Freud's psychology, and broke through the pessimistic dualism of the impulse-repression model of the mind.

The main methodologically oriented point arising from this comparison is the following: psychoanalytic theory, like Hobbesian theory, can be characterized as a balance of a *multiplicity* of forces, working in different, sometimes opposing directions. Virtually every phenomenon that Freud tried to explain—pathological symptoms, dreams, errors in speech and writing, and character traits—involved reference to this principle of tension and conflict, and the explanation always involved some kind of combination among the different forces, whether the combination resulted in overdetermination or in compromise. This general combinatorial principle, while modified in theoretical debate and reformulation, remains a central tenet of psychoanalysis.

Turning to Marx, we find certain formal theoretical parallels as well. Both Marxian and Freudian theories concern a system that maintains an equilibrium-in-tension between conflicting forces. For Marx the tension is expressed at bottom in contradictions between the mode of production and the social relations of production, but is manifested in the antagonism between two classes. For Freud the tension is between instinctual impulses (the id) and various personality establishments engaged in the management and control of these impulses (the individual's sense of reality, the superego). Both theorists stress, moreover, that the main strategy of control is a form of repression, politico-economic in the one case and psychological in the other. Furthermore, in each case the repressive forces are buttressed by a number of ancillary devices that lead to distortions of reality and consciousness. For Marx, one of the main functions of religion, philosophy, morality, and so on is to disguise the true interests of the subordinated class and to contribute to a false consciousness in them; for Freud, various mechanisms of defense such as projection, isolation, rationalization, and displacement distort the true nature of impulses and obscure them from the individual. For Marx, moreover, the structure of society results from the efforts of the dominant class to save itself from the destructive impact of societal contradictions; for Freud, the structure of the personality (character traits, symptoms, attitudes) is geared in large measure to saving the individual from the destructive impact of his or her inner conflicts. Finally, for both authors, freedom from repression is gained by an expansion of awareness (consciousness) of the conflicts besetting the system. For Marx, however, freedom expresses itself in the destruction of the system and the creation of a conflict-free one, whereas for Freud freedom expresses itself in the dissolution of symptoms and the increased capacity of the individual to redirect the previously conflict-bound energy into productive activity.

The general point emerging from this comparison is precisely the same as that emerging from the Hobbes comparison: both underscore the nature of the psychoanalytic perspective of the psychic system as one of individual coping with multiple, conflicting forces.

THE PSYCHOANALYTIC SITUATION AND THE GENERATION OF EMPIRICAL DATA

As a setting for therapy, psychoanalysis can be said to involve "tilted" or asymmetrical relationships between patient and analyst in a number of ways. The patient pays for services, the analyst receives the payments. The patient is free to terminate treatment voluntarily at any time, whereas for the analyst the burden of proof is on providing special reasons *not* to continue (persistent failure to pay, "untreatability," uncontainable acting-out, successful termination, and so on). The patient is placed in a supine position, symbolizing passivity and dependency, and cannot see the analyst, whereas the analyst sits behind and above and can observe without being observed; this suggests an asymmetry of power or control in the situation. All these points of asymmetry have been characterized frequently as facilitating in different ways the psychoanalytic work and the psychoanalytic process.

For the purposes of this essay, one of the most interesting asymmetrical aspects concerns the patterns of communication and the flow of information between patient and analyst. (It is interesting because these patterns generate the empirical data in the psychoanalytic situation.) Stated most plainly, the psychoanalytic situation is structured so that the analyst will know as much as possible about the patient, and the patient will know as little as possible about the analyst. This is attained by the rule of free association (saying everything that comes to mind on the part of the patient), the rule of abstinence or neutrality (not to be provoked or seduced, or become emotional in emotion-laden situations) on the part of the analyst, the taboo on personal contact outside the analytic situation, and the minimization of negotiation about the location, scheduling, and length of meetings, as well as negotiation about amount and mode of fee payment. The objective of these contrivances is to maximize the stability of the general parameters of the analytic situation and to minimize elements of structure in the analytic interchange, in order to permit the uncontaminated flow of information from the patient and the development of as "pure" a transference relationship as possible, unfettered by "real" knowledge about the analyst.

In such a situation, the analyst observes a flow of thoughts, gestures, silences, affective displays, interruptions, and attempted breaking of the "rules" and other provocations on the part of the patient. In observing these, the analyst is guided by one of the paramount assumptions of psychoanalytic theory and practice: that this otherwise unintelligible flow of events manifests systematic connections and has an overall pattern. This assumption, furthermore, is based on a further one—that the empirical material will manifest an (unconscious) preoccupation on the part of the patient with his or her central conflicts and the defenses against them. (Another allied assumption is that the common themes, being connected with core conflicts, will recur with frequency, however disguised.) The task of the analyst, then, is to free associate along with the patient, as it were, monitoring this process by attending to content, form, and affect, and identifying common themes that can be found in materials relating to the patient's past history, contemporary life situation, and the transference (as well as in the analyst's countertransference). The analyst's interpretations, while they may take a variety of specific forms, are ultimately aimed at raising the patient's level of awareness of these common themes, which is a precondition for his or her more adequate coping with the core conflicts and their associated affects.

The situation thus described is an unrealized ideal in many respects. The idea of fully free association is undoubtedly a kind of myth, as most patients, being adaptive, probably are in fact guided by their own internal considerations as to what may or may not be possible for them to deal with, and this constitutes a kind of gyroscope that shapes their efforts. Even the most abstinent analyst also communicates, for silence is a communicative phenomenon. In addition, interpretations are no doubt seldom so neutral as not to reveal subtleties of style and preference on the part of the analyst. Finally, countertransference reactions are forever threatening to break through and reveal further information about the analyst. Even represented as an ideal, however, this account of the asymmetrical structure of information flow tells us much about how the empirical data unfolds in the analytic situation.

THE CHARACTER OF CLINICAL INFERENCE AND EXPLANATION

We may link the foregoing points of discussion by pointing out that clinical inference and explanation in the analytic setting involves an *interaction* between psychoanalytic concepts and theoretical presuppositions on the one hand, and the flow of empirical data on the other. That interaction works out in something like the following way. Without the theoretical apparatus of psychoanalysis—or *some* theoretical apparatus—little if anything systematic could be gleaned from the flow of empirical data produced by the patient in the analytic situation. It is that theoretical apparatus that sensitizes the analyst to the content, associations, symbolism, and sequences of the events observed and permits him or her to make connections among them. For that reason the term "clinical inference" is likely to be misleading, because it implies an inductive movement from empirical data to conclusions or general principles. A better term would be "clinical assessment" or "clinical interpretation"—interpretation not in the technical psychoanalytic sense of "intervention" but in the cognitive sense of "assigning meaning to data"—because both of the latter terms capture the interplay between the data observed and the theoretical framework brought to bear on them.

The term "clinical explanation" involves the same kind of interplay. Recall the theoretical point made in the comparisons with Hobbes and Marx, that the psychoanalytic perspective, like those, envisions a system (in the former, a psychic system; in the latter, a social system) and posits a state of conflict and potential breakdown in that system. Whether psychic or social, the element of conflict is the same, and the notion of a multiplicity of forces at work is also the same. Such perspectives lead to, if not dictate, the distinctive criteria by which analysts *organize* the otherwise unstructured or little-structured phenomena that flow from the analytic process.

This clinical mode of inference—often referred to as the elucidation of ideographic patterns about individuals—can be contrasted with some modes of inference in the behavioral and social sciences and likened to others. More particularly, the clinical mode contrasts with what might be called the aggregative mode of inference, which typically is found in experimental work in academic psychology and statistical work in academic sociology. In the latter enterprises, the effort is to establish concomitant variations—or correlations—between distinctive traits or characteristics of aggregated groups of individuals, and to posit some kind of causal relations between the two on the basis of this association. As a rule—but not always, as the techniques of partial and multiple correlation reveal—the methodological aim is to strive for causal connections between two (or more) variables through their aggregated association, rather than through their idiosyncratic causal status as it is revealed in unique, patterned combination with a variety of other causal forces.

The approach taken in ethnographic investigation conducted by social or cultural anthropologists on individual cultures can also be compared to the psychoanalytic or clinical mode of inquiry. One point of discontinuity is that anthropologists in the field do not tend to approach their subject matter with any kind of presuppositions or hypotheses about discrete sets of variables, but, rather, rely on their investigations to produce complicated sets of connections among large numbers of attitudinal, symbolic, and behavioral phenomena that are linked together by meaningful association. Second, anthropologists do not represent themselves to their sources of information (informants) as therapists interested in change or improvement but rather as neutral, friendly researchers who also involve themselves to some degree with the lives of those they are studying. Third, the mode of inquiry is much more structured (interviews and observation) than the very unstructured psychoanalytic situation.

The main continuity between psychoanalysis and ethnography is in mode of explanation. The ethnographer is interested in cultural patterns, how these cohere or conflict, and how they shape the distinctive experiences, outlooks, and behavior of those exposed to those patterns. The pattern is clinical or ideographic in nature. "The social anthropologist," maintained Leach (1958, p. 11) "with his non-statistical prejudices, thinks of his data as being made up of 'systems of relationships.'" Because of this formal continuity, it is probably not accidental that one of the earliest and most active connections between psychoanalysis and the other behavioral and social sciences was with anthropology; this took the form of the "culture and personality" studies (Spindler, 1978) that thrived in the 1940s and 1950s and continue to some degree in later decades (LeVine, 1973). The thrust of many of these studies was to find coherent modes of child-rearing and derived psychodynamic patterns on the one hand, and the structure of religious systems, beliefs and attitudes, and common practices at the cultural level; an example is Whiting and Child's (1953) monograph on the relations between child-training practices and adult beliefs concerning the causes of disease. One point of kinship between the fields, I would argue, was their common preoccupations with the configurational mode of explanation; given this similarity, the problem for the culture-and-personality investigator was to locate correspondences among configurations.

As indicated in the foregoing remarks, the psychoanalytic method of investigation and inference is marked by a distinctive number of characteristics: it is gathered in the context of a special relationship between practitioner and patient, into which both have voluntarily entered; it is based on the presumption that the investigator will yield as little information about himself or herself as possible; the information is produced by the twin methods of free association on the one hand, in which the patient reveals—as far as is possible—anything and everything that comes to mind, and abstinence, on the other, in which the investigator withholds, as far as is possible, any emotional reaction or evaluative judgment about the materials produced; and the information is produced in the context of a mutual effort on the part of both analyst and patient to understand and gain insight into the patient's current problems, past experiences, and situation, with an aim to effecting an improvement in the patient's psychological well-being. While in principle "free," this method is in fact a highly contrived one, hemmed in by many special understandings and rules, it is a relationship not reproduced anywhere else in reality, though certain analogies can be drawn between the psychoanalytic situation and the doctor–patient relation generally (Parsons, 1951), the confessional relationship between priest and parishioner, and the relationship between friend and confidante.

What interests me most in this essay are the ways in which the psychoanalytic mode of investigation, with all its uniqueness and peculiarity, can be brought to bear on the understanding and interpretation of materials that are evoked in situations that *differ* from the psychoanalytic situation in important respects. There is every reason to believe that *all* human behavior in *all* situations is affected continuously by the kinds of psychodynamic processes enumerated above, yet these processes do not appear in such "pure" form as they do in the free association process, and their interpretation has to be modified accordingly. The thoughts I intend to put forward on this problem of the psychoanalytic interpretation of materials gathered in nonclinical settings are meant simultaneously to provide testimony about both the strengths and the limitations of the psychoanalytic method. My mode of proceeding will be illustrative, examining a number of different types of research efforts on the part of behavioral and social science investigators.

The Study of a Community Disaster

The first case to be considered is a follow-up study conducted by a sociologist, Kai Erikson, of the recovery, such as it was, of the citizens of Buffalo Creek, West Virginia, an Appalachian mining community that was stricken by a disastrous flood on February 26, 1972 (Erikson, 1976). The onset of the flood was sudden, its destructive impact and cost of lives great, and its effects profound and long-lasting. It was Erikson's mission to enter the community, interview its citizens, and write an account of the effects of the tragedy on their lives and their outlooks on the world.

There were a few respects in which Erikson's research falls within the scope of the psychoanalytic method, or at least is related to it. First, Erikson himself, while first and foremost a professional sociologist, is the son of an eminent psychoanalyst, Erik Erikson, who himself has contributed in a fundamental way to the application of the psychoanalytic method to the understanding of historical events and historical periods (see below). Surely this background was not lost on the son. In addition, Kai Erikson's own personal style is one that is open, receptive, empathetic, and nonintrusive, and therefore one that tends to evoke the greatest amount of spontaneous material from those he interviews.

Second—and in keeping with the analytic tradition—Erikson decided to record the memories, thoughts, feelings, and other reactions to the disaster as much as possible in the respondents' own words, thereby remaining true to the *individual contexts of meaning* in which these words were uttered; this is also in keeping with the analytic mode of representing clinical material—to place them in the complex of meaning that the patient gives them (while at the same time bringing the analyst's own psychodynamic logic to bear on their understanding).

Third, Erikson's enterprise carried forward a tradition that was not foreign to psychoanalysts: the tradition of analyzing trauma, grief, and loss under catastrophic situations. The work of Bruno Bettelheim (1943) on survivors in Nazi concentration camps comes most immediately to mind, but perhaps the most kindred line of research was that of Lindemann (1944), which concentrated on the bereavement experiences on the part of those related to or otherwise close to the victims of the famous Cocoanut Grove fire and panic in Boston in 1943. Lindemann was a psychoanalyst and was specifically interested in the phases of adaptation that characterized the mourners' experiences: initial denial of the event and the loss; a period involving a process of idealization of the lost one; anger at his or her disappearance; guilt, self-blame, and a sense of personal responsibility for "not having done enough" for the loved one in life; and a process of "grief work" on the part of survivors, which involved the emotional working-through of the strong psychic reactions that had been experienced, the gradual resumption of involvement in the routine round of activities in daily life, and the reconsolidation of existing and the building up of new personal relations with others.

Among other examples of work in this tradition are those of Grinker and Spiegel (1945), which dealt, in part, with the traumas of loss experienced by veterans in World War II occasioned by the violent deaths of their mates in battlefield situations, as well as the more recent research on Vietnamese war veterans by Lifton (1973), which dealt not only with these kinds of loss experiences but also with involvement in a war (in Vietnam) that was regarded as illegitimate by large numbers of American civilians and military personnel alike.

The fourth point of continuity between Erikson's research and the psychoanalytic method stems from the fact that Erikson was able to interview live persons, which is not always the case for those dealing with cultural products and with psychohistorical materials. Under these circumstances it is possible for the investigator, in interviewing, to probe and to discover the individual meaning contexts of those who have experienced the events in question, as it is in the psychoanalytic process.

There are three senses, however, in which Erikson's research diverged from that which is found in the classic psychoanalytic mode. The first is that Erikson used an interview method more structured than the analytic method (even though he was attempting to represent the respondents in their own words) and used a social-community framework as much as a psychological framework in interpreting his findings.

Second, Erikson represented himself as a "researcher" rather than an analyst, sought out his respondents rather than being sought out by them, and indicated to them the nature of his interest (the flood and its consequences for them). The respondents knew something about him—that he was a professor, that he was from Yale, that he was likely to be from a different social class from them, and that he had a number of specific points of interest in mind. A researcher, moreover, always tells some kind of story to his respondents with respect to the purpose of his or her own research. This story is usually partial in that it does not typically reveal to the respondents the nature of the interpretative framework he or she is bringing to bear (for fear of influencing the respondents in their responses); besides, the role of "researcher" in contemporary American life has become something of a well-institutionalized role, and informants are often satisfied with knowing no more about the stranger in their midst than that he or she is a "researcher." Be that as it may, the situation of the professional researcher is different in these few important ways from that of a professional psychoanalyst.

Third, and a very important point, at a certain phase of his involvement in the community Erikson let it be known that he himself was prepared to be something of an "expert witness" in a lawsuit brought by some of the surviving citizens of Buffalo Creek against the mine owners for their negligence that resulted in damage and loss to those citizens. While his respondents were aware in differing degrees of this special role he was taking, the fact that he was "on their side" against an antagonist might well have affected and skewed the nature of the information supplied by them (in ways I will explore presently). At the very least, it made a difference that Erikson was "on their side" in an important community conflict, more so than it would have been if he were "on their side" in a collective effort to be of help in diagnosing and improving their sense of psychological situations.

Erikson's account of the individual traumas experienced by the citizens of Buffalo Creek is completely consistent with Lindemann's account of the bereavement accounts of those who lost loved ones in the Cocoanut Grove fire, even though Erikson did not depict it as a series of recuperative phases. It includes the ingredients of numbing and denial; shock; being "muddled" and not being able to "reason things out"; confusion; a preoccupation with death and dying; an inability to act; an inability to understand why one survived and others didn't, and a great experiencing of guilt on that account; a ritual preoccupation with memories and precautions to be certain that the tragic event does not recur; and the scapegoating of others for causing the flood and the deaths of loved ones.

There were two features of Buffalo Creek as a community and a culture that highlighted some features of these individual traumas and downplayed others. The first concerns the kind of cultural tradition of Appalachia itself. In his first chapter Erikson notes that a culture—including that of Appalachian town life—always is organized around conflicting themes or possibilities, and that these different possibilities come into salience selectively. In particular, Erikson noted the contrasting themes of American independence and self-determination on the one hand, and helpless passivity or dependence on the other. The first theme is certainly a familiar one in American culture in general, but the second one is more foreign to American community life. At the same time, the villages of Appalachia had known decades of poverty, unemployment, and chronic reliance on welfare authorities for support. This specific ingredient of Buffalo Creek's cultural history probably highlighted the note of helplessness and passivity on the part of its survivors, largely because of its citizens' proneness to take up this mode as a way of life. This would also tend to minimize the community's ability to rebound in a constructive way, to rebuild its institutions and its sense of community spirit.

The recent social history of the community of Buffalo Creek also probably worked to produce the same result. In Lindemann's account, the bereavement process has a reconstructive aspect, namely the gradual substitution of new ties, loyalties, and social objects in the place of those that have been lost; it is the regrouping of the community into new lines of solidarity and a new web of object-relations. Because of the progressive decimation of the community of the population through decades of depopulation and out-migration, however, its collective and institutional resources—particularly its systems of extended kinship—had been progressively sapped and were literally unavailable to survivors as resources on which to rebuild in a time of community loss and crisis. Buffalo Creek was already in a state of fragility and disorientation when the crisis struck, and was at a great disadvantage from the standpoint of being able to regroup and re-establish community life after the disaster. This probably made the individual traumas worse than they would have been, and for this reason the survivors would be more likely to have become "stuck" at some stage of confusion, nervousness, helplessness, passivity, and isolation. Such is the subtle interplay between individual traumas and the capacity for communities to rebuild after the tragedy of catastrophe.

There was one additional feature of Erikson's involvement in the Buffalo Creek community that probably skewed the nature of his data and affected its flow. As we have seen, one of the inevitable concomitants of the bereavement-loss syndrome is the tendency to blame oneself and others for the otherwise largely incomprehensible events that catastrophic loss frequently brings. A natural disaster such as that experienced at Buffalo Creek, however, can be regarded in large part as an "act of God," of the working of mysterious, unpredictable forces in the universe, as beyond human control. Many of the citizens of Buffalo Creek did in fact experience the flood and its aftermath in precisely that way—beyond human control. At the same time, we should not forget the inevitable human capacity of survivors to personalize the event and blame someone for it. After the Cocoanut Grove disaster, the Boston press was teeming with scapegoating stories—that the busboy who mishandled the light bulb should not have been given that responsibility; that the nightclub owners were to blame for installing paper, inflammable palm trees in the nightclub; that the electrical inspection teams of the city of Boston had been negligent in their work, etc. (Veltford and Lee, 1943).

In the Buffalo Creek community, people tended to blame one another for the flood and the catastrophic loss of life it caused. Erikson's presence in the community, and most especially his ultimate willingness to join the legal effort to press charges against the mine owners, cast him into the important role of holding someone else responsible for the catastrophe, as against interpreting it as some kind of impersonal "act of God." In this way he probably compromised his role as more or less neutral "observer" and discouraged the passive victimized reactions of the aftermath of the disaster, as well as highlighting the vindictive element of the community reaction, however realistic or unrealistic this element might have been.

The Study of Authority in Formal Organizations

Two of the fundamental variables that inform psychoanalytic interpretations are the dimensions of intimacy and authority, particularly as these are manifested in family relations. In one respect the oedipal struggles that beset the young child's life can be regarded as reflecting a concern over his or her fate with respect to intimacy and authority. On the one side there is the (boy's) struggle with the father, who has, by virtue of his family position, a kind of monopoly over authority, for which the boy competes and strives, but ultimately surrenders to in the oedipal resolution. On the other side the young boy is in competition for his mother's affection, over which the father also appears to have something of a monopoly, at least as this is symbolized in terms of sexual access; the boy ultimately renounces his claim to sexual intimacy in the oedipal resolution as well, as he internalizes the incest prohibition and comes to regard his mother as sexually unavailable. In fact, then, it is possible to view the oedipal struggle—and perhaps struggles with siblings as well—as triangular struggles over two very scarce commodities in the family economy: intimacy and authority.

It is not a big step to suppose that these kinds of dramas will be operative in some sense in social organizations other than the family, since they occupy such a fundamental place in that special social organization. In particular, they ought to manifest themselves in *any* kind of organization in which authority and intimacy play a role. The case study I intend to examine in this section is just such an organization—a bureaucracy, a mental hospital as studied in the early 1960s by a number of social scientists (Hodgson, Levinson, and Zaleznik, 1965). As is well understood, a bureaucracy is, above all, the formal institutionalization of authority relationships, the subordination of the majority of subordinate staff members to a superior in the interests of the effective functioning of a goal-oriented enterprise (Weber, 1948 [1920]). While not explicitly built as a social form, all of us know that a bureaucracy, like all forms of social organization, is the setting for the development of all kinds of affective—including intimate—relations among those who are its members. It is the dynamics of authority and affection that interest us above all in the case to be examined. Before turning to it, however, it would be helpful to cite a number of other lines of research, which had developed earlier and which conditioned the questions asked by Hodgson, Levinson, and Zaleznik. To these strands of research we shall now turn.

One of the most interesting lines of research to emerge in the early 1950s in Harvard's Department of Social Relations was the investigation of the dynamics of small-group interaction carried out by R. Freed Bales and his colleagues and students (Bales, 1950). The line of this research that is of greatest interest in the present context is the development of leadership patterns in small groups. In one series of experiments Bales and his colleagues assigned various decision-making tasks to groups of Harvard undergraduates, who met as small groups over a sustained period of time. The kinds of behavior and the kinds of interaction undertaken by all members of the different groups were carefully recorded and plotted over time. One of the interesting developments that occurred in groups that appeared to be effective in their functioning over time was a certain differentiation of roles: the emergence of certain individuals who gathered information and made suggestions for action (idea specialists and instrumental leaders) on the one hand and certain other individuals who tended to joke, manage tensions in the group, and promote solidarity in the groups. The latter appeared to be the best-liked individuals in the groups, and they tended to form a special interactive alliance with the more instrumental members. Bales called these two types of specialist "instrumental leaders" and "expressive leaders," respectively, and the emergence and presence of each type appeared to constitute definite assets for the effective functioning of these experimental groups (Bales and Slater, 1955).

This line of research was soon generalized in two directions. Talcott Parsons, Bales's colleague at Harvard, argued that this differential of the basic adult family roles into the instrumental (father) and expressive (mother) role held one key to understanding the universal structure of the nuclear family, and together these constituted the basis for understanding the virtual universalization of the incest taboo in the family. The father and the mother were held to be a leadership dyad that formed a special solidarity relation with one another and provided the basis for the institutionalization of authority (instrumentalism) and intimacy (affect) necessary for the existence of the family as an effective socializing agency (Parsons, 1964 [1954]). In a comprehensive cross-cultural tabulation, Zelditch found that there was an almost universal differentiation of role structures along the lines of sex, with the father specializing in family authority and the mother specializing in intimacy or emotional functions (Zelditch, 1955), which appeared to constitute strong comparative and historical evidence for the universal significance of the authority and intimacy dimensions for social groups.

About the same time a separate but related line of research was being carried out in selected mental hospitals, which appeared to point in similar directions. The hospital is a structure based on a structural hierarchy of authority, organized to deliver health care to patients. At the same time it is an organization dedicated to providing emotional care for patients who are hospitalized in it. By and large such hospitals exhibit a kind of formal differentiation of roles, with the physicians responsible for determining what kind of treatment is to be administered to the patient population, and the ancillary staff (mainly nurses) responsible primarily for the direct caring of the patient population. In studies of mental hospitals (Stanton and Schwartz, 1954), the investigators appeared to find that the severity of patient pathology and the occurrence of patient "rumbles" could be traced directly and positively to the severity of disagreements and conflicts among staff members as to how a given situation in the hospital setting ought to be handled—findings which also seemed to point to the salience of the need to maintain a solid relationship between the instrumental and expressive authorities in the organization. In my own observations of the structuring of roles in colleges and universities, I noted a kind of differentiation of instrumental roles and expressive roles as well. Administrators are by and large charged with the enforcement of rules in the institution and with the exercise of discipline. The faculty, while certainly responsible for applying norms and standards in the evaluation of students (as authorities), are removed from the exercise of all other sorts of discipline and are expected to have the students' interests and aspirations in mind, and to support them. At the same time, the administration (authority) and the faculty (expressive) more or less back up one another in maintaining institutional goals and purposes.

Still another line of research—scarcely ever connected with the line just mentioned—concerns the styles of authority carried out in formal organizations. In what has become a classic in the field of bureaucratic research, Gouldner (1955) contrasted the leadership styles of two managers of a gypsum plant, one who succeeded the other as manager. The first mainly made minimal demands on his workpeople, using mainly permissive tactics to secure their cooperation in carrying out the tasks in the workplace, and always provided a good ear for their concerns. After his departure (through death), the second supervisor proved to be a stickler for rules, demanding compliance and generally assuming a "no-more-nice-guy" stance. The result of his arrival on the scene was an outpouring of dissatisfaction on the part of the workpeople with respect to his leadership style, along with a corresponding idealization of the departed manager, and ultimately the development of a wildcat strike on the part of the disgruntled workpeople. What the episode represented, in psychodynamic terms, was the sudden disappearance of the expressive role and the equally sudden imposition of the authority role, which led first to a basic instability of leadership and ultimately to its downfall.

It was more or less in the shadow of these traditions that Hodgson, Levinson, and Zaleznik undertook their investigation of the executive role constellation in a mental hospital, and the differentiation of roles among the executives. The hospital was a well-staffed one, and its atmosphere was one of excitement, dedication, ferment, and innovation. The basic executive role constellation comprised three officers of the hospital: the superintendent, the assistant superintendent, and the clinical director. The researchers attempted to draw out the distinctive administrative styles of the three, their relations with one another, and their relations with subordinates (though not with the patient populations).

The superintendent was the quintessential executive. He tended to be mainly responsible for external affairs of the hospital, its correspondence, and representing it to the larger community. In his internal relations with subordinates, he was perceived as having an approach that involved a "bluntness that was little short of brutality" (p. 105). He was very directive in his relations with both patients and residents. He was very much the "take charge" guy, and his interpersonal style was "gruff, and often disruptive, particularly to subordinates, who perceived almost everything he said or did as an edict" (p. 125). He was characterized behind his back by subordinates as "Ferocious Frank."

One of the interesting features of the hospital organization as studied by Hodgson, Levinson, and Zaleznik was that "Ferocious Frank" was in fact—from two and one-half years—the gruff successor to another superintendent, who had been regarded with respect and who was idealized as a benign leader in the early years of Frank's leadership. Frank was widely regarded as "a sneaky, no-good bastard, tactless, ignorant, blowhard, a jerk" (p. 252). Much of the heat generated by his arrival and subsequent style was defused by the managerial style of the second member of the trio, the clinical director. A soft-spoken man, he was noted for his consistently supportive style and his evident willingness to build the motivation, skills, and insights of future therapists. He had a consistent "open door" policy and was continuously attempting to bring young therapists to make their own decisions. Accordingly, he was dubbed "Mr. Helpful" and "Paul the Doll" by subordinates, and on the one occasion during the period of research when he cracked down on the "wild" therapeutic styles of some residents, it was widely assumed that he did not have it in his own heart to take this action but was simply carrying out the orders of the superintendent. By and large, however, he presented himself as a kind of "hick from the country"—naive, relaxed, and willing to help.

The third member of the triad, the assistant superintendent, was in charge of research coordination of the staff and occupied a kind of intermediate position between the superintendent and the clinical director. He insisted on performance and standards, and there was a clear competitive edge in his relations with the superintendent, but by and large he came across as one who was interested in the self-actualizing of the residents and other subordinates by encouraging their research and its development. He was relatively silent in meetings, always taking a back seat to the superintendent, and was somewhat more of an enigma to the subordinates in the organization, who tended to regard him as "Mr. Hi Guys." Hodgson, Levinson, and Zaleznik came to the conclusion that how the three played in this quite successful executive role constellation was fated by the subordinates who more or less effectively cast them in these roles out of an interest in their own authority needs, and the trio of leaders had little choice but to carry out their fated roles. In the end, moreover, these roles were regarded as cast into a somewhat familial mold, though the investigators were careful not to overstereotype them.

> The role types we refer to are the paternal-assertive, the maternal-nurturant, and the fraternal-permissive. These three role types are arche-

typical in their significance. There may be other types: for example, the rational-bureaucratic, in which the elements of an organizational role are suppressed. Also there may be many permutations and combinations of these types in the concrete behavior of individuals. (p. 495)

One of the advantages of this mode of investigation, as described, is that the investigators were able not only to talk with live subjects, who could free associate and present their own interpretations of their situations, but to gain *information* from others as well, particularly subordinates. The other advantage is that the investigators could make *direct observations* of the interactions among them, thus bringing an independent line of evidence to bear. At the same time, their investigations were impaired by the fact that the executives and their subordinates were in constant realistic interaction with one another, much of which was tacit and escaped their notice. What is interesting about the line of investigation, however, is the persistence with which these kinds of social leadership roles tend to emerge in all kinds of social organizations, no matter whether they are peopled by men or women. There seems to be a certain universal tendency for certain patterns of authority and intimacy to emerge in a social organization, and if these do not, then the organization proves to be ineffective or otherwise founders in its mission.

The Analysis of Cultural Products

Up to this point we have been concerned with types of research that involve the semistructured interviewing and observation of live individuals, in which data relevant to psychoanalytic interpretation can be gleaned, but which is gathered by investigators who cast themselves in the role of "researchers," a role which places some practical limitations on the extent to which the investigator can evoke the free-associative process, and some ethical limitations on the extent to which the investigator can reveal the innermost, sometimes reprehensible ideas, thoughts, and feelings of live subjects.

Dealing with a cultural production—a play, a novel, a painting, a poem—presents both advantages and disadvantages to the investigator from a methodological point of view. As often as not, the creator of the production is no longer alive, so this frees the investigator from the ethical restrictions mentioned before, though sometimes survivors and descendants of the creator of the cultural production may have special sensitivities that must be taken into account. On the other hand, a cultural production presents certain disadvantages. While there may be multiple preliminary sketches, earlier folios, and the like, the cultural product reveals itself as a finished and unalterable object to be contemplated and interpreted by the investigator. We will explore the implications of this limitation presently.

What kind of object is the painting, the novel, the play? It is a production that lies somewhere on a continuum that is marked by the dream on the one end and a logical, mathematical, or scientific report on the other. The dream is dominated by primary processes and content, and lacks forms, rules of language, and cognitive conventions; the formal report contrasts with the dream on all these counts. The cultural production is certainly a vehicle for the sublimated expression of primary process materials and neurotic representations. At the same time it typically is represented within certain structural limitations; the painter is restricted to certain chemical compositions (paints) and must work in two-dimensional space; the novelist and playwright operate within the conventions of acts and scenes, plot construction, and the portrayal of characters; the poet operates within the constraints of meters, stanzas, and other poetic forms. It is up to the psychoanalytically minded investigator to cut through them and dig for the expression of psychoanalytically relevant themes in the materials.

I mentioned that the cultural production typically resembles a dream in certain respects, but it cannot be analyzed in the same way as a dream. The main vehicle for analyzing the latter is through the free associations of the patient—his or her tracing it to day residues, affects, memories, other persons and objects, and transference materials. All this is unavailable to the psychoanalytically minded investigator. While I agree with Ernest Jones that a play or a novel cannot be regarded as "a finished thing-in-itself, something almost independent of the creator's personality" (Jones, 1954, p. 14), the deeper connections with the creator's personality are not directly available to the investigator. Given this inaccessibility, upon what can the investigator rely to derive psychoanalytic meanings from the production? The following sources of evidence come to mind:

1. Knowledge about the author's knowledge of associations. Those who create literary and other masterpieces are themselves often acquainted with other traditions (e.g., classical Greek, the Bible) and adorn their works with these kinds of allusions. The interpreter is led by them to the rich complex of meanings that may

be found in the classical stories and myths (at least those elements that the investigator believes to have been salient in the creator's mind at the moment of allusion).

2. Knowledge of the personal history and personality of the author. Because of the frequent availability of biographies, diaries, and personal reminiscences and survivors' reports about him or her, much information is available about his or her relations with parents, siblings, and lovers; about important anniversaries in his or her life; and, indeed, about his or her personality structure and neurotic preoccupations. If the investigator can legitimately assume that these genetic experiences and personal preoccupations will find their way into the creative productions of author—and this seems a most legitimate assumption—then the investigator can "free associate" *for* the author and make connections between the cultural product and his or her psychic life as revealed by the biographical information.

3. Knowledge derived from free associations by the investigator. In all likelihood the investigator, being an educated, cultured, and historically informed person, will have come to share in the language and culture of the creator and can, himself or herself, take the occurrence of a situation or event in the cultural production—for example, a love triangle, the manifestation of jealousy, the inheritance of land or title—in the context of its meanings as represented, and associate along lines of these meanings to other connotations and denotations that "make sense" to the investigator and presumably "made sense" to the creator. One important resource available to the psychoanalytically inclined investigator in this connection is the repertoire of meaningful connections and associations that are found in psychoanalytic theory itself. One of the reasons that Freud was able to make sense and find structure in dreams—which were otherwise composed of jumbled, unconnected, and otherwise nonsensical elements—was that he relied on certain more or less "universal" meanings of certain kinds of objects (serpent = penis; water = birth; oven = womb; salt = semen; urination = ambition) that derive from anatomical analogy, recurrence in folklore, etc. Controversial as these kinds of symbolic representations have become in the critical literature, they nonetheless constitute a set of criteria that guide the free associations of the psychoanalytic investigator.

4. Knowledge derived from the process of countertransference on the part of the investigator. Countertransference—affective reactions experienced by the analyst in response to material generated on the part of the patient—is one of the most powerful sources of information with which the analyst deals with the analytic material. This tool is also available to the psychoanalytic investigator of cultural productions, as he or she will be moved in one way or another—in a positive or negative emotional direction—by the material produced. To analyze these reactions, as well as the reasons for them, is a species of free association that leads the investigator to new and meaningful connections that the material evokes.

It should be acknowledged that all four of these kinds of inferential knowledge are indirectly produced and do not substitute for the process of continuous monitoring of the free associations of a living patient, and the continuous processes of learning, deepening, and correcting that thereby occur. To acknowledge this factor of indirectness also provides a clue as to why it is easier and more tempting to engage in "wild" analyses of cultural productions, analyses that are not continuously corrected by the subject itself. Because of this indirectness, moreover, psychological interpretations of cultural productions are among the weakest from the standpoint of being able to demonstrate them definitely, and whatever weight is to be given to them should not be one single observation, but should be based on the degree to which an extensive *range* of different types of indirect data are consistent with one another.

The first analyses of cultural productions were undertaken by Freud himself, notably in his analysis of primitive religious systems (Freud, 1955 [1912–13]), his analysis of Dostoevsky's theme of parricide (Freud, 1961 [1928]), and his analysis of the artistic productions of Leonardo da Vinci (1957 [1910]). It was also Freud who first suggested the fundamental psychoanalytic significance of Shakespeare's *Hamlet:*

> Another of the great creations of tragic poetry, *Hamlet,* has its roots in the same soil as *Oedipus Rex.* . . . In *Hamlet* the child's wishful fantasy [of parricide] remains repressed; and—just as in the case of a neurosis—we learn of its existence from its inhibiting consequences. . . . Hamlet is able to do anything except take vengeance on the man who did away with his father and took that father's place with his mother, the man who shows him the repressed wishes of his own childhood realized. (Freud, 1953 [1900], pp. 264–65)

The most extensive analysis of Hamlet, however, was to come from the pen of Jones fifty years later, in 1954.

Like Freud, Jones began with the surface phenomenon of the theme of Hamlet's inhibition, that is, his "hesitancy in seeking revenge of his father's murder" (p. 26). Jones rejects certain other interpretations as absurd, e.g., Shakespeare's need to prolong the play, his defense of certain religious systems, and that the act is such a repugnant one that almost no one could carry it out (pp. 26–39). After having rejected these reasons as implausible, Jones argues that the true cause for Hamlet's inhibition lies in "some special feature of the task that renders it repugnant to [Hamlet]" (p. 51). The other special reason why the play has such a powerful effect on its viewers is because the same conflict is in the presence of every one of them. Moreover, whenever a person cannot bring himself to do something that

> every conscious consideration tells him he should do—in which he may have the strongest desire to do—it is always because there is some hidden reason why a part of him doesn't want him to do it; this reason he will not own to himself and is only dimly if at all aware of. That is exactly the case with Hamlet. Time and time he works himself up, points out to himself his obvious duty, with the cruelest self-reproaches lashes himself to agonies of remorse—and once more falls away into inaction. (Jones, 1954, p. 60)

The power and weight of such an interpretation is difficult to establish, because it is derived from what does *not* happen, namely the vengeful murder of the uncle. If this phenomenon of inhibition were the only feature of Hamlet's psychological makeup, such an objection would be persuasive. But other ingredients in the play fall into place if we consider Hamlet's relations to other characters in the play, relations which reveal both the impulse and its inhibition in full ambivalence. For example, Hamlet is completely passive and submissive in his relation to his father, the ghost; he carps at his uncle and attempts to lure him into trapping himself into a commission of the crime, and is able to kill him only at the moment of his own death; but he is fully capable of sadism and ultimately the murder of another father-figure in the play (Polonius). In his relation to his mother as idealized in his father's eyes, he is completely inhibited ("Leave her to Heaven"); in his real life he is able to approach her bed but only hesitatingly; and in his relationship with Ophelia he develops a relationship that is at once lustful and sadistic. It is in this kind of application and interpretation that the psychoanalytic mode becomes most powerful and compelling. It permits the viewer to bring together a great many of the relations developed in the drama and to see them as standing in systematic relation to one another, as a kind of symbolic *family* of relations that cannot be understood except as a manifestation of the central conflict—and its ambivalence—of the major hero and protagonist in the play. It is also at this point that the psychoanalytic mode of interpretation fuses most closely with its aesthetic evaluation: the more subtly and ingeniously the author is able to work out the permutations and combinations of the central point of conflict in the play, the deeper and more powerful is the aesthetic impact of the cultural work.

The psychoanalytic interpretation of the play is also powerful because it involves not only the baring of the central conflicts of the main character—patricide, incest, and ultimately matricide—but also the widest range of defenses employed against these, in Hamlet's case the paralysis, inaction, and suicidal turning upon himself. The ultimate significance and value of the application of this distinctive kind of interpretation does not lie in the fact that it excludes all others by its particular force; the corpus of the psychoanalytic framework is so multifaceted and diverse that there can be a psychoanalytic interpretation of almost everything, and that interpretation can in most instances be regarded as one possibility. The unique power of the psychoanalytic mode of interpretation, then, is not its exclusiveness—any cultural production can be interpreted according to the most diverse levels and significance—but its ability to put into systematic place so many different facets of the creation that otherwise do not appear to stand in any special meaningful relation to one another. As in the case of the interpretation of a patient's character structure, the main power comes in elucidating *patterns* of attitude, outlook, defense, conflict, and behavior that otherwise do not bear any relationship to one another.

The Study of Psychohistory

One of the chronic debates among historians over the ages has to do with the relative degree to which larger social, cultural, and political forces shape the events of a nation's or the world's historical evolution, and the degree to which the actions of major figures, acting in accord with their motives, their impulses, and their understanding of their historical situation, affect that evolution (the "great man" theory of history). The debate is far from resolved, but the appearance of the psychodynamic interpretation of the role of major acting individuals in accord with their own historical biographies has lent a new twist to the debate.

The study of psychohistory is not really a new field, nor is it restricted to one particular mode of analysis. Historians such as Tocqueville have attributed at least some causal significance to distinctive features of the French temperament (Tocqueville, 1965 [1856]) and to the American spirit (Tocqueville, 1945 [1835, 1840]) in the development of distinctive historical situations and crises in those societies. The German historical school stressed the power of a given nation's *Geist,* or spirit—a notion that is at least partially psychological in character—as the driving force of historical change. In the hands of anthropologists and psychoanalysts alike, the notion of "national character" as determining the aggressive actions of Japan (Benedict, 1946) and Germany (Fromm, 1941) in World War II provided another set of examples of the personality-based interpretation of historical processes.

This particular mode of explanation has never enjoyed particular favor in the social sciences. My impression, moreover, is that the most telling and enduring criticism of it is a methodological one: that its arguments move too easily from the analytical level of a global-cultural or a mass-psychological character to rather more specific levels of historical levels and trends, and for that reason they lack historical determinacy and specificity as explanations, and hence can be regarded as interesting possibilities at best. Lowenberg (1971) singled out the phenomena of the mass malnutrition factor and father absence in Germany in World War I and suggested on that basis that for many the attraction to Hitler and the Nazi ideology might have constituted something of a psychological regression on the part of that particular generation. This kind of "demographic-correlational" analysis is also very suggestive as a way of linking mass psychological traumas with major historical events, but as it stands the correlations can be characterized as being vulnerable to the methodological problem known as the "ecological fallacy"—namely, that it is unknown that those individuals who were exposed to the presumed predisposing conditions were from the same subset of the population that lent support to the Nazi movement.

Still another variant of the psychohistorical mode of analysis is to select some major figure whose historical significance is beyond question (Woodrow Wilson, Joseph Stalin, Adolph Hitler, for example) and to "read back," as it were, into the personal biography of this figure and to divine the psychodynamics that propelled him or her into the fateful historical role that he or she played. The acknowledged master of this particular mode of psychohistory is Erik Erikson, who has selected the figures of Martin Luther, Mohandas Gandhi, George Bernard Shaw, Thomas Jefferson, and Jesus Christ, among others, to develop his penetrating insights. In keeping with this essay's focus on the methodological problems generated by a particular case, I have chosen Erikson's psychobiography of Martin Luther (1958). This was the first of his works of this genre and is regarded by many as being his most outstanding.

As is appropriate for the psychohistorian, Erikson's treatment of Luther was carried out with an eye focused both on the great sociohistorical transition associated with the man, on the one hand, and on his personal biography on the other. As for the former, Luther provided a "solution [which] bridged a political and psychological vacuum which history had created in a significant portion of Western Christendom"; Luther himself "at one time was a rather endangered young man, beset with a syndrome of conflicts [associated mainly with an identity crisis]" (p. 15).

Not surprisingly, Erikson focused on Luther's relation to his father and various father figures that loomed in his life. Luther's father was himself something of a bridge figure between the medieval and modern eras. Having deserted his peasant origins, he became a miner. He wished his son to forgo the priesthood and become a lawyer (a profession more befitting the looming mercantile and capitalist age). Luther's decision to go into the monastery was thus simultaneously a rebellious one and one which was reactionary in that it locked him into the pre-eminent institution—the church—of the older order. This decision reflected the negative side of a truly ambivalent relationship to his father, the positive side of which was reflected in his attachment to a number of senior religious figures during his period of religious apprenticeship. Erikson's treatment of Luther's great religious rebellion against the Pope and the Church, as well as his simultaneous embrace of the loving God in Heaven, with whom the true believer could relate to directly and lovingly, was a "splitting" of this ambivalence in his ongoing struggle between rebellious rejection and adoring love for his father. Erikson also interpreted Luther's preoccupation with sexual sin, as well as his continuous symbolic dialogue with the devil, as deep manifestations of Luther's relationship with his father, and with the elder Luther's own conviction that Luther could not honor his vows to celibacy. The whole of Erikson's treatment of the figure of Luther, by and large sympathetic, was couched in the trajectory of a life course, marked by a troubled and indecisive youth, a long moratorium preceding his full development of a confident identity, a mature adulthood marked by his leadership of a true religious rebellion, and his transition to a relatively calm older age, marked by a kind of secular conservatism and antirevolutionary posture.

The first methodological problem that arises in the kind of psychohistory undertaken by Erikson is the same that arises in connection with the analysis of the psychodynamic analysis of most cultural productions: the fact that most inferences about the religious and ideological writings of the historical figure are "given" in the historical record, and any symbolic interpretation of them must rest on associations made by the investigator to the creator's own biographical history and contemporary setting, as well as to the cultural context of his time. The data contained in the personal and social history of the great historical figure, moreover, are likely to be both fragmentary and distorted, both because of the unavailability of reliable written records of the time and because of the violence done to these records by generations of distortions perpetrated by admirers and detractors of the great figure over the generations.

A second methodological problem posed by Erikson's genre of psychohistory involves the bridging of the gap between the psychological level and the great social-political-cultural level that characterized the West in the sixteenth and seventeenth centuries. A moment's reflection should tell us that in the contemporary Europe of the time there were thousands of potential young Luthers about—rebellious and ambivalent young men of budding bourgeois fathers who were experiencing problems with their own youth and identities. What was it that could have made Luther, and only Luther, the "right man at the right time"? Would there not have been another like him if he had not appeared, who would have articulated the same bitterness and outrage against the abuses of the Catholic Church if he had not done so? Moreover, it is not clear whether the methodological strategy of "reading back" to the personal history of a figure whose greatness has been made great by subsequent history, and then attributing such force and salience to this single figure, is a valid one. Is this strategy no more than the personalization of a person who became the symbol of an age, and whose personal history was only a symbolic projection of future generations attempting to assess the historical significance of that age? All these queries represent, of course, the ancient ambivalence experienced by students of history about the relative importance of the larger historical process itself and those who shape it.

A Concluding Note

Whenever a truly novel and revolutionary method of generating new knowledge about the human condition is generated—and the psychoanalytic method was one of these—there emerges, as a concomitant tendency, something of an imperialist urge: to turn this method to the understanding of everything in the world—its institutions, its peoples, its history, and its cultures. This happened to the Marxian approach (there is a Marxist explanation of everything), to the sociological approach generally (there is a sociology of everything), and to the psychoanalytic approach (there is a psychoanalytic interpretation of everything). In this connection it is always legitimate to ask about the relative explanatory power of the method in settings and circumstances in which it was not invented. How well does it apply to these new settings and circumstances, and what are the emergent strengths and weaknesses of the method? It is to these questions that this essay has been directed.

References

Bales, R. F.
1950 *Interaction Process Analysis.* Cambridge, MA: Harvard University Press.
Bales, R. F., and Philip E. Slater
1955 "Role Differentiation in Small Decision-Making Groups." In *Family, Socialization, and Interaction Process,* edited by T. Parsons, R. F. Bales, *et al.* Glencoe, IL: The Free Press. Pp. 259–306.
Benedict, Ruth
1946 *The Chrysanthemum and the Sword.* Boston: Houghton Mifflin.
Bettelheim, Bruno
1943 "Individual and Mass Behavior in Extreme Situations." *Journal of Abnormal and Social Psychology,* Vol. 38, pp. 417–52.
Erikson, Erik H.
1958 *Young Man Luther: A Study in Psychoanalysis and History.* New York: Norton.
Erikson, Kai T.
1976 *Everything in Its Path: Destruction in the Buffalo Creek Flood.* New York: Simon & Schuster.

Freud, Sigmund

1953 [1900] "The Interpretation of Dreams." In *Standard Edition of the Complete Psychological Works of Sigmund Freud,* Vols. 4 and 5, edited by James Strachey. London: Hogarth Press.

1955 [1912–13] "Totem and Taboo." In *Standard Edition of the Complete Psychological Works of Sigmund Freud.* Vol. 4, edited by James Strachey. London: Hogarth Press. Pp. 1–161.

1955 [1922] "Group Psychology and the Analysis of the Ego." In *Standard Edition of the Complete Psychological Works of Sigmund Freud,* Vol. 18, edited by James Strachey. London: Hogarth Press. Pp. 67–143.

1957 [1910] "Leonardo Da Vinci and a Memory of His Childhood." In *Standard Edition of the Complete Psychological Works of Sigmund Freud,* Vol. 11, edited by James Strachey. London: Hogarth Press. Pp. 63–137.

1960 [1905] "Jokes and the Relation to the Unconscious." In *Standard Edition of the Complete Psychological Works of Sigmund Freud,* Vol. 8, edited by James Strachey. London: Hogarth Press. Pp. 9–257.

1961 [1928] "Dostoevsky and Patricide." In *Standard Edition of the Complete Psychological Works of Sigmund Freud,* Vol. 21, edited by James Strachey. London: Hogarth Press. Pp. 177–94.

1964 [1939] "Moses and Monotheism." In *Standard Edition of the Complete Psychological Works of Sigmund Freud,* Vol. 23, edited by James Strachey. London: Hogarth Press. Pp. 3–137.

Fromm, Erich

1941 *Escape from Freedom.* New York: Ferrar and Rinehart.

Gouldner, Alvin

1955 *Wildcat Strike: A Study of an Unofficial Strike.* Glencoe, IL: The Free Press.

Grinker, Roy R., and John P. Spiegel

1945 *Men under Stress.* Philadelphia: Blakiston.

Hodgson, Richard, Daniel J. Levinson, and Abraham Zaleznik

1965 *The Executive Role Constellation: An Analysis of Personality and Role Relations in Management.* Boston: Harvard Graduate School of Business Administration.

Jones, Ernest

1954 *Hamlet and Oedipus.* Garden City, NY: Doubleday.

Leach, Edmund R.

1958 "An Anthropologist's Reflections on a Social Survey." *The Ceylon Journal of Historical and Social Studies,* Vol. 1, pp. 1–11.

LeVine, Robert

1973 *Culture, Behavior, and Personality.* Chicago: Aldine.

Lifton, Robert

1973 *Home from the War: Vietnam Veterans, Neither Victims nor Executioners.* New York: Simon & Schuster.

Lindemann, Erich
1944 "Symptomatology and Management of Acute Grief." *American Journal of Psychiatry,* Vol. 101, pp. 141–48.
Lowenberg, Peter
1971 "The Psychohistorical Origins of the Nazi Youth Cohort." *American Historical Review,* Vol. 76, pp. 1457–1502.
Parsons, Talcott
1951 *The Social System.* Glencoe, IL: The Free Press.
1964 [1954] "The Incest Taboo in Relation to Social Structure and the Socialization of the Child." In *Social Structure and Personality.* New York: The Free Press of Glencoe. Pp. 57–77.
Smelser, Neil J.
1968 "Social and Psychological Dimensions of Collective Behavior." In *Essays in Sociological Explanation.* Englewood Cliffs, NJ: Prentice-Hall. Pp. 92–121.
1983–84 "Collective Myths and Fantasies." *Humboldt Journal of Social Relations,* Vol. 11, pp. 1–15.
1987 "Depth Psychology and the Social Order." In *The Micro-Macro Link,* edited by Jeffrey Alexander, Bernhard Giesen, Richard Münch, and Neil J. Smelser. Berkeley and Los Angeles: University of California Press. Pp. 356–87.
Smelser, Neil, and Erik H. Erikson (eds.)
1980 *Themes of Work and Love in Adulthood.* Cambridge, MA: Harvard University Press.
Spindler, George (ed.)
1978 *The Making of Psychological Anthropology.* Berkeley and Los Angeles: University of California Press.
Stanton, Alfred H., and Morris S. Schwartz
1954 *The Mental Hospital: A Study of Institutional Participation in Psychiatric Illness and Treatment.* New York: Basic Books.
Tocqueville, Alexis de
1945 [1835, 1840] *Democracy in America.* New York: Knopf and Random House.
1965 [1856] *The Old Regime and the French Revolution.* Garden City, NY: Doubleday.
Veltford, H. R., and S. E. Lee
1943 "The Cocoanut Grove Fire: A Study in Scapegoating." *Journal of Abnormal and Social Psychology,* Vol. 38 (Clinical Supplement), pp. 138–43.
Wallerstein, Robert S., and Neil J. Smelser
1969 "Psychoanalysis and Sociology: Articulations and Applications." *International Journal of Psycho-Analysis,* Vol. 50, pp. 693–716.
Weber, Max
1948 [1920] "Bureaucracy." In *From Max Weber: Essays in Sociology.* Edited, with an introduction by H. H. Gerth and C. Wright Mills. London: Routledge and Kegan Paul. Pp. 196–244.

Whiting, John W. M., and Irvin L. Child
1953 *Child Training and Personality: A Cross-Cultural Study.* New Haven, CT: Yale University Press.

Zelditch, Morris, Jr.
1955 "Role Differentiation in the Nuclear Family: A Comparative Study." In *Family, Socialization, and Interaction Process,* edited by Talcott Parsons, R. F. Bales, et al. Glencoe, IL: The Free Press. Pp. 307–52.

Index

Compositor: G&S Typesetters
Text: 10/13 Galliard
Display: Galliard
Printer: Thomson-Shore
Binder: Thomson-Shore